S. H. IRVINE

METHUEN'S MANUALS OF MODERN PSYCHOLOGY

EDITED BY C. A. MACE

THE STRUCTURE OF HUMAN ABILITIES

THE STRUCTURE OF
HUMAN ABILITIES

PHILIP E. VERNON
M.A., Ph.D., D.Sc.

*Professor of Educational Psychology
in the Institute of Education,
University of London*

LONDON: METHUEN & CO. LTD.
NEW YORK: JOHN WILEY & SONS, INC.

First published November 2, 1950
Reprinted 1951
Second edition 1961
Reprinted 1964

2·2

CATALOGUE NO. 2/5291/10 (METHUEN)

PRINTED IN GREAT BRITAIN BY
LUND HUMPHRIES
LONDON · BRADFORD

PREFACE

SOME acquaintance with the principles and results of factor analysis is nowadays necessary to the study and practise of educational, vocational, or other branches of applied psychology. The mathematical techniques of factorization are less essential for those who are not actually going to carry out analyses, and they are omitted in this book. Even without them the topic is a difficult one, but I have tried to present it simply and to show that it does have extremely important practical bearings. I assume only that the reader has had an elementary course in psychology and knows what an intelligence test and a correlation coefficient are. One section of the book which is inevitably more technical than the rest is relegated to an appendix.

My other chief aim is to bring together the large number of publications in this field, in Britain and America, which at first sight appear to give contradictory and confusing accounts of mental structure, and to show that they can be fitted into one consistent—even if incomplete—picture. This involves the reworking or reinterpretation of the results of many authors. Almost all the contributions from about 1935 to the middle of 1949 are critically surveyed (though less attention is paid to earlier literature), and several unpublished analyses carried out by British psychologists in the Services are described. The book does not, however, attempt to cover studies of personality factors, attitudes and interests, or other fields outside that of abilities.

Too many colleagues to mention by name have encouraged me to write this book, or have made useful comments on earlier drafts. I am indebted to them, also to my wife for her assistance in preparing the manuscript and index. Acknowledgment is due to the National Institute of Industrial Psychology for permission to reprint several sections of an article (Vernon, 1949a). It may be noted here that dates are inserted after authors' names as references to the bibliography.

P. E. V.

PREFACE TO SECOND EDITION

There have been several requests for the re-issue of this book since the first edition was exhausted, but it did not seem to me that the time was ripe for a complete revision. I have therefore preferred to bring it up to date by adding a chapter on developments in factorial work on human abilities from 1950 to 1959. Apart from this, a few minor corrections only have been made in the original text.

November, 1959.   P. E. V.

CONTENTS

FIGURES

TABLES

CHAPTER I

MENTAL FACULTIES AND FACTORS

Abstract. This chapter criticizes the ascription of human abilities and behaviour to hypothetical faculties, traits or powers of the mind, as exemplified in phrenology and in various educational and other theories. An ability or factor should be thought of as a class or group of performances, and it should be admitted only if a number of measurements in this class (e.g. test results) overlap or correlate positively with one another. The basic mathematical methods of factor analysis are quite straightforward. By means of them we can find what tests, examinations, etc., really measure, i.e. their factor content. The terms g, group factor, communality, specificity and variance are explained. Some of the limitations of factor analysis and its relations to other psychological methods are pointed out.

Faculties and Phrenology. The faculties or powers of the human mind have been for centuries a matter of interest, not only to the ordinary man who wishes to explain his own conduct and that of other people, but also to the philosopher, psychologist and educationist. Until recent years, however, their nature and numbers were matters of pure speculation. Casual observation and introspection are incapable of providing scientific proof of their existence, and in consequence many past theories of human abilities and qualities and their organization were entirely fallacious. One of the most popular doctrines of the early nineteenth century was the phrenology of Gall, Spurzheim and Coombe, which assumed that the strength of each faculty was indicated by the prominence of bumps on the appropriate parts of the skull. Thirty-seven faculties were recognized including Propensities (Amativeness, Combativeness, etc.), Sentiments (Self-esteem, Conscientiousness), Perceptive (Size, Colour, Number, Tune, Language), and Reflective (Comparison and Causality). We now know that traits and abilities are not located in particular parts of the brain, and that the growth of areas of the brain does not produce protuberances on the skull. Indeed it has been said that, 'The bumps on a man's skull tell you more about his wife's character than his own.' But the criticism which mainly concerns us is that Gall provided no evidence that these faculties are the fundamental ones, nor that they are independent or self-consistent. Is the sense of size really distinct from that of form; may not both depend on some more basic capacity? Is the person good at reading and spelling the English language necessarily good at languages in general? How about memory, reasoning, mechanical sense, and a host of other qualities absent from the list?

Faculties in Educational Theory. Unscientific faculty psychology permeates educational theory and practice even at the present day. School subjects or new methods of teaching are introduced because they are alleged to develop such and such a faculty. For example, Nature Study stimulates powers of observation, learning poetry develops the memory, and so on. A Board of Education circular in the 1930s justified physical training in schools not merely for its effects on the health of pupils, but because it enhances mental alertness, self-control and the team spirit. At one time it was thought that the reasoning faculty is only rudimentary in children up till the age of twelve, whereas memory is comparatively strong, hence primary schooling should concentrate on drill subjects. Scientific research has largely contradicted these assumptions. Children of three years and younger often reason out the solutions to problems that interest them; the capacity for learning new material increases with age and is much superior in the young adult to that of the seven-year child, as Thorndike has shown. This capacity, moreover, cannot be improved all-round simply by practising the memorization of poetry, multiplication tables or spellings. And an experiment by Sutcliffe and Canham (1937) disproved the view that extra physical training in school hours is of sufficient benefit to the mind to compensate for the loss of time from intellectual work.

Faculties in Popular Thought and in Vocational Psychology. Equally dubious is the view so often put forward by parents that their boy who is backward at school work makes up for it by being good with his hands, or the assumption that the quick worker is usually inaccurate. We tend to divide people up into types—the practical, the academic, the leader, the aesthete, etc., forgetting that most individuals are good at some practical things, not at others. The boy who would make a good carpenter would not necessarily succeed as a plumber, nor a machinist as a civil engineer. The influence of this type theory manifests itself when employers distrust the psychologist's paper-and-pencil spatial and mechanical tests for selecting tradesmen. Such tests, they think, are too 'theoretical' to pick the man with the practical 'flair' or to eliminate the 'ham-handed'. The whole field of occupational selection and guidance has indeed been befogged by unverified speculations about qualities underlying jobs. It is not only the layman who analyses a job as requiring 'dexterity, alertness and concentration'. Psychologists have carried out more systematic studies of jobs, but many, particularly in Germany, have been equally guilty of assuming that *names* like these represent distinctive and consistent abilities (cf. Vernon and Parry, 1949).

Definitions of Intelligence. It is psychologists again who, although they have been testing intelligence with some success for over forty years, have failed to reach any agreed definition as to what it is they are measuring. Binet frankly regarded it as a collection of faculties: 'judgment, practical sense, initiative . . . adapting oneself to circumstances'. His scale, however, was composed of tests which would differentiate older from younger children. The only criterion that they were measuring judgment, etc., was his own opinion. Several psychologists have considered intelligence as the ability to profit from experience, which contrasts with the mechanical, instinctive reactions of lower species. None of the commonly used tests appear to involve any such quality. In a famous symposium published in 1921, thirteen psychologists gave thirteen different views. Terman stressed capacity for abstract thinking, Dearborn capacity to learn, Colvin adjustment to environment, and so on. Actually there is much overlapping between such views, but further theoretical discussion will not get us anywhere. It will not tell us just how much they have in common, nor what is the real essence of intelligence.[1]

The Empirical Approach to Human Abilities, Based on Correlation. Psychologists nowadays tend to adopt a more operational or Behaviouristic outlook, though rejecting the wilder excesses of J. B. Watson's doctrines. They realize the fruitlessness of mental entities such as faculties, which can never be directly

[1] A useful summary of these and other definitions, and an explanation of Spearman's two-factor theory, are given by Knight (1933).

observed nor verified, and prefer to deal with concepts directly derived from measurable activities of human beings. An ability is inferred from the fact that some people carry out certain tasks more rapidly or more correctly than others. Whether it also depends on some power in the mind is a matter which interests metaphysicians but not scientists. The clue leading to a scientific solution of the impasse is provided by the term overlapping, i.e. by *correlation*. By means of correlation we can find whether the scores of a group of people on two or more tasks correspond or not, and therefore whether these tasks involve the same, or distinctive, abilities. If several tests presumed to measure a particular ability do not correlate positively with one another, that ability cannot be accepted as a useful conception. Take memory as an example. We all know that a schoolboy may have an excellent memory for cricket scores or names of motor-cars, and a poor memory for school work, and that a professor who remembers everything about his own subject may be absent-minded in daily life, or forgetful of names and faces. If these various kinds of memory are measured and inter-correlated and little or no agreement is found, it is obvious that there is no one general faculty of memory, but a lot of specific varieties. We need not demand that such tests correlate perfectly; they may show a limited amount of overlapping, and some may correlate more highly with the rest than others do. But only in so far as they do correlate can they be regarded as measuring a memory ability or *factor*. Otherwise each test is merely measuring the ability specific to that test and to no other. It follows too that any test can be regarded as divisible into two portions which we call its *communality* and its *specificity*, i.e. what it has in common with other tests and what is specific to it alone.

There is yet another possibility. Positive correlations between several tests designed to measure memory might arise if the tests were in fact all measuring some other, more fundamental, ability, say intelligence. Factorial technique enables us to examine this, and to discover whether or not there is overlapping over and above anything attributable to intelligence. We thus arrive at the definition of an ability given by the writer elsewhere (Vernon, 1940): 'It implies the existence of a group or category of performances which correlate highly with one another, and which are relatively distinct from (i.e. give low correlations with) other performances.'

ctors Are Not Mental Elements Like Faculties. From
xample it should be clear that a factor is a construct which
ints for the objectively determined correlations between tests,
ntrast to a faculty which is a hypothetical mental power. We
f we wish go on to theorize about the psychological nature and
n of factors. Better, we can conduct experiments to discover
what performances involve a factor, among which groups of
le it emerges, and what conditions affect it. But factors
ld be regarded primarily as categories for classifying mental
chavioural performances, rather than as entities in the mind
ervous system. Since by means of factor analysis we can
ce a large battery of tests to a few underlying factors there is a
in parallel to the analysis of chemical compounds into their
tituent elements. But this analogy should not be pressed too
or we shall see later that factors are much too fluid, too de-
ent on the particular groups and particular tests studied, to
ompared with elements. For example we might expect, and
ndeed find, that the factors in scholastic abilities are depend-
n how school subjects are taught. Some teachers emphasize
onnections between the various branches of mathematics, or
een a country's language and its literature and history, much
than others do, and this is likely to be reflected in the cor-
ons and factors.

entification of Factors. How factors should be identified
named is a somewhat controversial point. According to Guil-
(1940) the factorist studies the common material, formal and
tional features in the tests which are loaded with a factor and
this deduces its nature. Most factors are defined by material
verbal, mechanical information, etc.). The form of the test—
her apparatus or paper-and-pencil, choice-response or crea-
response—has not yet been proven to have much influence.
tional factors involve consideration of the testees' mental
esses, by means of introspections or job analysis procedures or
(e.g. reasoning, attention, etc.). Bentley (1948) and others
criticized the looseness of factorists' terminology, and the
ctivity of their guesses about the nature of some of their
rs. We agree with him that it is better to avoid names of
thetical functions or faculties, but would claim that the old-
oned procedure (still common among some vocational
hologists, psychiatrists, teachers and others) of assuming

Illustration of the Mathematical Fundamentals of Factor Analysis.

It is unfortunate that this approach to the analysis of abilities involves somewhat complicated mathematics, since this frightens or antagonizes many of the teachers, employers, and others who are most prone to discuss abilities unscientifically. Yet the basic principles are very simple, as the following hypothetical examples will show.

TABLE I.—CORRELATION COEFFICIENTS BETWEEN SIX PSYCHOLOGICAL TESTS

Tests	1	2	3	4	5	6
1. Vocabulary		+·76	+·79	+·45	+·41	+·34
2. Analogies	+·76		+·68	+·44	+·35	+·26
3. Classifications	+·79	+·68		+·49	+·39	+·32
4. Block Design	+·45	+·44	+·49		+·58	+·44
5. Spatial	+·41	+·35	+·39	+·58		+·55
6. Formboard	+·34	+·26	+·32	+·44	+·55	

Table I gives the correlations that might be obtained between six tests applied to a large group of children (Block Design and Formboard being given individually). Inspection suggests that the correlations between the first three and last three are relatively small, i.e. that ability at verbal tests is partially distinct from ability at practical or spatial tests. But the separation is incomplete. All the correlations are positive, showing that all tests have something in common, presumably of the nature of general intelligence. By the appropriate techniques we can find how far each test measures this general ability or factor which we shall call g, and Table II lists the loadings, saturations or correlations with g. Now if this was the only underlying ability, we could reproduce the test inter-correlations simply by taking the products of their g-loadings. For example:

$$r_{35} = r_{3g} \times r_{5g} = \cdot 8 \times \cdot 5 = \cdot 40$$

Such products are listed in Table II, and in Table III each product has been subtracted from the corresponding original correlation to show what overlapping, if any, remains. These are known as *residual correlations*.

TABLE II.—G-LOADINGS OF THE SIX TESTS AND THEIR PRODUCTS

	G-Loadings	Products 1	2	3	4	5	6
1. Vocabulary	·8		·56	·64	·48	·40	·32
2. Analogies	·7	·56		·56	·42	·35	·28
3. Classifications	·8	·64	·56		·48	·40	·32
4. Block Design	·6	·48	·42	·48		·30	·24
5. Spatial	·5	·40	·35	·40	·30		·20
6. Formboard	·4	·32	·28	·32	·24	·20	

TABLE III.—RESIDUAL CORRELATIONS AFTER SUBTRACTING THE OVERLAPPING ATTRIBUTABLE TO G

	1	2	3	4	5	6
1. Vocabulary		+·20	+·15	+·03	+·01	+·02
2. Analogies	+·20		+·12	+·02	+·00	—·02
3. Classifications	+·15	+·12		+·01	—·01	+·00
4. Block Design	—·03	+·02	+·01		+·28	+·21
5. Spatial	+·01	+·00	—·01	+·28		+·35
6. Formboard	+·02	—·02	+·00	+·20	+·35	

The residuals between the first three and last three tests are not all zero, but are so close to it that they can reasonably be attributed to chance errors in the original correlations. Within each group of three however the residuals are large, showing that distinct verbal and practical-spatial abilities are present. Each set can be analysed separately, and if the following loadings are multiplied out, they exactly reproduce the residual correlations:

	Verbal-factor loading			Spatial factor loading
1. Vocabulary	·5	4. Block Design		·4
2. Analogies	·4	5. Spatial		·7
3. Classifications	·3	6. Formboard		·5

Subsidiary abilities, over and above *g*, a... since they run through a limited group of t... name them by symbols, such as *v* for verb... than giving them ability-names which ma... preted. Similarly we use *g* to refer to the... general factor, instead of the subjective... intelligence.

The *communality* of any test, i.e. its... shown by the squares of its factor loading... loadings, their squares, the communality (... from 1.0, i.e. the *specificities*.[1] Thus we... bulary test measures 64 per cent. *g*, 25 per... ing 11 per cent. is specific. The Formbo...

TABLE IV.—COMPLETED FACTOR ANAL... LOGICAL TESTS...

	Loadings g	v	k	Squares of Loadings g	v
1. Vocabulary	·8	·5		·64	·25
2. Analogies	·7	·4		·49	·16
3. Classifications	·8	·3		·64	·09
4. Block Design	·6		·4	·36	
5. Spatial	·5		·7	·25	
6. Formboard	·4		·5	·16	
Variance	42·3	8·3	1...		

test, only 16 per cent. of what it measures... general factor, 25 per cent. to *k*, and 59... figures are known as the *variances* of the... variance of each factor is given in the bo... represent the importance or size of the fac... tests.

[1] Many factorists further subdivide this term i... variance of the test, and its true specificity. For... efficient of the Vocabulary test is shown to be ·94... and the variance of the factor specific to the test alo... logical statistics such as Guilford, 1936).

that a faculty exists and that certain tests measure it, is very much more subjective. Factorists do not, in fact, rely on hunches but always try to provide objective confirmation of a factor by carrying out further analyses with other populations and with enlarged batteries of tests, with a view to defining its content and extent more accurately.

Some Limitations of Factor Analysis. The mistake should not be made of identifying the whole of the psychology of abilities with factor analysis. Vocational and educational selection and guidance must take account not only of personality traits and interests which might profitably be expressed as factors also, but also of relevant experience, home circumstances and the like. And although there is a strong case for substituting objective tests for the subjective judgments of an interviewer, in practice it is seldom possible to carry out such guidance without an interviewer to bring together all the data and to interpret them to the candidates (cf. Vernon and Parry, 1949). Still more important for the development of psychological science are experiments on conditions affecting the performance of skills and of mental tasks, for example, investigations of the design of equipment, or studies of the learning process, of concept formation, of physical or mental fatigue and boredom, and so forth. Here factor analysis is largely irrelevant, since it deals only with the end products of human thinking and behaviour, and throws little light on how these products come about in individual human beings. Factors are indeed a kind of blurred average, for though they derive from the common features displayed by a large group of people, they may stem from very diverse mental and physical processes in different people. Analysis does not even usually tell us which factors an individual uses in any given performance, though it probably could do so. Thus one individual may score well at a test through high *g*, another might get the same score by virtue of some group factor, yet another through specific ability at that particular test.

The real need for factors arises as soon as we begin to discuss and name abilities or traits, and to compare the relative standing of different people on such faculties. Factor analysis is complementary, not opposed, to the approach of the experimental psychologist; but both are opposed to the layman's unscientific speculations about human qualities and their underlying nature.

It should be realized also that the 'map' of the mind so far

provided by factor analysis is very incomplete, although it represents a remarkable advance over what was known at the beginning
of the century. Factorial investigations normally require the
application of at least a dozen tests (Americans prefer forty to fifty)
to several hundred subjects, and the labour of calculating the
correlations and extracting the factors is almost too great to be
done without mechanical aids. Moreover, the results are so
affected by the particular tests used, especially when the battery is
small, and by the background, sex, age, and other characteristics of
the populations tested, that it is only by co-ordinating the findings
of numerous analyses that reasonable certainty begins to emerge.
Finally we shall see that different analysts often interpret the same
results differently, though the confusion to which this leads is more
apparent than real.

CHAPTER II

LANDMARKS IN THE DEVELOPMENT OF FACTOR ANALYSIS

Abstract. Some of the investigations which contributed most to the development of factor analysis from 1904 to 1947 are surveyed. Until the 1930s the predominant view among American psychologists was that all abilities are highly specific. In Britain, the importance of the general factor, *g*, was demonstrated by Spearman, but the existence of additional sub-types of ability or group factors gradually emerged from the work of Burt, Kelley, Stephenson, El Koussy, Alexander, and others. Results obtained from analyses among recruits during the 1939-45 war confirmed the hierarchical theory, to which this book is committed. This holds that there are certain main types of ability over and above *g* (in particular the educational and the practical types), and that these themselves can be subdivided into numerous minor group factors. Thurstone, Guilford, and other factorists in America from 1938 on, opposed the notion of a general factor and hierarchy. Instead they showed that test inter-correlations could be accounted for by a number of independent types of ability or multiple factors, not unlike the nineteenth-century faculties. However, more recent work suggests a *rapprochement* between the hierarchical and the Thurstonian viewpoints.

The Viewpoint of Early American Psychologists. In the late nineteenth century the method of correlation was devised, largely by Galton and Pearson, for measuring the agreement between two sets of scores. Some of the first applications of this method to mental functions were made by Wissler (1901) and Thorndike in America, with disconcerting results. Tests of reaction time and sensory acuity, for example, showed scarcely any correlation with the grades of college students. Apparently the 'alertness', 'concentration', 'sensitivity' or other qualities entering into these tests were not the same as the 'alertness', etc., involved in university work. Indeed for many years the notion of measuring mental ability in general was discredited in America. The experiments of William James, Thorndike and others on transfer of training reinforced the view that abilities are highly specific. If practice in learning English poetry does not improve the ability to learn French poetry, there can be no such thing as general memory. As Stratton put it: 'What you do to the mind by means of education knows its place; it never spreads. You train what you train.' Probably no American psychologist of the present day adheres to this extreme specific view, which Spearman called the *anarchic* theory of mental structure. Nevertheless it exerted a profound influence right up to the 1930s. Muscio (1922) in Britain, and Perrin (1921) in America obtained extremely small correlations between different tests of manual skills, and, in a well-known study of mechanical ability at Minnesota University, Paterson and Elliot (1930) showed that mechanical capacities are far from unitary. In the field of personality and character also different tests of the same trait often failed to correlate, one of the most striking investigations being that of Hartshorne and May (1928). These authors concluded that we should try to develop honest habits among children in each specific life situation, rather than to train honesty in general.

Spearman's Two-Factor Theory. During the period 1900–30 British psychologists, headed by Spearman, Thomson and Burt, followed a different course. It was in 1904 that Spearman published his correlations between sensory tests and estimates of intelligence which showed that: 'all branches of intellectual activity have in common one fundamental function (or group of functions), whereas the remaining or specific elements of the activity seem in every case to be wholly different from that in all others.' When correlations can be wholly accounted for by g, they tend to fall into what he called a *hierarchical* pattern.[1] Later he developed the *tetrad difference* technique of proving that no significant factors other than g and specifics are present.

The Abilities of Man (1927) contains the fullest account of Spearman's theories and of the numerous supporting investiga-

---

[1] This term refers to a steadily descending order of the inter-correlations and should not be confused with the hierarchical structure of group factors, described below. A useful and non-technical exposition of Spearman's views is given by F. C. Thomas (1935) in *Ability and Knowledge*. The whole development of factor analysis, particularly in America, is reviewed by Wolfle (1940) in *Factor Analysis to* 1940.

tions by himself and his students. In it he shows that neither the anarchic, nor what he calls the monarchic or oligarchic theories of the mind accord with the facts. The *monarchic* view reduces all abilities to a single capacity of general intelligence or 'common sense'. This would imply that they are all perfectly correlated, and would make no allowance for the unevenness of people's abilities along different lines. The *oligarchic* theory is the view that the mind is ruled by a number of separate powers or faculties. Spearman's *two-factor* theory satisfactorily explained the tendency for all abilities to overlap to some extent, and yet to show considerable unevenness. The pupil who is good at English is usually superior also in arithmetic, and even at handwriting or in physical health. At the same time each subject involves its own specific, or *s*, factor; hence some pupils may be relatively better at English than at number work, or vice versa. The specific factors in practical and physical abilities are larger, their *g*-saturations smaller, hence discrepancies in these abilities are much more common.

The two-factor theory provides a logical basis, also, for devising satisfactory tests of *g*. We need not, like Binet, choose tests or items which appear to involve judgment (or whatever we think intelligence consists of). Instead tests are taken which have been proved, by correlational analysis, to have high *g*-loadings. Each of these tests will have some specific content, but as these *s*-factors are, by definition, independent, when we combine several tests the various *s*'s will tend to cancel out, leaving us with a purer measure of *g*.

The Nature of *g* and of Specific Factors. Although Spearman wisely refused to identify *g* with intelligence or any other quality whose definition was controversial, he suggested that it depends on the general mental energy with which each individual is endowed. The *s*-factors he compared to a large number of mechanisms or engines, which could be activated by this energy. They are largely affected by education and training, whereas *g* is innate and ineducable. By studying the tests with high or low *g*-saturations he concluded that the outstanding psychological characteristic of the former is that they involve seeing relationships, or to use his own terms, *the eduction of relations and correlates*. In answering, say, an arithmetic problem, the pupil has to grasp the relations between the various data presented, and to deduce something new in order to reach an answer which bears the correct relations to these data. By contrast, if the pupil is asked merely to repeat the multiplication tables which he has learnt by rote, no new relationships are involved. Hence the g-saturation of the former task is high, of the latter low.

Thomson's Criticisms of Spearman. Some of Spearman's statistical techniques were strongly criticized by Thomson, and he argued that the two-factor theory was a possible, but not a necessary, inference from the statistical results (Brown and Thomson, 1921). The tendency towards positive correlation and zero tetrad differences could equally well be explained if abilities depend on a very large number of small causes in the mind (cf. Theory of Bonds, p. 31).

Spearman's Neglect of Group Factors. The chief criticism that would be raised nowadays against Spearman's views is that he failed to allow sufficiently for types of ability which, while less general than g, are certainly not specific. He admitted indeed that different number tests, also different mechanical, and certain other types of test, show residual correlations over and above g. But he ascribed this to the presence of common specific factors and insisted that such 'specific overlap' is very rare. Actually the notion of specific overlap is a contradiction in terms, and towards the end of his life Spearman did begin to recognize the existence of broad group factors such as the verbal and spatial, which arise from the overlapping of quite diverse s-factors. One reason why his own work, up to 1927, failed to yield evidence of group factors was that he and his followers were seldom able to test large populations. Hence any residual overlap that did appear was usually not statistically significant; it might have arisen from chance errors in the correlations. But Spearman was unduly cautious and did not admit that lack of statistical significance does not disprove the existence of additional factors; it only fails to prove it. A large-scale experiment was carried out by Brown and Stephenson (1933) with the avowed object of demonstrating the truth or falsity of the two-factor theory. Three hundred 10-year boys were given twenty varied tests. Some of the pairs of tests did in fact show correlation beyond that accounted for by g. But the authors attributed this to specific overlap, and on eliminating the disturbing elements they were naturally able to prove that g was the sole factor present. Some years later Blakey (1940) re-analysed the correlations by Thurstone's method, without omitting any of the awkward overlap, and concluded that verbal, perceptual and spatial group factors were present, though their variance amounted only to 12.9 per cent. as compared with 41.2 per cent. attributable to *g*.

It is noteworthy that if Spearman's strict view was correct, educational or vocational guidance with the aid of tests would be impossible. We could not measure aptitude for linguistic or mechanical work by linguistic or mechanical tests, since both types of test would predict nothing but *g*. In fact the only tests worth using would be the purest *g* ones. By means of these we could determine the general level of occupation or education for which an individual was suited, but could not differentiate between different types of ability at this level. The only possibility would be to apply tests covering the specific factors in each prospective job. Thus an assembly test might measure the *s*-component of mechanical assembly work, but would throw no light on aptitude for lathe operating or other mechanical jobs.

In point of fact Spearman has proved much more nearly right than vocational and educational psychologists would wish him to be. We shall see later that group factors are generally more limited in scope than general, and highly specific, ones, so that it is indeed very difficult to differentiate types of aptitude.

Burt's Analysis of Scholastic Attainments. As early as 1909 Burt had obtained suggestive evidence of a sensory discrimination group factor beyond *g*, and in subsequent years he explored the fields of imagery, temperament and scholastic attainments. His memorandum on *The Distribution and Relations of Educational Abilities* (1917) was a landmark since it provided clear evidence (which Spearman continued to ignore) of verbal, numerical and practical group factors in school subjects,[1] in addition to a general factor. Also he arrived at the fundamental formula for the *Simple Summation* technique of analysis, later rediscovered by Thurstone and named the *Centroid* method, and developed techniques of assessing group factors. The verbal factor appeared to be two-fold, one part including the more complex or literary subjects—Composition, History, Geography and Science, the other including the

---

[1] Slightly earlier (1915-16), Carey inter-correlated the school examination marks of up to 500 children, and found a distinctive practical factor in Writing, Painting and Needlework. There were indications also of a verbal factor in Composition, Reading and Spelling, but Geography, Science, History and Arithmetic appeared to depend only on the general factor.

simpler word-reading and spelling attainments.   The practical group included Handwork, Drawing, Writing Quality and Speed. Substantially similar results were obtained with 613 ten-year children in 1939, except that the two types of verbal ability appeared to have amalgamated.   For the average school subject the variance attributable to the general factor was 27·9 per cent., and to group factors 20·7 per cent.   Another interesting point was that the general factor correlated highly, but not perfectly, with an intelligence test.   This suggested that general scholastic ability is largely made up of g, but involves in addition such qualities as interest and industry.

Kelley's *Crossroads in the Mind of Man* (1928).   In America, Kelley studied the inter-correlations of batteries of tests given to three groups of over a hundred pupils, aged around 13, 9 and $3\frac{1}{2}$–6 years.   By means of an elaborate and rather difficult technique which has seldom been used since,[1] he established much the same pattern of verbal, number, rote memory, spatial, and speed factors at each level.   The general factor was still the most prominent in all groups, but Kelley accorded it a much less important role than Spearman, interpreting it as heterogeneity due to differences in age or maturity, race, nurture, sex, etc.

The Minnesota Study of Mechanical Ability.   This investigation by Paterson and Elliot (1930) represents another assault on the two-factor theory.   The finding that the average correlation between some twenty-six tests applied to 13-year boys was only $+\cdot17$ is often cited to show that mechanical and motor abilities are highly specific.   But actually the low correlations occurred chiefly among physical tests such as Dynamometer, Steadiness and Agility, and among certain questionnaires or assessments of interests, which are likely to be unreliable at this age.   Table X (p. 102) shows considerable overlapping among the twelve more important measures in the main experiment with 100 boys.   What the investigators did show (cf. Carter, 1928) was that a single general factor as defined by Spearman, and substantiated by the tetrad difference or other techniques, does not fit their results.   But they admitted the presence of group factors, though they did not commit themselves as to their nature.   They claimed also that mechanical ability or abilities are almost independent of g, but then they were considering only a single verbal group test which, according

[1] Except by McDonough (1929).

to later work, probably involves almost as much v as g. Further their group is likely to have been fairly highly selected, and we shall see below that g-saturations are always reduced when all the testees are high (or all low) in g. Further deductions from these figures are given on p. 101f.

Group Factors Established by Stephenson and El Koussy. Two more investigations employing Spearmanian techniques deserve special mention. In 1931, Stephenson gave seven verbal and eight non-verbal intelligence tests to 1,037 girls, aged around ten to twelve. Correlations between the non-verbal tests could be accounted for by a single factor, which he identified with g. The verbal tests were more complex, but their correlations with one another and with the non-verbal tests, could be accounted for by g and a verbal group factor. It should be pointed out, however, that Stephenson's results do not disprove the alternative of another group factor of a spatial-perceptual nature in the non-verbal tests—that is a structure similar to that of Table IV. In terms of variances (roughly calculated by the present writer) Stephenson's solution was:

	g	k	v	Communality
Average non-verbal test	38%	0%	0%	38%
Average verbal test	36%	0%	13%	49%

A solution which would be more favoured nowadays, and which maintains the same communalities, would be:

	g	k	v
Average non-verbal test	31%	7%	0%
Average verbal test	44%	0%	5%

The symbol k for the spatial factor was first applied by El Koussy (1935) who gave twenty-six tests to 162 boys aged 11 to 13. He showed by tetrad analysis that eight of these obtained loadings on such a factor with about the same variance as their g-loadings. According to introspective evidence all these tests seemed to require visual imagery for their successful solution. Other tests employing visual material, together with Cox's Mechanical Explanations and Completion (i.e. mechanical comprehension) tests, and school marks in woodwork and drawing, gave only low correlations with this factor (cf. p. 66).

18 · The Structure of Human Abilities

Thurstone's Multiple Factor Analysis. In 1931 Thurstone developed the centroid technique of analysis and applied it to measures of attitudes and to ratings of personality traits, where it was natural to expect—not a general factor and small subsidiary group factors—but a number of components of more nearly equal variance. The differences between two-factor, group-factor and Thurstonian multiple-factor analyses may be illustrated by the diagrams in Fig. 1. According to the third diagram, no factor runs

1. Two Factor Analysis   2. Group Factor Analysis   3. Multiple Factor Analysis

Test	General Factor	Specific Factors	Test	General Factor	Group Factors A	B	C	Specific Factors	Test	Multiple Factors A	B	C	D	Specific Factors
1	+	+	1	+	+			+	1	+				+
2	+	+	2	+	+			+	2	+		+		+
3	+	+	3	+	+			+	3	+	+			+
4	+	+	4	+	+			+	4	+				+
5	+	+	5	+		+	+	+	5		+	+	+	+
6	+	+	6	+		+		+	6	+	+			+
7	+	+	7	+		+		+	7		+			+
8	+	+	8	+			+	+	8			+	+	+
9	+	+	9	+			+	+	9			+		+
10	+	+	10	+			+	+	10			+		+

Fig. 1. Two-Factor, Group-Factor and Multiple-Factor Analyses

through all the tests. Each covers a different, though often overlapping, set of tests. Thus the content of some tests can be ascribed to one factor only, while others show significant loadings on two or even three factors. Note that the blank entries in the diagram are not usually zero loadings, but are so small that they can be attributed to chance. In a group-factor analysis, however, every test has a general factor loading and a loading on one (or occasionally more than one) group factor. In each type of analysis, every test shows its own specific factor.

Alexander's Investigation. Apparently the first application of Thurstone's method to abilities was that of Alexander (1935), who gave large batteries of verbal and non-verbal intelligence tests and certain performance tests to groups of about one hundred Scottish primary school boys and girls (11–12 years), American secondary and technical school pupils (16–17), and adult women in a delinquent institution. For the technical school group he also had school examination marks. Actually the multiple factors that he obtained conformed quite closely to a group factor pattern. Thus in addition to g, there was a v factor in the verbal tests, and some of the more complex and constructive performance tests gave a practical group factor, which he called F. It was on the basis of these results that Alexander developed his performance test scale, consisting of Cube Construction, Kohs Blocks and Passalong, for measuring 'concrete' or practical ability. Another important finding in the third group was that the measures of school attainment showed a separate group factor of their own, thus confirming Burt's results, mentioned above. He called this factor X, and identified it, very plausibly, with the influence of personality and interests, i.e. with something in the nature of industriousness which affects all school work.[1]

Thurstone's Primary Mental Abilities. In 1938 Thurstone published the first of his long series of investigations of human abilities, namely an analysis of fifty-six tests given to 240 college students. This seemed to reveal a complete break with Spearman, since there was no g at all, but—much as in the personality field—a series of distinct multiple factors. The eight main or primary factors were identified as:

V Verbal P Perceptual Speed I Inductive Reasoning
N Number M Rote Memory D Deductive Reasoning
    W Word Fluency S Space or Visualization

Note that American multiple factors are usually assigned capital letters, while British g and group factors receive small letters. Though their content and derivation are very different, the status of these primary factors is closely similar to that of nineteenth-century faculties, against which Spearman had battled

---

[1] Numerous previous writers had, of course, interpreted discrepancies between I.Q. and E.Q. as due to emotional influences. In effect the X factor is much the same as the A.Q.—the accomplishment or achievement quotient. Alexander claimed yet another factor, Z, of doubtful reliability, which has since been identified by Yela (1949), after re-analysis, with Thurstone's or Meili's perceptual synthesis factors (cf. pp. 58, 89).

for over thirty years. Spearman (1939) was quick to point out that, as all Thurstone's tests were positively inter-correlated, they could equally well be analysed to yield a large general factor and smaller group factors. Such alternative analyses of Thurstone's figures were, in fact, carried out by Holzinger and Harman (1938) and Eysenck (1939). The latter's g obtained a variance of $30 \cdot 8$ per cent., and the combined group factors $23 \cdot 5$ per cent. The content of the group factors corresponded quite closely to that of Thurstone's primary factors, just as in Fig. 1/3 the multiple factors A, B and C cover much the same tests as the group factors of Fig. 1/2. Although Thurstone's solution of the factors underlying the tests is as legitimate mathematically as a general $+$ group factor solution, he has not disproved the existence of a g. In effect he has divided it up among his seven group factors. The arguments for and against these alternatives (which are much less irreconcilable than might appear at first sight) are examined in the Appendix.

Subsequent American Work. Almost all factorial psychologists in America[1] have followed Thurstone's lead, and their results, like his, can readily be fitted into the picture of mental structure advocated in this book. With their vastly greater resources for applying huge batteries of tests to large groups, and for doing most of the donkey-work of calculation by machine, it is natural that they should be responsible for most of the advances of recent years in this field.

Thurstone, aided by his wife and students, have greatly extended the above investigation. Several of the primary factors have been studied in more detail, by analysing the original tests for a factor along with others which helped to define it more accurately, or showed how it could be sub-divided. And comprehensive batteries, similar to the original one, have been given to high-school and younger pupils, even to 5–6 year olds. The results at different ages have been remarkably concordant. Thus the first six factors in the above list were clearly identified when sixty tests were analysed among 710 pupils aged around 14 years (Thurstone, L. L. and T. G., 1941), though Deduction disappeared and Induction seemed to be better named R (Reasoning). P was also somewhat unstable, and has been omitted from the battery of

[1] With the exception of Holzinger, and R. B. Cattell, the latter a pupil of Spearman.

Primary Mental Abilities tests issued for measuring these factors. One noteworthy difference, however, is that the primary factors among children tend to be less independent. Since they correlate with one another moderately highly, they themselves can be analysed in the same way as tests are analysed, and they usually reveal a kind of super-factor, or what Thurstone calls a second-order general factor.[1] Though he does not go so far as to identify this with g, he admits that it constitutes a bridge between his own and Spearman's viewpoints. He now describes primary factors as 'facilities' in the mind, or 'media of expression', and regards second-order factors (of which g may be one) as more central (Thurstone, L. L., 1948). This theory is strongly reminiscent of Spearman's general energy and specific engines.

The U.S.E.S. Investigations. In 1945 there appeared the first report on large-scale researches by the United States Employment Service, Division of Occupational Analysis, into the development of a set of differential aptitude tests (cf. Staff, Division of Occupational Analysis, 1945). Various batteries of about twenty tests (fifty-nine in all) were given to nine fairly large and representative groups of adult applicants for employment, totalling 2,156 persons. On analysis, the most stable or consistent factors, which recurred in most of the groups were:

V Verbal	P Perceptual	T Motor Speed
N Number	Q Clerical	F Finger Dexterity
S Space	L Logic	M Manual Dexterity
	A Aiming	

also a general factor.

The best tests for measuring each factor have been issued as a battery, lasting about three hours, and from a testee's profile or pattern of factor scores, it is hoped to predict the type of occupation for which his aptitudes fit him (Dvorak, 1947).

Factorial Studies in the U.S.A.A.F. During the 1939–45 war, large-scale testing of recruits occurred in Britain and America, and factor analyses were often carried out on populations of a thousand or more. Particularly extensive use of the technique was made by Guilford and his collaborators in the U.S. Army Air Force (Guilford 1948ab, Guilford and Lacey 1947, Davis 1947, Melton 1947). Studies of the job of the pilot and of other air-crew personnel

---

[1] The mathematics of oblique (i.e. correlated) factors are clearly described in the later editions of Thomson's textbook (first published 1939).

suggested what abilities might be worth testing. Elaborate and extremely ingenious tests for measuring each of these were devised, and factorization was applied to discover which were consistent and distinctive. By this means pilot aptitude itself was largely broken down into factors objectively definable by appropriate test batteries, instead of into subjectively determined qualities. More then twenty factors are claimed :

Carefulness

Integration I, II and III

Length Estimation

Memory I, II and III

Mathematical Interest and Training

Mechanical Information

Perceptual Speed

Pilot Interest

Planning Ability

Psychomotor Co-ordination

Psychomotor Precision

Psychomotor Speed

Reasoning I, II and III

Spatial Relations I, II and III

Social Science Interest and Training

Verbal

Visualization

Factorial Studies in the British Services: Hierarchical Group Factor Theory. In this country, where most work was done on less selected samples of the population such as Navy and Army conscript recruits, the importance of *g* was amply confirmed (Vernon, 1947a). In eight analyses, *g* was found to cover more than twice as much variance as all group factors combined. Table V shows an analysis of thirteen tests given to 1,000 Army recruits,

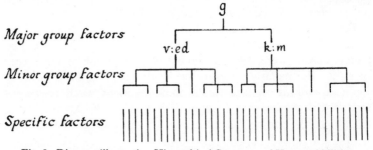

Fig. 2. Diagram illustrating Hierarchical Structure of Human Abilities

and brings out a feature which appears to be highly characteristic of mental structure, namely hierarchy. After the removal of g, tests tend to fall into two main groups: the verbal-numerical-educational on the one hand (referred to as $v{:}ed$ factor), and the practical-mechanical-spatial-physical on the other hand (referred to as $k{:}m$ factor). If the analysis is sufficiently detailed, i.e. if sufficient tests are included, these types themselves sub-divide. The $v{:}ed$ factor in Table V gives minor v and n (number) group factors. In other analyses (e.g. Table IX), $k{:}m$ splits similarly into mechanical information, spatial, and manual subfactors. Thus a first approximation to mental structure is provided by the hierarchical diagram of Fig. 2, resembling a genealogical tree. Its advantages and limitations form the subject of the next chapter.

TABLE V. SIMPLE SUMMATION AND GROUP FACTOR ANALYSES OF TESTS GIVEN TO 1,000 ARMY RECRUITS

Tests	Unrotated Centroid Factors					Group Factors					
	I	II	III	IV	h²	g	k:m	ed.	v	n	h²
0 Progressive Matrices	·77	+·23	+·10	—·16	·68	·79	·17				·65
Dominoes (non-verbal)	·80	+·09	+·19	—·12	·70	·87					·75
Group Test 70, Pt. I	·74	+·16	+·03	—·08	·58	·78	·13				·62
4 Squares	·63	+·35	—·00	+·01	·52	·59	·44				·54
8 Assembly	·37	+·54	—·15	+·28	·52	·24	·89				·85
2 Bennett Mechanical	·69	+·33	—·17	+·07	·62	·66	·31				·54
25 Verbal	·88	—·24	—·26	—·14	·92	·79		·29	·45		·90
Dictation	·79	—·42	—·25	—·11	·88	·62		·54	·48		·90
14 A.T.S. Spelling	·81	—·32	—·20	—·11	·80	·68		·41	·43		·82
21 Instructions	·89	—·06	+·11	—·15	·82	·87		·23	·09		·82
3A Arithmetic, Pt. I	·84	—·29	+·22	+·23	·89	·72		·49		·39	·91
Arithmetic, Pt. II	·86	—·16	+·12	+·13	·80	·80		·38		·16	·82
23 A.T.S. Arithmetic	·84	—·21	+·26	+·14	·84	·77		·36		·32	·82
Variance per cent.	59·8	8·5	3·1	2·2	73·5	52.5	8·7	8·4	6·9		76·5

The Relations Between Group-Factor and Multiple-Factor Analyses.

Table V also serves to illustrate some of the resem-

c

blances and differences of centroid and group-factor analyses. In a centroid analysis the first factor represents the highest common element in all the tests. It is not usually the same as g, but is a kind of average of the particular tests applied in the investigation. Subsequent factors, II, III and IV, are known as *bipolar*, since roughly half the tests receive positive, half negative, signs. These successively divide the tests into contrasted groups, and although they may have no psychological meaning as they stand, yet they do usually reveal what group factors are present. Often this classification by bipolar factors tells us all we need to know, and in several examples in subsequent chapters the original, or *unrotated*, centroid factors alone are quoted. But it is preferable to transform the first and the bipolar factors into a series of factors where all the tests have either positive loadings, or zero or insignificant negative loadings, by means of what is called *rotation of axes*. This of course redistributes much of the variance of the first factor among the remaining ones. Actually the aim of rotation is to maximize the number of zero or insignificant loadings on each factor, so that as much as possible of the variance of each test is confined to a single factor. Thurstone calls this *Simple Structure*. Often such rotation does yield a general factor running through most or all of the tests, and smaller factors each confined to a few tests, in other words a group-factor pattern. But true group-factor analysis is carried out by assessing g-loadings first, and then analysing the residual correlations in each group of tests, as in Tables I–IV. A clear and much fuller account of these different types of analysis, and their inter-convertibility, is given by Burt (1944; cf. also 1938, 1939a, 1940a, 1949).

Other Methods of Analysis. This historical résumé must not omit to mention, however briefly, certain other approaches to factor analysis which have been less widely applied than general or group factor, and simple summation or centroid, methods. Broadly speaking they are more accurate mathematically, but do not provide appreciably more psychological information about the make-up of the analysed tests, which would compensate for their much greater complexity and tediousness of calculation. They include Burt's Weighted Summation, Lawley's Maximum Likelihood, Hotelling's Principal Components, and Kelley's Principal Axes, methods. Explanations may be found in Thomson's and Burt's textbooks.

CHAPTER III

HIERARCHICAL GROUP-FACTOR THEORY OF THE STRUCTURE OF ABILITIES

Abstract. The strict hierarchical picture of mental structure is an over-simplification. For the results of any factor analysis depend largely on the composition of the population tested (e.g. its degree of selection), and on the number and kind of tests studied. Since by choosing suitable tests almost any specific factor can be turned into a group factor, it is suggested that only those group factors shown to have significant practical value in daily life are worth incorporating in the picture. It is doubtful whether group factors differentiate merely as a result of ageing or mental growth. Rather, their pattern or structure changes according to the type of education and training. Thomson's theory of bonds gives a useful explanation of *g* and of ability group factors, but the influence of temperament and personality, physique, sex, age, interests, etc. should be taken into account. The fallacies of the layman's conception of theoretical *vs.* practical, and other opposed types of abilities are discussed.

The Hierarchical Diagram Should be Regarded Only as an Approximation. The hierarchical theory which was outlined at the end of the preceding chapter, was first put forward by Burt, under the influence of McDougall. In a recent article (1949) Burt describes how it originated, and shows that it applies in the fields of temperament and of anthropometric measurements, as well as to abilities. Though it is certainly an improvement both on the original two-factor theory and on the 'neo-faculty' theory of American writers, it has numerous limitations and implications which we must now discuss. The more technical arguments for preferring it to the American viewpoint are given in the Appendix.

A diagram such as Fig. 2 would be obtained only if an extensive battery of tests, covering—or at least sampling—most of the varieties of human abilities, could be applied to a very large and representative sample of the population. With one or two hundred testees the correlations are usually too unreliable for more than two to four group factors to be established at a time. In general a minimum of three tests is needed to define a factor, hence only a few factors can be resolved in any one investigation with a limited battery of tests. Further, if such a battery consists only, or predominantly, of a specialized type of test (e.g. all tests of sensory-motor abilities), the g and major group factors may fail to reveal themselves. The diagram is, in other words, a hypothetical integration of all the factorial investigations that have been carried out, rather than an established fact. It is considerably expanded, and corrected, in Figs. 3, 4, 5 and 7.

Broad and Narrow Group Factors. Nevertheless there is ample evidence to support the view that group factors are almost infinitely subdivisible, depending only on the degree of detail to which the analysis is carried. Indeed, by including sufficiently similar tests, any specific factor (in Spearman's sense) can become a group factor. The only truly specific element is the unreliability or error variance of the test. Thus in a complete factorial investigation the communality of each test should approximate to its reliability coefficient. It is even possible, when analysing specialized tests, for a specific factor to become a general one. For example, a reaction time test analysed in a battery of paper-and-pencil mental tests might obtain a g and major group factor variance of about 10 per cent., specificity 90 per cent. On including two other kinds of reaction time, a small group factor would appear, while in a battery consisting only of such tests, a general reaction time factor with 30 per cent. or higher variance might be found; and we should be unaware that this was composed partly of 'higher' factors such as g and $k{:}m$. Thus there is no absolute distinction between general and specific factors as Spearman believed.

An important problem, as yet unsolved, is how broad a group factor should be before it is accepted as a useful element in our picture of mental structure. Some of the primary factors of Thurstone, Guilford and others—rote memory, for example—are so narrow in content that it may be more harmful than helpful to name them. It is unlikely that the rote memory tests which make up Thurstone's M factor have any predictive value for the rote memory in which teachers are interested (cf. Carroll, 1943; Wittenborn and Larsen, 1944). Only if it were possible to establish a common factor (over and above g and $v{:}ed$) in rote memory tests and in the learning of spellings, multiplication tables and poetry, would the notion of a rote memory group factor be acceptable. The same stricture holds for most of the manual dexterity, sensory-motor, and co-ordination factors that have so far been proposed. At the present moment the writer cannot think of any objective basis for distinguishing between acceptable group factors, and narrow factors confined to the highly specialized types of test which psychologists delight in constructing. But he would suggest that factors which fail to contribute at least 5 per cent. to the variance of some measure of educational or occupational proficiency or other capacity in daily life should be relegated to the latter category. If, for example, g and v tests alone predict the ability to learn and retain poetry to the extent of a correlation of ·60 (i.e. a variance of 36 per cent.), then the addition of tests of rote memory to the predictive battery should raise the correlation to at least ·64 (variance 41 per cent.) if the factor measured by these tests is to be acceptable.[1] Such a criterion involves subjective judgment as to what constitutes a 'capacity in daily life', and is beset with many difficulties. But it appears preferable to a judgment of the broadness *vs.* narrowness of the tests which yield a distinctive factor.

Relative Importance of Factors at Different Levels. The hierarchical group-factor viewpoint implies that most of the variance of human abilities in daily life is attributable to g and to highly specific (or very small group) factors, and that the role of the broader group factors is rather meagre. If our diagram could be worked out completely to cover all human abilities, the g-variance might amount to about 40 per cent., the major and minor

---

[1] This suggestion recalls Thomson's (1939) argument that factor analysis is of little use in vocational or educational psychology, because the predictive value of tests can be established much more efficiently by multiple correlation technique. The writer would agree that the content of a test as determined by factor analysis at the present time often fails to reveal its true predictive value, because the test's specificity may embody other group factors which are particularly relevant or irrelevant to some job. For example a test of graph-reading is very useful in selecting radar operators, but when analysed it usually appears to consist purely of $g + n +$ specificity. More detailed analysis would however break down part of the specificity into a minor group factor for graph-reading, i.e. a sub-division of n. This is the line that Guilford and Lacey followed in the U.S.A.A.F. After considerable experience of multiple correlation, the writer has come to the conclusion (Vernon and Parry, 1949) that it is much too efficient. It does not, like the factorial approach suggested in this note, sufficiently allow for the chance errors in the validity coefficients of selection tests, and prohibits the inclusion of two or more rather similar tests in order to improve the reliability of prediction.

group factors to some 10 per cent. each, and the remaining 40 per cent. would consist of very narrow group factors and unreliability. This means that, fairly good predictions of ability in education, industry, or everyday life, can be achieved by g tests alone, and that somewhat more ground can be covered by tests of the main group factors. But only by much more detailed experimentation on tests relevant to particular jobs, or by work-sample methods (i.e. trying candidates out on the actual work), can much more than 50 per cent. accuracy be obtained. This explains why Stanford-Binet or Terman-Merrill I.Q., or all-round intelligence as measured by reliable group tests, have considerable practical value both among children and adults, whereas more specialized tests add something but not very much in educational and vocational guidance.

Effects of Range of Ability and Selection on Factor Patterns. However, these quantitative estimates of the importance of different 'levels' of factors are dangerous, since so much depends on the degree of heterogeneity of the people concerned. When the same tests which, among unselected recruits, gave g and group-factor variances of 50 per cent. and 20–25 per cent., respectively, were analysed among high-grade mechanics or officer candidates, g often fell to 15 per cent. and group factors rose to 35 per cent. Similarly it has often been observed that the g and $k{:}m$ content of manual dexterity tests sinks almost to zero among such selected groups as technical school pupils or college students; such tests no longer correlate at all with paper-and-pencil tests of mental abilities. Since the people receiving any special type of education (e.g. grammar school or university), and those engaged in any one job, almost always constitute a strongly selected group, there is usually more scope for tests of major and minor group factors and less for g tests, than the preceding paragraph suggests. (The relatively unpredictable portion is however generally larger among such groups.) It also follows from Thomson's (1939) demonstration of the effects of selection on factors that not only the general degree but also the type of selection is important. For example, if a battery of mechanical and other tests is applied to a group of men with engineering background, and to another group with the same range of g but without experience, the factor patterns are liable to differ (cf. Chapter X). This accounts for many of the discrepancies between the results of different investigators, and makes it extremely difficult to fill out the details of our diagram accurately. We cannot expect to reach a final and complete map of the structure of abilities, since it necessarily varies with the kind of population studied.

Differentiation of Specialized Abilities with Age. The relative prominence of *g* has often been thought to depend considerably on age. The writer at one time accepted the view that *g* tends to differentiate into more specialized abilities during adolescence and early adulthood. This view is advocated by Garrett (1946), who summarizes several confirmatory investigations. But most of these compare college with high school, or high school with elementary school, populations, hence the smaller *g*-variance in the older groups may be due merely to their greater selectivity.

Clark (1944) did choose groups of eleven-, thirteen- and fifteen-year pupils with the same distribution of group test I.Q.s, and found a decline in the average inter-correlation of the Primary Mental Abilities tests from ·488 to ·393. Other studies such as those of Swineford (1947), Reichard (1944) and Doppelt (1949) fail to support the theory. Anastasi (1936) summarizes a large number of investigations and shows that, though there are strong indications of alterations in factor patterns with age and training, the evidence for differentiation is far from unanimous. McNemar (1942b) carried out fourteen factorizations of Terman-Merrill scale items at mental age levels ranging from 2 years to 18 years. His results are irregular and show no sign of any consistent trend towards greater differentiation at later ages. This might be criticized on the grounds that the later items are less diverse in content than those for young children. However Balinsky (1941) factorized an identical battery of tests, namely the Wechsler-Bellevue scale, among groups aged 9, 12, 15, 25–9, 35–44 and 50–59, all with average I.Q. 100. He obtained the following first factor variances: 38, 36, 24, 20, 33 and 45. These suggest differentiation from 9 to 30 and then greater integration. But he neglected to ensure the same degree of heterogeneity among the testees at all ages, and when correction is made for this, his first factor variances show much the same irregularity and lack of any clear trend as McNemar's.[1]

---

[1] It is difficult to see how a crucial investigation of this problem could be planned even if strictly random samples could be tested at several age levels. For as Emmett (1949) points out, the content of the tests should be equally

Particularly striking are Williams's (1948) results from the application of the same battery of ten intelligence, spatial and mechanical tests to samples of 250 boys, carefully chosen to be representative, at the ages of 12, 13 and 14. Here the first factor variances were 51, 56 and 62 per cent., respectively, indicating that secondary education tends to produce greater integration, not specialization, of verbal and practical abilities. In a research by the writer the standard British naval battery of five tests was given to 1,171 boys leaving school at 14, and the results were compared with those of 265 seamen recruits who had also left at 14 in the same district some four years previously. Scores tended to rise with age on the spatial and mechanical tests, and to drop on the arithmetical ones (cf. Vernon and Parry, 1949), but the average inter-correlation and g-saturations were almost identical. The only significant change was a drop in the correlation of mechanical arithmetic with mathematics (from ·642 to ·379). The correlation of k:m tests with these educational tests were slightly lower, but with a verbal reasoning test (mainly a measure of g) they were slightly higher. Similarly, two parallel groups of about 240 naval artificer apprentices aged 15+ and 18+ took nine varied tests, and most of the correlations were slightly higher in the older group, although the nature of the group factors altered considerably (cf. p. 116).

Another approach to this problem was to calculate tetrachoric inter-correlations among ten tests, first by contrasting the top 25 per cent. of a group of 993 Army recruits with the bottom 75 per cent., secondly contrasting the top 75 per cent. with the bottom 25 per cent. If abilities are more differentiated among the more able and intellectually mature, the former correlations should be lower than the latter, but actually the reverse occurred. Many more men were very high on all tests than were very low on all tests, and the first factor variances were 75·6 and 66·3 per cent., respectively.

From these and other bits of evidence the writer would conclude that there is no general tendency towards differentiation, except perhaps in early infancy, and that everything depends on the type of educational and vocational training. Usually when abilities are

appropriate at all ages, otherwise reliability is affected, and with it the first factor variance. This condition may have disturbed both Williams's and the writer's results reported in the next paragraph.

practised at school or in jobs they tend to become more specialized, though sometimes the teaching is of such a nature as to increase integration. Again regression or de-differentiation may often occur as the effects of past training wear off. It is conceivable that secondary schooling is more fragmentary in America than in Britain, and so apt to produce more differentiation between 12 and 18 than is usual here. But undoubtedly the main reason for the apparent reduction in the importance of g in adults is that the testees are more homogeneous in ability.

It is because the majority of American investigations are conducted with college students, aircraft pilots, high-school pupils and other selected groups, that their results so readily fall into independent primary factors, instead of g and group factors. But when more heterogeneous adult groups have been studied, a g has usually appeared. Thus Anastasi (1948) quotes American Army studies which showed almost as high correlations between verbal, numerical, spatial and mechanical tests as between different numerical, or different mechanical tests. An analysis of the U.S. Navy battery gave a g with variance of over 30 per cent., together with smaller mechanical, spatial and educational group factors (Staff, Test and Research Section, 1945). The emergence of a g in the Division of Occupational Analysis's investigations has already been mentioned.

Psychological Nature of Factors. We must next consider the nature of g and the group factors a little more closely. Thomson has shown that the statistical fact that test inter-correlations can be largely accounted for by a single factor does not prove that such a factor represents any unitary power, or organ of the mind. It might also arise if the mind is thought to consist of an immense number of 'bonds', including inherited reflexes, acquired habits and associations, etc. A person's performance at any one test would involve the activation of a large number of such bonds, and if a miscellaneous set of tests is given, the extensive sampling of bonds would result in the positive correlations that actually tend to occur. But he agrees that factors are useful concepts for describing the content of the various kinds of samples that may be taken, provided that they are not reified into organs or faculties. In this book we accept Thomson's view, and hold that factors over and above g arise, partly perhaps from hereditary influences, but mainly because an individual's upbringing and education imposes a certain grouping on his bonds. The *v:ed* factor is, as we shall see, a rather strongly unified group because our society gives a fairly uniform education to all its members. It does not readily break down into separate verbal, number, speed, reasoning, attention, memory or other factors because the abilities covered by these names tend to be developed differently in different schools and homes, though partially distinct minor group factors can often be established, especially in fairly homogeneous groups such as university arts students. On the practical or *k:m* side there is, as Anastasi points out, less cultural standardization, hence the *k:m* pole is more heterogeneous and amorphous than *v:ed*. It would appear to be not so much a positive practical ability as an aggregate of all non-symbolic capacities, or of bonds that are not usually affected by primary schooling. Nevertheless, evidence is given below that not only mechanical and spatial, but physical and manual, and some non-verbal *g*, perceptual and performance tests all have something in common over and above *g*. The kind of test which is most strongly saturated with this factor is the mechanical assembly test, presumably because this epitomizes, as it were, non-scholastic activities. A rather significant point is that boys and men (at least in Western European civilization) tend to surpass girls and women on most aspects of *k:m*, whereas females tend to be superior in the linguistic aspects of *v:ed*. Though this might be attributable to cultural norms, it suggests the operation of hereditary influences. Thus it cannot be due to upbringing that girl babies usually start to talk earlier, or that boys and men have on the average greater physical size and strength.

Modifications of the Hierarchical Picture. It follows that there is no need to regard the hierarchical or genealogical principle as pre-eminent. Minor group factors are not always 'descendants' of *either* v:ed *or* k:m. And we shall see later that several factors cut across this dichotomous grouping, scientific ability, for example. Probably also there are other group factors which split off from *g* but are not subdivisions of either type. Auditory and musical abilities seem to constitute one such cluster, and others are mentioned in Chap. VIII. It is merely because *v:ed* and *k:m* have the widest practical importance, and have received most investigation, that they alone are listed in Fig. 2.

Temperamental and Other Influences. In yet another respect the diagram over-simplifies matters. It does not allow for

personality, physique and other factors which have complex inter-
actions with ability factors. Physique and physical health constitute an important dimension (or set of dimensions) which certainly affects practical abilities; and physical defects of the senses
in particular react on educational attainments. Sex influences not
only $v:ed-k:m$, but also most of the lower-order group factors, such
as manual, imagery, etc. (Burt and Moore, 1912). Age is important
in spite of the conclusions reached above. Thus among adults the
spatial, manual and physical aspects of $k:m$ tend to decline, whereas
specialized mechanical skills and information probably go on increasing almost to senility (cf. also deterioration, p. 57). Cattell
(1946) has pointed out that g is somehow associated with such personality traits as conscientiousness and with cultured interests.
Terman's work on gifted children, and studies of mental defec-
tives, confirm this. Apparently therefore the bonds established by
character training, and by the development of sentiments and
attitudes are linked with the bonds responsible for our cognitive
or intellectual activities. Doubtless interests greatly affect our
more specialized abilities. It is known also that the fluency factor,
measured by tests of richness of association with words or pictures,
is connected with extraverted or cycloid trends, and that such
physical or manual capacities as visual acuity, dark adaptation,
agility, and finger dexterities are impaired among neurotics (Slater
and Slater, 1944; Eysenck, 1947). Again Eysenck finds speed *vs.*
accuracy in mental and manual operations to differ among hysteric
and dysthymic (anxiety or obsessional) neurotics.

Clearly then we are very far from a complete theory of the
structure and nature of human abilities, and though it is useful to
analyse them in isolation as though they were purely cognitive or
motor, we should not forget that they are abstractions from the
total personality structure.

Conclusions Regarding g. Finally it may be seen from
Thomson's theory that g is not a fixed, purely inherited, quantity.
Thomson interprets it as the total number of bonds. Presumably
this is largely dependent on some psycho-physiological and innate
property of the higher nervous system, but there is no reason why
the number should not be affected by the use made of the mind,
and by organic conditions such as brain injury and ageing. This
fits in with modern research on the highly individual nature of
mental growth (cf. Dearborn and Rothney, 1941; Fleming, 1948),

on the effects of schooling and the intellectual stimulus provided by people's jobs (cf. Vernon and Parry, 1949), and on deterioration of mental efficiency in pathological conditions.

Compensation Theories. We have considered the relation of the hierarchical theory to Spearman's and Thurstone's views. How does it stand *vis-à-vis* the popular notion of compensation, and of opposed *types* of people? Actually it admits a large measure of truth in the contrast between the theoretical or academic and the practical, since they roughly describe our two major group factors. But these abilities are not inversely correlated, i.e. opposed, and they are independent only when the influence of g is ignored. Thus in fact the majority of children who are superior educationally are also above average in mechanical ability, in doing things with their hands, and even in physique, because of the common influence of g. The Norwood Report's separation of academic and practical-technical types of children is unsound for several reasons, but chiefly because the child with high g who is likely to do well at a grammar school would also do well at a technical school (cf. Burt, 1943). So far, however, we have been talking about average tendencies; and as correlations between intelligence, educational, practical and physical tests are far from perfect, they admit of many exceptional individual cases. Thus there is a proportion of children who are suited to grammar school education not because their g is very high, but because of strong $v{:}ed$ factor, and such cases may well be poor in $k{:}m$ factor, and therefore unsuited to technical education. There are many cases too who are exceptionally well-developed physically, or good at athletics or at certain manual skills, whose $g + v{:}ed$ are low, who therefore conform to the layman's stereotype. But it is none the less true that such cases are much rarer than those who are above average, or below average, all round.

There are several reasons why the compensation theory gains such wide credence. First, whenever g-saturations or correlations with educational attainment are low, bright or dull children will tend to be nearer the average in non-educational activities. The child who is very high in intelligence and school work will usually be less high in manual, practical or artistic work, and the scholastically dull pupil will on the average be less retarded in non-scholastic fields. This can readily be deduced by studying the scatter for a low correlation (cf. Vernon, 1940, p. 154).

Secondly, the groups with which we are most familiar above the age of 11+ are selected ones, and as already pointed out this reduces the g-loadings and exaggerates the group factors. Hence it is quite conceivable that in a grammar school there may be an inverse, or at least a negligible, correlation between, say, mathematical attainment and football. But if we could study the whole range of 15-year pupils we should find that grammar school pupils are usually superior to secondary modern pupils not only in mathematics, but also at football.

Thirdly, we are concerned here only with abilities, not with interests. The latter probably show much stronger contrasts than the former. Thus the adolescent with keen interests in reading or other v:ed activities is frequently (perhaps more often than not) weakly interested in mechanical or athletic activities, and it may be that he devotes so little time to them that his potentially superior ability at such activities deteriorates. Nevertheless, the university professor with his high g can usually, if put to it, do better at things in which he is not much interested such as cooking a dinner and washing up without breaking the crockery, than can a low-g domestic servant. And it is by no means fanciful to suggest that the victories of the Jews in Palestine in 1948 over the Arabs (who tend to be more bellicose in interests) was largely due to their superior g and v:ed.

'Slow but sure' is another popular compensation theory, which likewise ignores the influence of g and other factors that tend to make the quick worker more rather than less accurate. However, it is considered in more detail in Chapter VII, and is shown there to possess a modicum of truth.

The notion of types of people, as distinct from types of ability, should also be discouraged. As Burt (1943) points out, there is no more justification for talking of an academic or practical type of child than for a tall or a short type. Just as the majority are intermediate in height, so there are many more who are about equally able in educational and practical activities than there are extreme cases. Ability types themselves are abstractions, since many abilities when factorized will be found to be loaded on two or more group factors, i.e. to be intermediate. But the grouping is more clear-cut than in the case of individuals, because it is often imposed by school syllabuses and other cultural institutions or norms.

Note that our insistence on g does not involve any denial of special talents in individual cases. Apart from such rarities as idiots savants, there certainly exist children and adults of mediocre g and educational attainment who develop outstanding talents in the fields of art or scientific invention, or become leaders in business, politics, warfare, etc. Such talents can to some extent be attributed to the possession of strong group factors, but personality influences, drives and interests are probably still more important. The analysis and measurement of such influences by psychologists is far less advanced than that of abilities. Thus the warning given at the end of Chapter I against regarding factors as covering the whole psychology of human achievements should be reiterated.

CHAPTER IV

ANALYSES OF EDUCATIONAL ATTAINMENTS

Abstract. School marks yield a different structure from objective psychological tests because of the X-factor—a complex of personality traits, interests and background. This, together with g and $v:ed$ form the major influence in all educational attainments in unselected groups of children and adults, though differentiation according to subject-matter can readily be established in selected secondary school pupils or university students. The more drilled and mechanical aspects of v (verbal) and n (number) abilities differentiate most clearly, but there is insufficient evidence to justify contrasting 'rote' with 'reasoning' attainments. Many *a priori* classifications of types of reading and number ability lack empirical substantiation. For example word-knowledge (vocabulary) and comprehension in reading come to much the same thing. However, mechanical, rate, vocabulary and comprehension aspects are partially distinguishable at advanced levels.

The Industriousness Factor in School Marks. The psychologist's v, n and other factors are usually based on tests which are fairly pure measures of the abilities at which they are aimed. A good vocabulary test, for example, should measure g, v, a small error component and very little else. Educational attainments, especially when measured by school or other examinations are naturally more complex, and we have already seen that a somewhat ill-defined factor of industriousness $+$ interest, which Alexander calls X, plays a prominent part. Similar factors, variously called interest, study, or 'halo' have been reported in American investigations by Holzinger and Swineford (1939), Sisk (1940), Carroll (1943) and Comrey (1949). Because of this, selection for secondary or other higher education by means of g, v, n or other psychological tests alone is usually less successful than selection which also takes account of previous school work (cf. McClelland, 1942). At one time some psychologists did propose that children most likely to benefit from advanced schooling would be those with the highest innate intelligence, rather than with the best attainments, but we realize now that this was short-sighted.

Although interesting attempts have been made to measure or assess personality factors relevant to scholastic success, it is doubtful whether any are practically applicable on a large scale. When teachers' judgments are studied, some are found to give excellent predictions, but others are less competent than objective ability tests. The overall result (if we may accept McClelland's findings) is that such judgments add nothing worthwhile to estimates based on tests *plus* school marks, since anything of value which the average teacher knows about the industry, etc., of his or her pupils is already embodied in the marks. At the moment, therefore, we know little about X, though further research would certainly be profitable. In particular we would like to know how far it depends on:

(a) home background; (b) the 'tone' of the pupil's school; (c) the stimulatingness of, or good teaching by, his teacher; (d) the pupil's interests; (e) his temperamental characteristics.

Overlap of School Examinations and Psychological Tests. That psychological tests and school marks often measure rather different things is shown not only by the imperfections of objective tests in picking good and poor scholars, and by Alexander's work, but by such investigations as the following. Bradford (1946) presents data for 105 technical school boys on five varied subjects and nine paper-and-pencil or performance tests. There is a general factor with 24 per cent. variance and a bipolar with 16 per cent. separating all the school marks from all the tests. Another bipolar, distinguishing the more technical subjects and performance tests from the more linguistic subjects and tests has a variance of only 4 per cent. Drew's results (cf. p. 111) are similar. Blackwell (1940) compared mathematical achievements of 100 secondary school boys and 100 girls with scores on spatial and verbal tests specially designed to measure the reasoning processes believed to be involved in mathematics. By rotation of axes she arrived at factors in which all types of measure are represented, but a study of her unrotated factors suggests that here, too, the mathematical marks, the spatial and the verbal tests, fall into relatively distinct clusters. However, it is probable that the contrast is most marked in highly selected groups. For in a research by Kerr (1942) with 527 relatively heterogeneous twelve-year pupils, five school subjects and four tests yielded no such factor as Alexander's or Bradford's. Instead a clerical test fell in a cluster with English and Language marks, and an intelligence test in the Maths-Science cluster. Art marks and spatial-mechanical tests provided additional group factors of their own. Comrey (1949) also reports complex overlapping between test factors and courses of study among West Point cadets. It should be noted that only when results such as these are obtained is differential diagnosis, i.e. the prediction of suitability for different types of school course, possible.

Unitariness of *v:ed*. We would expect attainment measures to correlate highly with one another because of their common g and X content. But there seems to be a common *v:ed* ability in addition, since the isolation of distinctive sub-factors for different subjects is remarkably difficult among representative groups of adults and children. For example in the investigation of Army recruits in Table V, the correlation between spelling and dictation tests was no higher than the correlation of either with the verbal ability Test 25. (Descriptions of this and other tests used in the Services may be found in Vernon, 1947b, or Vernon and Parry, 1949.) Apparently spelling ability is little if at all differentiated among average adults from the fluency + vocabulary ability on which this test probably depends, although according to Thurstone (1948) spelling is a highly distinctive factor among college adults. Though verbal and numerical abilities are usually separable, as in Burt's original research and in Table V, they tend to show a good deal of overlap, over and above g. Thus in Schiller's (1934) investigation of twelve tests among 395 pupils aged around nine years, the correlation between Arithmetic Reasoning and Computation was no higher than the correlations of both tests with four reading tests and tests of verbal g.

Sub-divisions of *v:ed*. *V:ed* breaks down more readily into specialized abilities in populations that are more homogeneous in educational level, such as technical schoolboys or college students. Kerr's (1942) research, already mentioned, gave a factor differentiating linguistic from mathematical-scientific subjects, though its variance was far smaller than that of the general factor. Again Wilson (1933) analysed three sets of School Certificate marks and found, in addition to a general factor (presumably a mixture of $g + X + v:ed$), group factors for Arithmetic-Algebra-Geometry, for French-English and History-English, for Art-Needlework and

D

Art-Handicraft. The mean general and group factor loadings both approximated to ·53, i.e. about 28 per cent. variance.

It might be supposed that group factors tend to become more prominent relative to general educational ability with older pupils. Yet Wolf (1939), when trying to develop aptitude tests for different types of courses at Yale University, found almost as high correlations (averaging ·45) between first-year examinations in arts and science subjects as between different arts or different science subjects (average ·59). Among postgraduate student teachers Vernon (1939) still found the general educational component predominant. His correlations can be most simply analysed into a *v:ed* factor with 26 per cent. variance, and separate group factors for science subjects—Psychology, Arithmetic, Hygiene, Nature Study—and practical subjects—Speech Training, Teaching Skill, Physical Training—with combined variance 12 per cent. The remaining subjects—Education, Geography, English and History, depended entirely on the general factor. Among Army engineering cadets, nine tests of attainment in different branches of mathematics and physics and two intelligence tests were analysed. The marks were found to depend only to $5·3$ per cent. on g, but to $49·3$ per cent. on a mathematics-physics educational factor. Additional group factors, covering $18·5$ per cent., involved:

(1) Lower maths—Arithmetic and Algebra.
(2) Higher maths—Trigonometry, Calculus, Co-ordinate Geometry.
(3) Physics—Mechanics, Heat, Light, Electricity.

The unitariness of *v:ed* is illustrated too by the success with which verbal or mathematical tests predicted ability among Service recruits at almost all jobs involving theory or bookwork, except the most highly specialized such as radio mechanics (cf. Vernon and Parry, 1949). Similarly recruits who had held clerical jobs as civilians were usually excellent at verbal or mathematical jobs such as telegraphist, electrical mechanic, etc. No doubt there is a limit to this; thus a man who made a good interpreter would not necessarily be equally capable at the higher maths and physics needed by an electrical mechanic.

Rote *vs.* **Reasoning Attainments.** We have seen that a classification of attainments into linguistic and mathematical-scientific emerges fairly readily, together with further divisions at more advanced educational levels. Another type of classification has been suggested, namely into attainments involving rote knowledge, including spelling *and* mechanical arithmetic, and attainments involving more reasoning such as reading comprehension, composition, *and* mathematics. Burt first made this distinction among linguistic subjects, but failed to confirm it in his later investigation of a larger group of ten-year-olds (p. 15). Sutherland (1941), working with 134 eleven-year-olds, found, in addition to *g*, *v* and *n*, a small group factor in spelling, mechanical arithmetic and a number series test, which he tentatively labelled a memory factor; also an 'induction' factor in problem arithmetic and number series. Conceivably this represents a distinction between the stages of schooling, the 'rote' subjects being those that are studied earliest in the school career. Possibly also there is a link with Thurstone's *W* (word fluency) and *V* (verbal reasoning) factors. But it seems equally likely that the distinction arises merely from the higher *g*-content of the 'reasoning' subjects. At least there is no conclusive evidence so far against this explanation.

It follows that *v* and *n* are most readily isolated by rather elementary tests. Thus Thurstone (1938a), Coombs (1941), Guilford and Lacey (1947) and others regard computation ability as most representative of their *N* factor. Similarly Vernon (1949b) found a mechanical reading and a spelling test to be more *v*-, less *g*-saturated than two silent reading comprehension tests among 15-year-olds. In the Services rote arithmetic (the first part of naval or Army Test 3) and spelling or dictation were always much more strongly opposed to *k:m* tests than was mathematics (the second part of Test 3). In any moderately selected group the correlations were apt to sink to zero or negative values. It follows also that, in primary schools, children are much more likely to show unevenness or specific backwardness in elementary arithmetical or verbal attainments than they are in problem arithmetic and composition, or other higher, more *g*-saturated, subjects.

Arithmetical-Mathematical Ability. Let us turn now to possible divisions within the mathematics or the English fields. Most factorial studies tend to show much less differentiation than educationists are apt to suppose. In spite of the different *g*-saturations of mechanical arithmetic and mathematics among recruits (approximately ·55 and ·77, respectively), the correlations between these tests were always so high that a broad arithmetic-mathematics group factor appeared unavoidable. Oldham (1937–8) claimed that Arithmetic, Algebra and Geometry yielded separate group factors among secondary and central school pupils, but it is difficult to see how her figures substantiate this. Although she used tests specially designed to avoid overlapping between the subjects, she obtained a common factor covering, on the average, 57 per cent. of variance, very little of which was attributable to g (cf. also Wilson's results, p. 39). More detailed testing could no doubt transform the s-factors for Algebra, Geometry, etc., into group factors; but they would still be quite small. In other words, pupils with special flairs for, or special disabilities at, particular branches of mathematics are rather rare. What Oldham's figures did demonstrate, however, was the great amount of variation in correlations in different school classes, which could be ascribed to the way the subjects were taught, and to the interconnections that teachers had established in their pupils' minds. Effects of teaching on the structure of educational abilities was shown too in a study of 500 naval Air Mechanics, who took an ordinary school mathematics examination on entry to a training establishment, and, a few months later, an exactly parallel 'progress' test. They were coached in similar problems throughout the period. Both examinations were factorized along with naval tests, and the entry one resembled the mathematics part of Test 3 in its loadings, the progress one resembled the arithmetic part. The coaching had transformed the ability from the 'reasoning' to the 'rote' type.

An interesting point established in Sutherland's (1941) research, mentioned above, was that the familiar or unfamiliar setting of arithmetic problems does not affect their factor content. According to his rotations, tests involving familiar or unfamiliar situations obtain g, v (i.e. general educational) and n loadings all close to ·5, together with small loadings (·3) on his tentative 'induction' factor. No investigations, to the writer's knowledge, have shown any differentiation between mental and written arithmetic, or between money or other types of sums.

Another research which attempted to define the essence of N was that of Coombs (1941), who analysed thirty-four tests among 223 high school pupils. He included several tests based on letters of the alphabet or shapes, which were designed to measure the same kind of functions as arithmetic tests. Actually their N loadings were all close to zero, showing that the ability is specifically related to numbers. Nevertheless, they did bear out the hypothesis that N involves the application of a set of highly stereotyped and practised rules. Tests based on shapes, i.e. relatively unfamiliar symbols, gave even lower saturations than those based on letters. Another conception, that of serial response, did not seem to be crucial; for it was actually the simplest two, three and four digit addition tests which had the highest loadings of all. However, Guilford and Lacey's work indicates that, in high-grade groups such as aircraft pilots, the tests which give the purest measures of N must not be too mechanical. For they report higher saturations for subtraction and division than for addition and multiplication sums. This is borne out by the experience of British Army psychologists.

Reading Ability or Abilities. As in arithmetic, so in English there are no definitely established classifications of sub-types of ability. We talk of literacy and illiteracy as though they constitute a general factor in all verbal subjects, and very likely we are correct. But we do not even know how far the reading and writing components of literacy are distinctive, nor whether creative composition, knowledge of grammar, sentence structure and punctuation, or spelling are separable components of writing (cf. Vernon, 1949b). Harris (1948) lists correlations between fifteen reading, writing and English measures in four groups of about fifty American Indian pupils. But they are far too irregular for any definite factors to emerge other than a strong $g + v{:}ed$ one throughout, and possibly a contrast between the reading tests on the one hand and the usage and composition tests on the other.

In the field of reading many different batteries of tests have been published. Each author analyses the total complex of reading skills into different *a priori* components, for none of which is any empirical justification offered. For example, Burt and Schonell provide tests of word pronunciation, continuous prose, speed and comprehension. Gates's tests for Grades 3 to 8 claim to measure Reading to Appreciate General Significance, to Understand Precise Directions, to Note Details, etc. Trigg's series for Grades 7 to 12 includes Vocabulary, Visual and Auditory Comprehension, Rate of Reading three types of material, and two tests of Word Attack. Hall and Robinson (1945) state that the correlations between Gates's tests, which are supposed to measure distinct skills, are as high as those between tests by different authors which are supposed to measure the same skill. When moderate or low correlations are found among tests aimed at different aspects of reading, this is often due merely to the unreliability of the tests, and not to any real distinction between those aspects.

Mechanical Reading. The existence of only moderate correlations between mechanical (e.g. word-pronouncing) and silent reading or comprehension tests is fairly well established; but we have already suggested that this may be due mainly to the higher g-content of the latter. Vernon (1938) correlated several reading tests and teachers' marks among Scottish primary school pupils, and found his Graded Word test to have a higher reading factor saturation than either a comprehension or a speed test. Within the field of mechanical tests, there is some evidence that recognition tests differ from pronouncing ones. Thus Dunlop (1942) reports a correlation of ·83 between Vernon Word Recognition and McLaren Word and Picture Matching tests, among 6-year children, but correlations of ·64 and ·67 between these and the Burt-Vernon Graded Word tests. There is as yet no justification for subdividing oral reading into speed *vs.* accuracy factors, or into ability with regular phonic and irregular words, or into pronunciation of isolated words *vs.* complete sentences, though these are all possibilities.

Silent Reading. American investigators seldom use mechanical (individual) tests, but are more interested in differentiation among silent reading tests. There is fairly strong evidence for partially distinct speed of reading, vocabulary or word knowledge and comprehension of sentences and paragraphs, factors at the high school and college levels, though at the same time there is a strong general factor. Gates (1921) quotes correlations for several groups of children (eight to fourteen year) in a single school for four reading comprehension tests, three rate tests, one oral, two vocabulary, and a group intelligence and a directions, tests. The averaged figures, shown in Table VI, indicate that all types measure much the same thing at this level. Thus different comprehension tests correlate more highly with rate measures (from other tests) and with intelligence than they do with one another. However, both rate and vocabulary show some specific overlap, i.e. they constitute partially distinct group factors. And another test (omitted here) based on reproduction of material read, gave very low correlations with the rest.

Hall and Robinson (1945) claim to have separated speed, vocabulary and accuracy in a study of 100 college students, together with an independent factor of ability to read and understand charts and tables. And they criticize reading tests which commonly involve a mixture of factors. Langsam (1941) similarly factorized twenty-one tests among 100 17-year students and obtained five factors which she identifies, not very convincingly, with Thurstone's V, P, W, N and I. The perceptual factor covered most of the speed of reading tests, W the vocabulary tests, and I the tests involving logical organization and selection of ideas. Her first, general V, factor had about twice the variance of all the other reading factors combined.

TABLE VI. AVERAGED CORRELATIONS BETWEEN DIFFERENT TYPES OF READING AND INTELLIGENCE TESTS (GATES, 1921)

	Compre-hension	Rate	Oral	Vocabu-lary	Intelli-gence
4 Comprehension tests	(·52)	·55	·56	·51	·59
3 Rate of Reading tests	·55	(·59)	·52	·47	·50
1 Oral Reading test.	·56	·52	( )	·39	·53
2 Vocabulary tests	·51	·47	·39	(·69)	·52
Intelligence and Directions tests	·59	·50	·53	·52	(·61)

Davis (1944) also attempted to sub-divide reading ability and criticized tests which involve a mixture of factors. From a survey of the literature he arrived at the following *a priori* components:

(1) Knowledge of word meanings.
(2) Recognition of appropriate meanings for words in particular contexts.
(3) Following the organization of a passage and identifying antecedents and referents in it.
(4) Recognizing the main thought of a passage.
(5) Answering questions that are directly answered in a passage.
(6) Answering questions that are only indirectly answered.
(7) Drawing inferences from a passage about its contents.
(8) Recognizing literary devices used, and getting the tone or mood.
(9) Determining the writer's purpose and point of view.

Tests of these components were devised and given to 421 students without time limits, in order to eliminate any speed factor. On factorizing Davis claimed to isolate two main independent factors—word knowledge (chiefly in 1) and reasoning (chiefly in 6 and 7), together with several smaller factors corresponding to some of the other components. However, Thurstone (1946) re-analysed the data and showed that all correlations could be well accounted for by a single general factor, a blend of word knowledge and comprehension.

Other Reading Factors. Gans (1940) finds that success in selecting reading matter for help in solving a problem is separable from comprehension. Feder (1938) claims that reading factual material for information, and reading for inference, are distinct. But, in common with many other investigators, he fails to show that these are consistent factors in themselves. Artley (1943, 1944) reviews researches on reading tests in different fields of knowledge and concludes that although they show considerable overlapping, there are wide variations between pupils' or students' abilities in different fields. Here, too, the unreliability of the tests has seldom been properly controlled. Artley himself obtained a correlation of ·785 between general reading vocabulary and vocabulary in a special field—Social Studies. It is noticeable also in Hall and Robinson's research, which included reading tests in several fields such as Geology, History and Art, that none of the factors differentiated the tests according to subject matter. However Greene (1941) lists correlations between vocabulary tests in eight fields: Human Relations, Commerce, Government, Physical Science, Biological Science, Mathematics, Fine Arts and Sports. These average only ·27, whereas the average reliability of the separate tests is ·84. Tests containing technical (e.g. mechanical) matter also appear to show the influence of content fairly readily. Thus those devised in the U.S.A.A.F. received mechanical loadings of the same order as their V-loadings. Comprehension tests are liable to show more overlapping than vocabulary ones, and there is a real danger in the exclusive use of objective achievement tests of the comprehension (multiple-choice) type for assessing pupils' or students' knowledge. All their marks are likely to be greatly influenced by a general vocabulary + comprehension ability at such tests (cf. the discussion of test ability factors, p. 76f).

Conclusions. No further factorial evidence seems to be available regarding the practical subjects that Burt distinguished, though we shall see in later chapters that the *k:m* factor probably links up with scientific ability, and that there may be an aesthetic discrimination factor relevant to certain subjects. Fig. 3 attempts

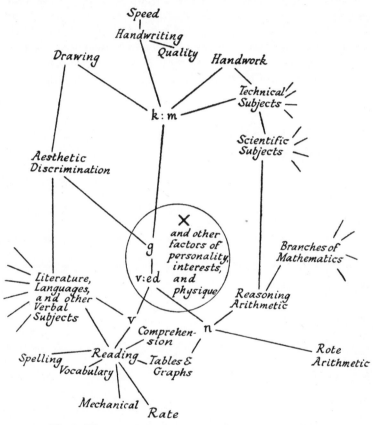

Fig. 3. Diagram of the Structure of Educational Abilities

to portray the main findings so far. Although the picture that it gives of mental structure is certainly an advance on Fig. 2, it still cannot hope to do justice to the complex interconnections of different subjects, and to their variations among groups of different educational levels, or taught by different methods.

Note that *g*, *X* and other relevant personality, interest and physical factors, together with $v:ed$ are placed in a central 'complex' which constitutes general educational ability. This affects all branches of all subjects. The influence of particular interests, traits or physical conditions on particular subjects, could not be shown. $V:ed$ subdivides into v and n, which branch into the various linguistic and mathematical-scientific subjects. Each such subject, it may be assumed, would yield its own small group factor if appropriately investigated. An attempt has been made to place the more specific attainments, those which are usually least dependent on general educational ability, furthest from the centre; also to place furthest apart those attainments which tend to show the lowest correlations.

CHAPTER V

INTELLECTUAL FACULTIES

Abstract. The general conclusion of this chapter is that, though small group factors can be isolated fairly easily in many types of specialized cognitive tests, no intellectual faculties beyond g and v are yet established as having much educational or vocational importance. W (word fluency), F (ideational fluency), I or L (inductive or logical reasoning) and many other minor factors have been partially separated in selected groups, though often coalescing into $g + v$ in other researches. The f group factor may be linked with certain personality trends. If there is a separate imaginative or creative ability, it seems impossible to measure it. The discovery of other abilities may well be stimulated by clinical research with mental patients, but so far there is no evidence that the commonly used deterioration and other clinical tests measure new factors. Apart from rote-memorizing and attention-to-directions group factors, memory and attention must also be regarded as unsubstantiated faculties.

Introduction. Most modern psychological textbooks avoid using such terms as memory, attention, imagination, reasoning, etc., as though these constituted separate faculties. But we have seen that they still bulk largely in the layman's and the educationist's discussion of human mental make-up. Very commonly, for example, objections are raised to objective or new-type attainment tests because they are said to measure memory for facts, and fail to bring out the understanding of principles, or the capacity for applying knowledge, or the originality and constructiveness, which find expression in the old-fashioned essay examinations. Similarly these tests and ordinary timed verbal intelligence tests, applied at eleven years, are said to select the 'slick' type of pupil for grammar school education and to handicap the pupil with more profound intellectual qualities who would make a better scholar. While it is by no means proven that none of these 'types of mind' or faculties exist, the evidence summarized below shows that they should not be accepted until experimental demonstration is forthcoming. Indeed the only thoroughly established ability of this kind, over and above g, is the v-factor, which we will consider first.

V **factor and its Sub-divisions.** Verbal ability is usually inextricably bound up with education, and impregnated with our X-factor. For example two representative groups of Army recruits, totalling 1,570 men, took a test designed to measure v, a test of clerical ability and an arithmetic-mathematics test; they were also assessed for education received. The inter-correlations of these four measures were all so high and so similar, lying between ·753 and ·807, that they obtained almost identical factor loadings. Since the educational assessment was based merely on length of schooling, without any allowance for goodness of schools attended or for education obtained by private study, it would seem that v is determined more by upbringing than by any special linguistic aptitude (cf., however, p. 32).

A number of American investigations do throw some further light on its nature and on possible sub-divisions. Unfortunately these are less revealing than they might be since American V usually embodies such a large admixture of g. Thus some writers regard it as essentially verbal reasoning, though the majority seem to agree that it is most effectively measured by straightforward vocabulary tests.

In heterogeneous populations it is a broad and closely integrated factor. Thus Cureton (1947), who studied large groups of school pupils and U.S. Army clerical workers, claims that there is no factor in paragraph reading, verbal analogies, proverb-matching, mixed sentences and reasoning tests which is not covered by vocabulary tests. Thurstone, however, claimed independent verbal, word fluency and inductive reasoning abilities in his 1938 research, and has since extended this division down to the six-year level (T. G. Thurstone, 1948). Among children he admits that all these factors overlap with one another, and with the N factor. Eysenck's (1939) group-factor analysis of Thurstone's data likewise revealed separate v and word fluency group factors, though Holzinger and Harman's (1938) group-factor analysis was less congruent, since it grouped the chief W tests under a 'completion ability' factor.

On the other hand Woodrow (1939b) found no W, only a single V, when he analysed fifty-two tests given to 110 students, although several possible tests of fluency were included. Incidentally he also found that four of the five component tests of the George Washington Social Intelligence Test measure scarcely anything but V.[1] The Division of Occupational Analysis's (1945) list of factors also omits W; but some of its verbal tests obtained loadings on the perceptual and speed, as well as the V and general factors. The Spearman-Holzinger unitary trait study also yielded a single v among 13-year children, though some of the minor group factors such as imagination (i) or mental speed (a) may correspond to Thurstone's W (Holzinger, 1934–5). Johnson and Reynolds (1941) analysed ten verbal tests and identified the two factors that emerged as flow of responses, and selection of correct responses, which appear to correspond to W and V. Thornton (1939) mentions a fluency factor in his research into tests of persistence; but it seems to be merely the verbal and g element in the tests he happened to use.

More recently Thurstone (1948) has stated that three verbal factors should be distinguished, and suggests that they are selectively affected in different types of aphasia:

V=understanding of verbal material.
W=fluency in finding words to fit a restricted context.
F=ideational fluency with words.

This conclusion seems to fit in reasonably well with the several investigations of verbal tests listed below, though it is quite impossible to reconcile them all. Since they involved extracting and rotating up to ten factors with populations of one to two hundred students, it would be hopeless to expect consistent results. Fruchter (1948) re-analysed the correlations of twenty of Thurstone's original tests and found, in addition to V, W and the other primary factors, a 'speed of calling up pertinent associations' factor in Inventive Opposites, Controlled Association and Completion tests. Taylor (1947) describes four verbal factors:

Verbal comprehension (in Sames-Opposites, Sentence Completion and Mixed Sentences tests);
Verbal versatility, or ability to express an idea by several differ-

---

[1] The writer has found moderate overlapping between this battery and extraversion-introversion questionnaires. Possibly this connects with Cattell's (1936) statement that fluency tests give good predictions of 'surgency'.

ent combinations of words (in Similes, Making Sentences from Initial Letters, Completing Unfinished Stories);

Word Fluency, involving no reference to the meaning of words (in Anagrams, Words ending with 'tion', Words beginning with S, etc.);

Ideational Fluency or production of words through meaningful associations (in Writing Themes, Names of Things that are Round, Adjectives to Describe a House, etc.).

Finally Carroll (1941) discovers eight verbal factors, though one of these may be largely motor (Maximum and Normal Speed of Oral Reading), and another is concerned with coherent oral expression. He narrows down V to ability to learn and retain conventional linguistic responses (e.g. Grammar, Vocabulary, Spelling, Rhymes), and separates a Verbal Relations factor (Recognition of Roots of Words, Rearrangement of Syllables), and a third somewhat amorphous factor. W he splits into A—speed of word association in a restricted context (e.g. Colour Naming, Suffixes, Dis-arranged Words), E—rate of production of syntactically coherent discourse (e.g. Number of Words in a Written Theme, Number of Relevant Words in Describing a Picture), and a third Naming factor or ability to attach appropriate names to stimuli.

Oral Fluency. There seem to have been few factorial studies of speech characteristics apart from Carroll's. Gewirtz (1948) applied a number of oral fluency tests to thirty-eight 5-6½ year children, and suggests that there are different fluency abilities in restricted and unrestricted contexts. Most of the correlations between tests of his first type (Finding Rhymes, Words to Follow 'In the —', Children's Names, etc.) appear to be wholly attributable to $g + v$ as measured by Stanford-Binet and a Mixed Sentences test. But the fluencies shown in describing one's own home, in giving adults' names, and in saying as many things as possible, yield a distinct factor. All tests tended to correlate positively with behaviour ratings on Gregariousness, Competitiveness, Curiosity and Originality, negatively with Social Apprehensiveness and Patience.

Fluency and Personality. Fluency has been approached from a different angle by a number of London psychologists—Hargreaves (1927), Cattell (1936), Stephenson and Studman (1934), etc. They have been interested in it mainly as a temperamental trait, which differentiates various types of mental patients, or which may be related to the popular conception of extraversion, rather than as an ability. The tests generally used for measuring it include Numbers of Words Beginning With—, Names of Animals, Numbers of Four-letter Words, Inkblot Responses, Associations with Pictures, Writing Themes, Normal Speed of Reading, etc. Several of these use non-verbal stimuli, though the responses are verbal, and Taylor (1947) suggests that they are factorially complex. Certainly they correlate positively, but Hargreaves doubted whether they embody any common factor over and above g, speed, and memory group factors. Holzinger (1934–5) included a number of them in the unitary trait study, and found that they resolved chiefly into g and v in one group of children. In other analyses he does claim a small distinctive imagination group factor (i). Another possibility which requires investigation is that W derives merely from the simpler and more highly drilled, less g-saturated aspects of verbal ability, i·e· that $W = V - g$.

Creativeness. How about an imaginative, creative or constructive faculty? So far our evidence suggests that, apart from g and v there is nothing but this rather dubious fluency factor, or set of factors. An aesthetic discrimination or literary taste factor is mentioned below (p. 93), though this too appears to be very small when g and v are held constant. Knowledge of grammar, punctuation and sentence structure might constitute another partially distinct aspect of v. If all these were measured it is doubtful whether any further creative factor in the writing of English could be isolated.

Obviously this answer will not satisfy teachers, but the difficulty in distinguishing such a factor is that it is almost impossible to measure creativeness reliably. The disagreement between examiners when marking the 'higher' (as opposed to the more factual) qualities of essay papers is notorious. True, the work summarized in Chapter VIII shows that some consensus of opinion as to the aesthetic merit of literary, visual or musical compositions can be established, but no one has yet extended this method of investigation to pupils' or students' compositions. They are still marked mainly for g, v and knowledge factors.

It is desirable here to distinguish between the pedagogical and psychometric viewpoints. The writer entirely agrees that the exclusive use of objective intelligence and attainments tests for selection at 11+ has had a most undesirable backwash, stimulating teachers to confine their instruction to the sort of problems set in these tests. Everything possible should be done to encourage creative work, including the writing of continuous prose, and to develop inquiring and reflective attitudes of mind. But it is a different matter to claim that any generally recognizable quality of originality exists and can be marked or measured, when it depends so largely on subjective taste.

We also lack any proof that such a quality is really relevant to secondary school work. The writer is very willing to be converted by experimental evidence, but doubts whether predictions which take creativeness into account would be any more accurate than predictions based on objective tests + ordinary school marks to cover the X factor.

Reasoning. Spearman himself admitted specific overlap, or a small group factor, in logical reasoning, though this was based only on two tests, given to sixty-three students, and so need not be taken very seriously. Thurstone's primary factors included one main type of reasoning denoted as I (Induction), and two more uncertain factors— D (Deduction) and R (Reasoning). In younger groups these appeared to amalgamate, and Thurstone's followers such as Davidson (1945), Taylor (1947), Fruchter (1948) and others have usually found only one. Now reasoning ability is one of the commoner definitions of intelligence, and we would therefore expect, if we allow a g factor, that g would include the whole of the variance of reasoning factors, together with part of that of V, N, S, etc. Both Holzinger and Harman (1938) and Eysenck (1939) show that this is the case, and that in only two tests out of Thurstone's fifty-six is there some specific overlap which might be termed logical reasoning. Holzinger does mention an additional Analogies group factor, but it is probably insignificant. In their work at the high school level, the Thurstones admit a high correlation between I and second-order g, though this was not confirmed in another experiment which included a wider variety of induction and deduction tests (Thurstone, L. L., 1940; Thurstone, L. L. and T. G., 1941). Among British investigators Ormiston (1939) claimed a logical reasoning factor in three verbal reasoning tests, but her method of rotation of axes was dubious. As already mentioned, Sutherland (1941) found a small induction factor; this too might have been better incorporated in g. Dempster (1948) describes a bipolar factor separating 'Reasoning' from 'Appraisal' tests in more than one investigation, but he does not give sufficient information about the tests or correlations to enable us to assess its status.

More convincing is the Division of Occupational Analysis's discovery of a Logic factor in several verbal and non-verbal tests involving formal rational solutions to problems, in addition to their general factor content. But it is clear that the investigators rotated their factors in such a way as to minimize g. In the absence of published figures, we cannot tell whether a different set of rotations might not have absorbed most of this into g. Since the General Aptitude Test Battery issued by the Division omits this factor, it is apparently regarded as having no vocational importance. The same may well be true in the educational field. A small reasoning or logic group factor could be isolated from specialized tests, but it would be unlikely to add anything to measures of g, v and n in the prediction of the reasoning ability desirable among secondary pupils or college students.

U.S.A.A.F. Investigations of Reasoning. The most elaborate work is that of Davis and Guilford among U.S.A.A.F. candidates and trainees. Davis (1947) tried out fourteen tests designed to measure 'practical judgment' on 150 high school boys. Tests with mechanical or spatial content were, as usual, differentiated from verbal ones, but the latter appeared to yield separate group factors of:

(1) Logical reasoning in Syllogisms, Reading or Arithmetic Problems.
(2) General vocabulary.
(3) Pure judgment and reasoning judgment.

It is difficult to discern the difference between (1) and (3), but Davis suggests that the latter requires the calling to mind of pertinent information, in other words that Judgment involve something in the nature of Fluency. In default of analyses along with g and W tests, it seems unsafe to draw any conclusions. Davis stresses the complexity and the number of independent factors involved in reading, but this may be due merely to his use of Kelley's factorial technique on highly unreliable tests.[1] Actually

---

[1] The Principal Axes technique inevitably turns every specific factor (including error variance) into an independent common factor.

E

the average correlation of tests falling *within* groups (1) and (3), namely ·249, is scarcely any higher than the average of ·223 *between* these groups.

Guilford and Lacey's (1947) list of reasoning factors includes the following, in addition to V, N, mechanical, spatial and other influences in certain tests:

General reasoning in mathematics tests and several verbal judgment and non-verbal tests.

Reasoning II in non-verbal analogies and Gottschaldt Figures.

Reasoning III in spatial reasoning tests and decoding (cypher) tests.

Planning of routes on maps, through mazes, and in electrical circuits.

Judgment in practical situations, making common-sense decisions.

They point out that none of these conforms to logical categories like Thurstone's Induction and Deduction. Considerable caution is needed in evaluating Guilford's factors, since many of them were established only in smallish groups (2 to 300) of highly selected aviation students, and are of doubtful reliability (cf. p. 131). It is noticeable that in the larger analyses with populations of several thousands (which admittedly included few reasoning or judgment tests) only a single General Reasoning factor emerged, and even this tended to overlap with V. Only one analysis was carried out on a relatively unselected group of 689 high school boys. This was re-analysed by the present writer, using group-factor technique, and it was found that a g (with some 22 per cent. variance) + group factors for verbal, mechanical and spatial-perceptual tests (totalling some 12 per cent.) gave almost as good a fit as Guilford's six multiple factors—V, Mechanical, Visualization, General Reasoning, Reasoning II and Judgment.

Reyburn and Taylor's Experiment. One investigation which appears at first sight to provide crucial disproof of a single g and evidence for several distinctive intellectual faculties, is that of Reyburn and Taylor (1941). Ten varied intelligence tests were analysed among 1,497 South Africans, aged 12–18, and although all correlations were positive, many were so low that the only statistically satisfactory solution was a set of five multiple factors. The content of these was very puzzling, only one—a verbal factor—appearing to coincide with the findings of other investigators. Yet with so large a number of carefully tested subjects, we cannot afford to ignore this. The writer would suggest that the wide age range has distorted the coefficients, and is responsible for their generally low level. For example an Absurdities test and Porteus Mazes which would normally correlate to about ·4 in a twelve-year group, correlates here only ·047, probably because ability at Absurdities may go on increasing up to 18, whereas ability at Mazes may reach a maximum and even begin to decline before 18. Another disturbing condition is that about half the group was English-speaking, half Afrikaans. The correlation would be reduced if the former were superior in Absurdities, the latter in Mazes.

Factors in Mental Deterioration. A case might be made out for a factor distinguishing what Cattell (1943) calls fluid and crystallized abilities. The former is an individual's effective intelligence at new problems, which declines with age and is reduced by brain injury and other pathological conditions. The latter consists of long-established discriminatory habits which are less, or not at all, subject to deterioration. Since, however, the most representative tests of the former type are those most saturated with g such as Matrices, Abstraction, Wechsler Similarities, etc., whereas tests of the latter type include Vocabulary, Information, Comprehension and Arithmetic, there do not seem to be sufficient grounds for positing any new factors beyond g, v:ed and (as will be shown in Chapter VII) speed. Indeed, susceptibility to deterioration might provide us with a useful external criterion, beyond the purely statistical one, as to which tests are most representative of g.

Neuropsychiatric Faculties. This brings us to a thorny topic. What do the innumerable clinical tests employed by neurologists, psychiatrists and clinical psychologists measure? Neuropsychiatric literature is extremely prone to talk of such faculties as memory, concentration, conceptualization and orientation, and to state that one or more of these is affected by organic disorders, lesions or psychoses. Numerous unstandardized tests are employed in addition to scientific scales like the Wechsler-Bellevue, for example Serial Sevens, Bender Visual Gestalt, Vigotsky Blocks, Repeating a Story in Own Words, Naming Six Large Cities (cf. for example, Curran and Guttmann, 1945). It is argued that even though many of these may not yield accurate measures of established factors, they provide valuable clinical insight into the patient's disturbed intellectual functions. In the writer's view (Vernon, 1949c), research with such tests should have considerable exploratory value in suggesting distinguishable mental capacities, but it should be followed up by factorial studies like that of Thurstone in the field of perception (p. 89). The two approaches should be complementary. The argument that every patient is a different individual who cannot be measured and fitted into a neat factorial framework is dubious. For if it is true, then the clinician should not talk about conceptualization, concentration, etc., as these also differ in every individual. If he is going to use such concepts in describing large numbers of patients, their distinctiveness and consistency must be objectively demonstrable. There can be no doubt that many such tests measure nothing but g and v and valueless specifics. At the same time the factorist may have much to learn from the clinician. Many syndromes such as impaired retentivity for recent events, the decreased 'insight' of the paranoiac, etc., are thoroughly established and should provide pointers to factors which would be worth measuring (cf. Hsü, 1948).

One attempt to analyse clinical tests is that of Halstead (1945, 1947). He claims that thirteen tests given to fifty patients yield four distinctive aspects of intelligence, or else (applying Holzinger's group-factor technique) one general and three group factors. The general factor which he calls C (Central Integrative) obviously corresponds to g, being highest in a group intelligence test, an Abstraction test, Speech Discrimination, etc. But it seems doubtful whether the other factors are statistically significant. They have no clear psychological meaning, and Halstead fails to show that they are differentially affected by different psychopathological conditions.

Other Analyses of Intellectual Qualities. An original view of intellectual qualities has been put forward by Meili (1946; cf. also Myers, 1947). Though using Thurstone's centroid technique, his factors are somewhat uncertain, being based mainly on individual tests given to several small groups of subjects (thirty to fifty) of of various ages. He rejects g, and is not concerned with such factors as V, N, or S, which he regards as arising from the external characteristics of the tests. Instead he finds four main factors which are aspects of, or together make up, intelligence, namely:

(1) Plasticity: the breaking down and reorganization of structures. This seems to resemble Thurstone's second perceptual factor closely (cf. p. 89).
(2) Complexity: ability to realize complex intellectual structures.
(3) Fluency. This corresponds to Thurstone's unrestricted or ideational F factor.
(4) Globalization: uniting separate data into a single whole, an essentially creative capacity.

It will be interesting to see whether these can be confirmed by more extensive investigations.

One other tentative approach to the analysis of intellect which deserves mention is that of Earle (1948). He has not used factor analysis, but has compared the results of numerous intelligence and other tests given at 10 to 13 years with the subsequent performance of the children at various types of secondary school course, and so arrived at a working classification. Though regarding g as the main source of individual differences in scholastic abilities, he considers that the following sub-types or group factors tend to differentiate, probably under the influence of interests and temperament.

(1) Knowledge of words and comprehension of sentences.
(2) Logical reasoning, seeing relations between objects and ideas, recognizing and describing attributes of persons or things.
(3) Seeing relations between, and carrying out operations with: (i) numbers, (ii) shapes.
(4) Comprehending the structure and functions of shapes, mechanisms and other objects; dealing with practical problems.

Clearly Nos. (1) and (4) correspond to v and $k:m$ factors. No. (3) links k and n. This seems doubtful at so early an age, though it does occur among older pupils and students (cf. p. 73). No. (2) is the faculty which has been criticized in this chapter. A large-scale analysis of Earle's Duplex tests, which yield scores for g and for these types of ability, is badly needed.

Memory. One of the most popular faculties, both among educationists, psychiatrists and laymen, is memory. Spearman (1927) admitted that g enters into many learning and reproductive activities, but regarded retentivity as an entirely distinct mental function. Moreover, he did not expect overlap between retentivities for different materials, except in so far as the materials were closely similar. Ingham (1949) gives a valuable review of the complexities of measuring learning ability and retentivity, and concludes that Spearman was not far wrong. But *g* does enter into all memory activities, particularly when the material is meaningful, and a fairly broad rote memory factor can be recognized in addition.

As early as 1920, Smith and McDougall found correlations of ·53 between two tests of logical memory, and ·61 between two of habit memory, but coefficients around zero between tests of these two types. A memory for prose test partook of both types. They claimed thus to substantiate Bergson's distinction between habit and meaningful memory. These results were obtained with forty-one students only and they have not been confirmed, but it is likely that the correlation between their logical tests represents *g*, and that the overlap between their habit tests is due to a separate factor. Several subsequent researches cast doubt on the existence of any memory factor or factors. Thus in Holzinger's unitary trait study (1934–5) the memory tests resolved into *g*, *v* and *a* (mental speed). But in a later publication Holzinger (1938) demonstrated a group factor in immediate memory span for words, sentences, digits and pictures. Eysenck and Halstead (1945) applied fifteen of the commonly used clinical tests of 'memory' to sixty mental hospital patients, and found that a single factor, identical with *g*, accounted for the whole of their overlapping. However, this result was at least partly due to the unusual heterogeneity of their patients in *g*. Again, Bryan (1934), working with 200 kindergarten children, found as close correlations between eleven memory tests and Stanford-Binet and Vocabulary as among the memory tests themselves.

Nevertheless a large number of investigators have obtained clear rote memory group factors, including Thurstone, L. L. (1938a, 1940), Thurstone, L. L. and T. G. (1941), Woodrow (1939b), Carroll (1941), Wittenborn (1943), Taylor (1947), etc. Most of these factors were based on digit or sentence span, paired associate or recognition tests, none of which bear much resemblance to learning, retention, or recall in everyday life. Kelley's (1928) factor, found among 13-year, 9-year and kindergarten groups, extended to verbal, numerical and visual material. But the tests for each type of material were exactly similar in form. Words, numbers or pictures were shown to the children, who then picked out which items they had seen on their answer sheets. Anastasi (1930, 1932) obtained a small but significant group factor in several paired associate tests and in recognition tests of previously presented words, syllables and forms. But as soon as she tried to extend this to learning and retention of logical material, delayed memory for words, reproduction of movements, and Seashore's tonal memory test, the correlations mostly became negligible. Since she worked with somewhat homogeneous groups of college students, none of the tests except those for logical memory showed appreciable correlations with a verbal g test. In the U.S.A.A.F. also rote memory factors were readily established, but a delayed memory test for logical and visual material showed no loadings on these factors, only on V and Visualization (k).

The broadest factor so far described is that of Ingham (1949), who gave eight paired associate tests, individually, to eighty Army recruits, and included nonsense and meaningful words, pictures and forms. Each test was scored in four ways, for immediate memory, for speed of learning, for retention after thirty minutes (given a constant amount of initial learning), and for time saved in relearning. A single memory factor, as well as g, ran through all these scores. The average variance of both factors was 12 to 13 per cent., but g was more prominent in learning and immediate memory scores, and the memory factor more important in retention and saving scores.

Some sub-divisions of rote memory have been discovered. Thus Guilford and Lacey found different factors among paired associates tests and tests involving study and immediate recall of details on maps. The Thurstones (1941) state that the factor involved in tests involving temporal sequence differs from that in paired associates. Carlson (1937) attempted to study rote *vs.* logical, and visual *vs.* verbal memory factors. But as his material consisted solely of word-recognition tests, the general factor at which he arrived and the sub-factors for 'vocal', 'visual' and 'meaning' tests can only be accepted as specialized rote factors. Similarly Brener (1940) factorized seventeen tests of memory span among forty students and obtained, in addition to a prominent general factor, some rather doubtful group factors, one of which seemed to be mainly verbal, another visual or spatial. Some further work on sensory memory tests is described in Chapter VIII.

Attention. Finally we must consider the evidence for a faculty of attention or concentration. At one time Burt (1909) and Mc-Queen (1917), finding that tests which demanded the greatest attentiveness tended to have high g-saturations, concluded that g and attention are identical. Holzinger (1934–5) did discover a group factor (t), over and above g in certain tests involving listening to the experimenter and following directions. For example, the tester reads 'D 2 3' and the subjects count mentally and write down F I, the second and third letters after D. He admits that it was the smallest of his group factors, and the most irregular in his different groups of subjects. Woodrow (1939b) used oral and written directions tests, and found a distinctive factor in these and in tests of arithmetic, cancellation and copying figures off a chart. This would appear to bear a close resemblance to Thurstone's perceptual speed (clerical) factor, discussed later. However, Wittenborn (1943), in an investigation with 175 Air Corps trainees, included several complex oral directions tests demanding sustained concentration. For example, lists of digits were read out (on phonograph records), testees having to write a cross if the first in a list was the largest, the second the smallest, or to make appropriate responses to odd or even numbers. Other tasks were based on lists of vowels and consonants. These tests gave a prominent factor distinct from P, M, S and N. How far it involves g and v was not indicated.

Much the same concept is implied by Guilford and Lacey's work on 'integration'. They claim not one, but three integration factors in tests where subjects have to learn a number of rules and hold these in mind while deciding the appropriate responses to problems. Thus the best test of the $I1$ factor shows aircraft carriers flying various flags, and the carrier from which planes should take off depends on the numbers of flags, the directions of the ships relative to the wind, and other instructions. $I2$ factor appeared in a printed directions test and other tests involving quick adaptation to new instructions. $I3$ occurred in certain planning and reasoning tests where numerous considerations had to be integrated. It appeared to represent breadth rather than strength or flexibility of attention. While we can admire the ingenuity of the tests devised by U.S.A.A.F. psychologists for measuring the mental traits considered important in aircrew, and the care with which they were validated, we can legitimately ask for confirmatory evidence from less highly selected groups before we accept these as distinctive and practically useful group factors.

Many teachers appear to think that most of their troubles would be ended if they could develop their pupils' attentiveness. Probably however what they mean by attention can be resolved into:

(a) $g + v$ or in other words the children's mental ages. For it is well known that lack of concentration is most prominent in younger classes.

(b) the X factor, which includes the pupils' interests in each school subject. As already pointed out this is a function of the school or teacher as well as of the pupil, and wandering of attention should often be attributed to the teacher's failure to make a subject sufficiently interesting rather than to the pupils' traits.

(c) a relatively tiny group factor such as that isolated by Holzinger, Woodrow and Wittenborn. It is conceivable that their tests might give valuable predictions of educability, over and above g and $v{:}ed$ tests, but the only evidence so far is negative (Wittenborn & Larsen, 1944). More probably their attention-to-directions group factor is, like the rote memory factors, confined to too narrow a type of test to have much spread to other attention situations.

CHAPTER VI

VERBAL AND NON-VERBAL FACTORS IN INTELLIGENCE TESTS

Abstract. All intelligence tests measure some group factor or factors based on their type of material, in addition to g and specifics. $V:ed$ factor is very prominent in verbal tests, in Stanford-Binet and Terman-Merrill, but this enhances their predictive value for most educational and occupational purposes. Spatial or k tests are nowadays distinguished from intelligence tests, but there is no clear dividing line, and non-verbal g tests—abstract or pictorial —usually show a small spatial-perceptual component. At the same time the group factors are seldom sufficiently marked to justify using intelligence tests as measures of abilities other than g. The Stanford-Binet, for example, does not give reliable diagnostic indications of verbal, numerical, memory, spatial or other abilities.

Research findings are often contradictory since the incidence of spatial or perceptual factors varies with the selectivity of the subjects and their sex, the ease of the tests, and with the pre-suppositions of the factorist. The theory that k does not differentiate till about 14 years is not borne out. K contrasts strongly with n in children and dull adults, but they tend to link up at high-grade levels, presumably because of scientific education. The only subfactor branching off from k that is well established is perceptual speed in matching or identifying details of shapes or pictures. This may link with the clerical group factor—a sub-division of v, though both are rather unstable. Perceptual speed is not responsible for the non-g content of tests like Progressive Matrices.

V **in Verbal Intelligence Tests.** Most psychologists were content to test intelligence by means of verbal problems until the 1930s, on the quite plausible grounds that the highest achievements of man's intellect are usually reached through verbal symbols and concepts. Nevertheless it was realized quite early that performance at such tests was influenced by linguistic development and education, and many investigations such as Gordon's with canal boat children proved this. Hence scales of performance tests, and group tests based on shapes or pictures, were constructed as early as 1917 in an attempt to give the non-English speaking or illiterate recruit, the deaf child and other verbally handicapped individuals, a fair chance. Kelley showed in 1927 that an ordinary verbal group test measures to the extent of 90 per cent. the same thing as a summed battery of scholastic achievement tests. This might of course be attributed to the achievement tests depending over-much on g, particularly if the instructions and the form of the objective items are unfamiliar to the pupils. Hence correlations with attainment as measured by ordinary school marks are usually somewhat lower. But at least as likely an explanation is that intelligence tests involve much the same linguistic capacities as achievement tests. A study of conventional intelligence test batteries shows indeed that they often include vocabulary and sentence completion items, that is precisely the same kind of material out of which silent reading tests are composed.

Recent research indicates that nearly half the communality of many group verbal intelligence tests consists of v rather than g, but that some types of test are less v-saturated than others (cf. Vernon, 1947b). Abstraction tests, for example, whose problems are based more on letters and on word forms than on meanings, seem to have a g-variance of some 65–75 per cent., and v only 5 per cent. Number Series tests, again, have quite small n-loadings. Presumably the size of the group factor depends on the extent to which it is fostered at home or in school. Hence it is large in any test depending on comprehension of words and sentences. And it might become equally large if schools set out to train pupils in answering Abstraction and Number Series problems. There can be little doubt that the coaching for group intelligence tests which is nowadays so common at 11+ has reduced the g-variance and increased the group-factor variance of such tests.

Factors in Non-Verbal Intelligence Tests. Next the problem arises whether similar group factors are present in non-verbal tests. Here there is a vast quantity of somewhat conflicting evidence, and it will be far from easy to pick our way through it to clear-cut conclusions. As already mentioned, Kelley (1928) found a distinctive factor both among 13- and 9-year pupils in two tests involving memory for shapes and two based on turning shapes around imaginally. Even among kindergarten children, though the results were less definite, a spatial factor appeared in a test of memory for shapes and a simple formboard. The Thurstones (1938a, 1941, 1948) included numerous spatial tests in their primary mental abilities investigations and obtained a factor which they call S, obviously the same as El Koussy's k, even as early as 5 to 6 years. It was most marked in tests involving imaginative manipulation of shapes. Both Eysenck and Holzinger and Harman, reworking Thurstone's figures, agree that such tests measure g and k or S, the average variance of both factors being in the neighbourhood of 25 per cent.

At the same time the distinction between spatial and other non-verbal group tests is by no means as clear as El Koussy (cf. p. 17) believed. Tests such as Cube Counting and Paper Formboard appear to involve imagination of shapes, and have obtained large k-loadings in many experiments. Yet they were originally designed as parts of the Army Beta test for measuring intelligence non-verbally, and were included by Stephenson (1931) in the battery whose inter-correlations he attributed solely to g (cf. p. 17). Emmett (1949) recently reanalysed El Koussy's figures and showed that several visual tests, together with mechanical tests and wood-work marks, have almost as high k-loadings as the original eight tests. Though Alexander (1935) and Drew (1947) accept Spearman's and Stephenson's assumption that non-verbal g tests depend only on g, their results accord at least as well with the view that they contain a small spatial component. In numerous analyses in the British Services, the Progressive Matrices test and the National Institute of Industrial Psychology's Group Test 70 have obtained small k:m loadings (cf. Tables V, VII, IX). Probably it is the spatial and not the mechanical aspect of k:m ability which is involved (cf. Table IX). Williams (1948), on the other hand, found distinctive verbal, mechanical and spatial group factors in his investigation of 12 to 14 boys, but his non-verbal g tests were loaded only with g.

Spatial Factors in School Subjects. Another dubious point is whether k enters into geometry or other school subjects. From his extensive work in developing intelligence tests for the selection of college students, Brigham (1932) was one of the first to note verbal, numerical and spatial group factors in such tests. And he found much higher correlations between spatial tests and subsequent performance in drawing (descriptive geometry and mechanical drawing) than between spatial tests and other subjects, or between verbal tests and drawing. Similarly Smith (1948), who used several of El Koussy's tests and obtained results analogous to his among 100 13-year-olds, claims k-loadings in art, geometry and engineering drawing, though not in handwork, marks. On the other hand Blackwell (1940) and Holzinger and Swineford (1946) do not find any overlap between spatial tests and geometry, apart from g. The one point on which all workers agree is that girls or women are poorer than boys or men in k, and the sex difference has been used as a sign that a test is measuring this factor.

Reasons for Divergent Results. No doubt different methods of factorization and different arbitrary rotations account for some of the discrepancies in the results of different investigators. The use of groups of subjects of differing degrees of selectivity also probably plays a part. It is not unlikely, for example, that k is less differentiated from g among duller testees. Subjects of different sex, age, training and general ability may often tackle the same test items by different methods (cf. Thurstone 1938b). Thus many of the items in the Matrices test can be done largely by verbal logic, or by spatial imagery, and possibly even by visual matching (perceptual factor). Hence the irregular appearance of k in tests supposed to measure g is not surprising.

Space Factor and Age. The role of the age factor has been stressed by Slater (1940, 1941, 1943), though again there is no general agreement. In a series of researches he applied verbal, non-verbal g and spatial tests to 82 and 211 children aged 11+, 161 aged 13+ and 89 trade apprentices aged about 18. In the third group there was a clear k-factor, which extended through almost all the spatial, and the mechanical, tests. But he claims that, in the younger groups, the only factor besides g is a verbal one, and that spatial tests measure just the same thing as non-verbal g tests. He concludes that k tests cannot be used at 11, or even at 13, for selection for technical education. It should be recognized however that, just as in Stephenson's research (cf. p. 17), it would be equally legitimate to postulate a separate group factor in the spatial and the non-verbal g tests. Although he obtained a good fit with two factors there is nothing to stop us extracting a third. Adcock (1948) has done this, using both Thurstone's multi-factor, and group-factor, techniques. He finds clear v and k factors in addition to g. According to his results the non-verbal g tests, Matrices and Group Test 70 Parts I and III, have some 7 per cent. of k-variance, whereas the definitely spatial tests have about 16 to 30 per cent. variance. Emmett (1949) similarly, after grouping together several of Slater's tests, found three statistically significant factors, and some though not all of the non-verbal g tests certainly involved k. Another feature of Slater's investigations was that his younger groups consisted half of girls, half boys, whereas his older group was all male. Several researches, described later, indicate that k is less differentiated in females than in males. Emmett suggests also that most of the tests were not well suited to young children.

The evidence for a space factor around 11–13 and earlier, from El Koussy's, Kelley's, Thurstone's and other investigations is indeed overwhelming. Kerr (1942), Dempster (1948), and Williams (1948) may also be cited. Peel (1949) gave nine tests to three groups of 70–80 boys and girls aged around 11, $12\frac{1}{2}$ and $13\frac{1}{2}$, and in each group his second, bipolar, factor contrasted two performance tests with three verbal tests. A spatial test based on detecting faults in patterns, not on manipulation of shapes, approximated to the performance type, and two non-verbal g tests were usually intermediate between the verbal and practical-spatial. Emmett (1949) factorized four verbal and numerical, three non-verbal and two spatial tests among 178 eleven- and twelve-year boys. The spatial tests yielded a distinct factor, one which involved three-dimensional judgments gaining a higher loading (and less g) than the other which involved two-dimensional. The non-verbal g tests did resemble the spatial tests more closely than the verbal ones, but after rotation they appeared to depend solely on g. He also refactorized Mellone's (1944) figures, which had suggested the presence of a spatial factor in picture tests given to 218 seven-year boys, but not among 196 girls. The same factor did now appear among girls, though it was smaller and rather irregular. Omitting two educational tests the g and k variances were $24 \cdot 3$ and $12 \cdot 1$ among boys, $26 \cdot 6$ and $9 \cdot 4$ among girls.

Pictorial Intelligence Tests. Though several of Mellone's picture tests were clearly spatial (e.g. Mirror Images and Cube Counting), and others with very low k-loadings were non-spatial (Substitution and Directions), yet others which were more pictorial than manipulative were found to measure k as well as g. No investigation seems to have discovered a pictorial factor in pictorial group intelligence tests (though Burt suggests the existence of such a factor in certain performance tests; cf. p. 109). Most of the picture tests like Mellone's, Otis Alpha, Cattell, etc., seem to be rather unreliable measures of g and to possess large specific components, or else to evoke a small amount of k.

Perceptual and Clerical Group Factors. Another possibility, which we must next consider, is the existence of a perceptual group factor, distinct from k—a specialized ability to solve problems based on abstract diagrams, which might enter into such non-verbal g tests as Progressive Matrices.

A P factor of Perceptual Speed was first described by Thurstone in tests involving rapid visual inspection and identification of letters, numbers, words and shapes. In a more extensive study of this factor (1938b), the most saturated tests included selecting common word associations, classifying words under headings (e.g. flowers, clothing, etc.), picking out the highest number in a column, and other tasks of a kind often included among clerical tests. Cancellation and arithmetic tests also obtained small loadings. But non-verbal material of the same type seemed to be more saturated with S (k) than P. Other investigators, however, such as Dvorak (1947) and Guilford and Lacey have concluded that the factor is most prominent in tests involving the matching of pictures or shapes. In fact the Division of Occupational Analysis postulates two separate factors—Q in tests of a clerical type, simple arithmetic and coding, and P in matching figures or distinguishing slightly different pictures and shapes. A few tests such as comparing lists of numbers partook of both P and Q, but there is as yet no evidence as to whether they are linked.

In a British Army investigation, a clerical factor was discovered as an offshoot of $v{:}ed$. An analysis of twenty tests among 300 clerks yielded g, $k{:}m$, v and n factors with variances $28 \cdot 3$, $3 \cdot 3$, $5 \cdot 4$ and $6 \cdot 7$ per cent., and a clerical factor with variance $7 \cdot 7$ per cent. in four clerical tests and in the A.T.S. spelling and arithmetic tests which involve the checking of right answers. Jorgensen's (1934) correlations among some 150 college students likewise indicated a small group factor in spelling and in four clerical subtests, beyond g and v. But in more heterogeneous groups the factor seems to be absorbed into $v{:}ed$. For example, there was no sign of it in the investigation of Table V, although three tests suitable for measuring it (together with two perceptual g tests) were included. It is note-worthy that in the Thurstones' researches with fourteen-year-olds, P appeared only irregularly and tended to merge into Word Fluency or Space. Again in an analysis of sixteen of Thurstone's Primary Mental Abilities tests by Goodman (1943), the tests meant to measure P resolved chiefly into V or S.

A fundamental investigation by Thurstone into types of perception does not seem to throw any light on the nature of non-verbal P. It is described in Chapter VIII. But several other researches must be mentioned here.

Other Investigations of the Perceptual Factor. Ten non-verbal reasoning tests were given by Blakey (1941) to 286 15–18 year pupils and five factors extracted. There was no sign of a k factor, although several of the tests were spatial in character. The only clear factor besides g was one that differentiated four tests involving matching or identification of patterns and pictures, and a type of substitution test, from the rest. Probably the tests, and Blakey's other factors were rather unreliable, and they may have been distorted by the wide age range. Thus no firm conclusion can be drawn here, except that non-verbal P and k are somehow connected.

During the war, an investigation was made of fourteen tests among 500 candidates for naval radar which included, besides verbal tests, Matrices, Group Test 70 (all parts), an Oscilloscope Reading test involving rapid matching of oscilloscope pictures, Test 2 Mechanical and four spatial tests. The intercorrelations of these eight tests were almost wholly accounted for by g and $k:m$, but there was a slight contrast between the first three and the last five, which might mean either that Matrices, 70 and Oscilloscope involve less k than the others, or that they bring in a distinct P factor. As Matrices and Test 70 Parts II and III are given with fairly generous time limits (Matrices often with no limits), this might well obscure any factor of perceptual *speed*. However, Test 70 Part I and Oscilloscope Reading are speeded tests, and these showed no residual correlation.

Correlations between thirteen American tests for radar operators among 100 trainees are given by Lindsley (1943). An analysis by the writer suggests that, in addition to a prominent general factor and a group factor in several tests of graph reading, there is a distinctive perceptual factor in the Oscilloscope Reading test mentioned above and in three tests depending on identification of irregular visual shapes.

In another analysis of R.A.F. aircrew aptitude tests, mostly borrowed from the U.S.A.A.F., a definite perceptual or observational factor appeared in three tests involving matching of aerial photographs, of photographs and maps, and of aircraft silhouettes, and (to a smaller extent) in table and dial reading tests. It also showed some loadings for mechanical information and comprehension tests and aviation information. This very wide content suggests that it derives mainly from aviation interests and A.T.C. training, rather than from any primary psychological aptitude. However, the same three matching tests form the basis of Guilford and Lacey's perceptual speed factor, and in the U.S.A.A.F. it is linked, not with aviation interests, but with several tests usually presumed to involve k. No test of the clerical type had loadings of more than about $\cdot 30$ with this factor.

The most relevant study is one where seventeen tests were analysed among 645 ground recruits—a group fairly representative of the general population. This included Test Obs-C—the aircrew test of matching silhouettes (which closely resembles the Division of Occupational Analysis's P tests)—two tests of dial or scale reading, two non-verbal g tests, a clerical and three k tests. The results shown in Table VII do indicate the presence of a perceptual-clerical factor, but its variance is so small (an average of 3 per cent. in seven tests, whose mean communality is 68 per cent.), that it cannot be regarded as having much statistical or practical significance. In a subsequent group-factor analysis of the same battery, not yet published, it appeared chiefly in scale and dial reading tests, clerical and Obs-C. Though not present in non-verbal g tests, it was shown to affect a few of their easiest items.

We may conclude then that there probably is a non-verbal perceptual or observational factor in certain visual matching or identification tests, which may be fairly prominent among selected groups but is very small in unselected populations. It would appear to be an offshoot of, or to be linked with, both the spatial or k factor and the clerical sub-factor of $v:ed$. But it probably does not play any important part in non-verbal or perceptual g tests, particularly when these are of a power rather than a speed variety.

Conclusions Regarding Intelligence Tests. In general, no test can claim to measure nothing but g (and error variance). The type of material used for expressing intellectual ability, whether verbal or non-verbal, always imposes some group factor, though this may be fairly small if the material is unfamiliar, as in verbal abstraction tests and visual tests of the Matrices type. Possibly pictorial tests are least likely to be biased either verbally or spatially but so far these have been constructed only for young children, and seem to be too unreliable to provide a promising source of *g*

TABLE VII. ANALYSIS OF 17 TESTS AMONG 645 R.A.F. GROUND RECRUITS. (Rotated Centroid Factors; loadings less than ·075 omitted)

Test	g	n:ed	v	Perc.	k	Mech Inf.	h²
Calculations test	·61	·70					·87
Arithmetic test	·62	·67				·08	·84
Test 119, Scale and Graph Reading	·88	·33					·87
Test Ins-A, Dial Reading	·80	·32					·74
Test V-4, Verbal	·67	·40	·40	·09			·78
Gen-A1 and SP 14, Spelling tests	·59	·31	·45				·65
Gen-A2, Reading Comprehension	·59	·29	·38	·14		·17	·63
SP Test 21, Clerical	·74	·35	·25	·22			·79
Obs-C, Matching Aircraft Sil-houettes	·59			·34	·30		·56
G-5, R.A.F. Matrices, and Progressive Matrices	·69	·27		·11	·30		·66
K-6, Spatial test	·66	·18			·57		·80
SP 4, Squares spatial	·52	·16			·51	·15	·57
Group Test 80, spatial	·68			·09	·44		·66
SP 117 E & M, Electrical and Mechanical Information	·51	·21			·13	·55	·62
Mec-C, Mechanical information	·67	·17		·15		·52	·78
Mec-B, Mechanical Diagrams	·70		·08		·12	·42	·69
SP 122 Practical Problems	·63				·25	·33	·57
Variance per cent.	43·8	10·7	3·5	1·4	6·3	5·5	71·1

tests for older children and adults. For most scholastic, and many vocational, purposes verbal group tests are far more useful than any non-verbal tests, because scholastic attainment is itself so largely a matter of *v:ed* as well as *g*. Non-verbal tests, whether pictorial or abstract, may be fairer to persons whose education has been disturbed, but they will seldom give as good predictions of educability or trainability. Their main use should be for research purposes, where it is desired to separate off group factors from *g*.

Stanford-Binet and Terman-Merrill Scales. Several analyses of these scales have been carried out by Burt (1939b), Wright

(1939), McNemar (1942b), Burt and John (1942) and Hammer (1948). These agree in showing that a general factor carries most of the variance, but that there are numerous small group factors whose make-up depends on the age level, i.e. the particular series of items, chosen. Most usually found are a verbal factor (e.g. in vocabulary), numerical (in digits, counting, and giving change), or alternatively an immediate memory factor, and a spatial-pictorial factor. It is doubtful whether any of these are sufficiently clear-cut or sufficiently consistent over a wide age range to justify testers in using the scales diagnostically, e.g. in claiming that a child is 'good on the verbal side', or 'weak in memory'. So far no one appears to have analysed the scale among children with other reference tests. If this were done it would almost certainly be found that the general factor is partly composed of v. Thomson's (1940) analysis of Stanford-Binet and eight performance tests among eleven-year-olds suggests that its g variance is about 50 per cent. One might guess therefore that the rest consists of $v:ed$ 25 per cent., other group factors 10 per cent., specificity and unreliability 15 per cent. Alexander included Stanford-Binet in his factorial study of adult women, and analysed it into g 44 per cent., v 27 per cent., F (practical) 4 per cent., specificity 25 per cent. The group-factor content certainly differs at different ages, which means that the test does not always measure the same thing. Nevertheless it seems to be as useful as, or more useful than, any group test among children, partly because its g and $v:ed$ content is so high, partly perhaps because it is less affected than group tests by artificial 'formal' factors (cf. p. 76).

The Spatial Factor and Mathematical-Scientific Ability. Some further work on the space factor may be appended here. Among children and dull or average adults, k and n tests are strongly opposed, apart from g (cf. p. 34). But at high-grade levels an interesting alteration occurs (as Brigham seems to have realized in 1932). Both k and non-verbal g tests tend to link up with mathematical ability, and n becomes detached from the $v:ed$ cluster. Probably this is due to the influence of science training both on mechanical-spatial and mathematical abilities. Thus among Vernon's (1939) Training College students, Stephenson's non-verbal g test correlated more highly with arithmetic and science subjects, a verbal g test with education, geography and history. Similarly among Army engineering cadets, the correlations of advanced mathematics and physics were greater with Matrices, while the more elementary arithmetic and algebra correlated more highly with the verbal Group Test 33. Finally, among 540 candidates for the higher Civil Service, the two factors shown in Table VIII bring out the main features of ten psychological tests, four examinations and two gradings of education. The first contrasts all the tests with the educational measures, while the second contrasts verbal tests and academic

TABLE VIII. ROTATED CENTROID FACTORS FOR TESTS
AND EXAMINATIONS TAKEN BY 540 CANDIDATES FOR
THE HIGHER CIVIL SERVICE

Test	Tests vs. Academic	v vs. $n:k$
CISSB Test 70/1	·55	·09
Reading Comprehension	·55	·15
Verbal Fluency	·24	·58
Current Affairs	·15	·37
CISSB Test 6, Verbal	·12	·43
Qualifying Intelligence Test	·47	·40
Qualifying Verbal	·40	·24
Qualifying Instructions	·35	·00
Qualifying Orientation	·54	—·11
Qualifying Cube-Counting	·54	—·17
Arithmetic Examination	·57	—·25
Examination, General Paper	—·05	·29
English Precis	—·09	·28
English Essay	—·14	·27
Length of Education rating	—·11	·40
Education Standard rating	·01	·47

measures with spatial tests and arithmetic. An additional group factor, not shown here, linked the General Knowledge paper with the Current Affairs test.

Sub-divisions of the Spatial Factor. Attempts have been made to sub-divide the spatial factor. Both with nine-year and kindergarten children, Kelley (1928) obtained a factor which appeared to involve memory for shapes rather than imaginative manipulation. Peel (1949) observes that some non-verbal tests possess a distinct aesthetic quality and wonders if this might prove relevant to the selection of craftsmen, as contrasted with technicians. He is investigating this further. The Thurstones in their high school study (1941) noted a small factor in several tests apparently involving visual pursuit, e.g. Mazes, but they have not followed this up.

At a very different level, namely, highly selected aircrew, Guilford claims three spatial relations factors, a visualization factor, a length-estimation factor, and perceptual speed. Visualization occurred mainly in mechanical comprehension tests, though also in some k tests such as Paper Folding, and a test based on verbal descriptions of painted blocks of cubes. $S2$ is confined to Thurstone's Hands and Flags tests. $S1$ was found in psychomotor tests of reaction time and complex co-ordination, in instrument and dial reading, and in certain spatial group tests; and $S3$ was another rather curious mixture. In his later publications Guilford (1948ab) appears to identify Visualization with the conventional k and to define $S1$ as appreciation of spatial directions from the body (up down, to from, right left). But when Guilford and Zimmerman (1948) constructed tests for measuring these two factors separately, they correlated to about ·5 among college students. Thus until much more confirmatory research is available, one would suggest that this plethora of spatial factors is more confusing than helpful.

The relationship of k to mechanical abilities is discussed in Chapter X. An attempt to incorporate the main findings of this and the previous chapter in a diagram of mental structure is given at the end of Chapter VII.

PRACTICE, DIFFICULTY, SPEED, AND OTHER FACTORS

Abstract. Several unintentional factors, or extraneous conditions which influence factor content, are considered in this chapter. The form of the test item has not been shown to be of great importance, but it is possible that all objective (selective-response) tests embody a formal factor, which detracts from their educational or occupational value.

Factor content is found to alter with practice, but no clear trend is discernible, unless the practice is directed towards stimulating some ability. The more difficult, and the easier items of any one test may be answered by different methods by the more and less able testees, or else measure different abilities. Wrong responses to some tests may likewise show different factor content from right ones; and their predictive value should be followed up separately.

Speed of work can be partly distinguished under appropriate conditions from level, accuracy, or power, both with intelligence tests and (more readily) with simpler cognitive or motor tests. There is little evidence so far that a speed factor disturbs the predictive value of ordinary time-limit tests, except perhaps among adults of wide age range.

Factors Deriving from the Form of the Test. We have seen that there is little ground for the supposition that there exist a number of intellectual faculties, of educational importance, which are not covered by objective intelligence and attainment tests. The discrepancies that occur between verbal intelligence or attainment tests and school performances were attributed mainly to a temperamental or interest factor, X. Another possibility, which merits investigation, is that the *form* of objective tests, as distinct from their content, introduces an extraneous group factor of 'test ability', and that this reduces the predictive value of such tests. Guilford (1940) considers that formal factors are unimportant, citing Smith's (1933) work, where fourteen tests were analysed among 186 students. Roughly one-third each were verbal, numerical and spatial; also about one-third were in completion (creative) form, one-third analogies and one-third classification. Using tetrad analysis, Smith concluded that any differentiation according to form is obscured by the stronger content factors, or else by unsuspected specific linkages. However, it is possible to apply Burt's group-factor method to the correlations unaffected either by content or form, and to extract a g with some 35 per cent. variance. This leaves verbal, numerical and spatial content factors with about 15 per cent. variance, and Analogies and Classification formal factors with about 7 per cent., but no group factor for the creative tests. Thus this research suggests a 'test ability' factor or factors in the selective-response tests only. If this is confirmed, it would help to explain why the Stanford-Binet and Terman-Merrill scales appear to have better predictive value in daily life than do multiple-choice group tests. We know that larger practice effects occur on most group tests than on Terman-Merrill, and that these effects tend to spread from one test to another (cf. the summary in Vernon and Parry, 1949). Presumably testees become sophisticated to the instructions and the kinds of items used in all selective-response tests of intelligence, English, or other attainments; and as they differ in their degree of sophistication, this creates an artificial group factor.

Further evidence of formal factors was obtained by the writer in an analysis of forty-two items of the Progressive Matrices test, along with twenty-one other tests which served to define the factorial content of the items. The communality of the item factors approximated 40 per cent., and of this only some 24 per cent. could be regarded as content factors (g, v, k, perceptual, etc.). Both figures are unusually low because the testees were a rather homogeneous group of 640 recruits. But the difference between them, 16 per cent., probably gives a fair estimate of the variance attributable to formal factors. Part of this amount represents a 'difficulty' factor (cf. below), introduced by the imposition of a time-limit; for some testees spend more time on the early items, some more on the later ones. The rest appears to arise from a common form factor in all the items and from separate formal group factors in each of the sets of items of which the test is composed.

Effects of Training and Practice. Several investigations have shown that factor content may be modified by training(pp. 42,116). Anastasi (1936) claims that group factors can be produced or obliterated by experience, on the basis of a study of five tests among 200 children. After taking two forms of the tests, the children were given specialized training in new methods of answering three of them; e.g. they were shown how to employ spatial devices in certain reasoning tests. Some ten days later they took two more forms of the tests, and the inter-correlations and factor patterns showed marked alterations.

The effects of practice without directed training are somewhat obscure. McNemar (1936) found higher correlations between five psychomotor tests after three of them had been practised intensively. The first factor variance rose from 29·8 to 37·5 per cent. There was little alteration in a second, bipolar, factor. Woodrow (1938) had tests of arithmetic, anagrams, cancellation, length estimation, drawing 'gates', and others practised by fifty-six subjects for thirty-nine days, and then factorized initial, final, and gain scores. In another research (1939a), eighty-two subjects practised four tests sixty-six times, and initial and final scores were analysed along with several tests of known factor content (given once) which helped to identify the factors. Both studies showed marked differences between the loadings of initial and final tests. Woodrow concluded that not only their common factor, but also their specific factor content had largely altered. He failed to find any general improvement factor, but the gain scores tended to correlate positively with N and P, that is with the factors underlying the operations which were practised. They also showed negative correlations with his Attention factor. This suggests, quite plausibly, that the least 'attentive' subjects were able to gain most with practice.

Heese (1942) gave an adding test and five psychomotor tests ten times to fifty students, and found positive but low correlations between the gain scores. Like Woodrow he denies a general improvement factor, but the three rotated factors that he prefers seem to have little meaning. In another study by Greene (1943), four parallel forms of twelve miscellaneous tests (aiming, tapping, mazes, etc.) were given to 394 14–15 year boys. The first and last forms were analysed separately. The last forms showed more overlapping and stronger group factors (communalities of 49·7 and 59·4 per cent., respectively), and it is claimed that the factor patterns altered. But in the absence either of the original correlations or of the unrotated factors, it is difficult to say what, if anything, this investigation proves. Melton (1947) presents a factor analysis of seven psychomotor tests among 350 aircrew candidates, where several trials were given and were treated as separate variables. He claims that the factor content of the tests altered considerably even over five to ten minute periods, some factors showing higher and some lower loadings as the trials progressed. But in view of the low reliability of the scores for separate trials it would appear, to the writer at least, that there is no more alteration than might be expected by pure chance.

Alterations of Factors with Difficulty. Several writers have drawn attention to 'difficulty factors', but their significance in practical mental testing has not yet been worked out clearly. Hertzman (1936) studied the correlations between the scores on the easier and the more difficult halves of seven tests and, though he did not arrive at any factors, was able to show that the two halves often measured somewhat different abilities. Ferguson (1941) points out that if items in a test (or sub-tests in a battery) are homogeneous in content yet different in difficulty, a spurious factor or factors will be introduced, over and above the general one, contrasting the difficult and easy items (or tests). This assumes that inter-correlations are calculated by product-moment or point coefficients. Wherry and Gaylord (1944) show that this can be overcome by substituting tetrachoric correlations, and recommend that this technique of correlation should be generally adopted for factorial investigations, unless all tests yield normal score distributions. However, this is not the whole story. Thus Guilford (1941) analysed correlations (using tetrachorics) between the ten sets of items in Seashore's Pitch Discrimination test, and found that the most difficult sets (5 to 0.5 cycle discriminations) measured quite different factors from the easier sets (30 to 8 cycles). One would have thought these sets to be highly homogeneous in content, but it is clear—either that the difficult ones measure a different pitch ability from the easy, or that the more able subjects use different methods of discriminating from the less able.

An investigation by the writer of intelligence and educational tests at 75 per cent. and 25 per cent. difficulty levels (cf. p. 30) yielded much the same pattern of group factors among the more and less able, but showed larger group factor content, relative to *g*, among the latter. Shaefer (1940) makes the interesting suggestion that the perceptual *P* factor emerges only at a fairly low difficulty level; more difficult items of the same kind (or the same items answered by less able testees) presumably bring in reasoning or other 'higher' factors. He does not say whether he has experimental evidence, but he may be inferring from the different results of presumed *P* tests when given to adult students and to high school pupils (p. 70).

While we shall probably continue to base our studies of test content chiefly on product-moment correlations between (approximately) normally distributed scores, we should certainly not neglect the indications of these researches that content may differ considerably at different levels.

Factors in Right and Wrong Answers. Another fruitful suggestion of Guilford's is that right scores and wrong scores on the same tests should be analysed separately, unless they correlate with each other more highly than, say, ·80 (when corrected for attenuation). In several U.S.A.A.F. studies, scores based on the numbers of wrongs had different factor loadings from scores for rights, and different validities for aircrew selection. It follows that, with multiple choice or selective-response tests, guessing corrections should not be applied arbitrarily. The most appropriate weightings for rights and wrongs should be determined by follow-up research. In several of the A.A.F. tests of careful numerical or clerical work, a separate factor appeared, mainly in the error scores, which Guilford and Lacey identify as 'Carefulness', though they fail to provide any external evidence of its nature. It would be worth following up error scores on tests given at 11+, to see if they improve selection for secondary schools, and help to eliminate the hypothetical 'facile-ness' to which grammar school teachers object (cf. p. 49).

Speed. By far the most important and most controversial of these supplementary or unintentional factors is that of speed. Ever since group tests were introduced complaints have been raised against the speed element. These have not been stilled by frequent demonstrations that scores on speeded tests correlate to about ·90 or more with scores on the same tests given without time limits, nor by Spearman's suggestion that different individuals have different preferential rates of work which do not affect their actual ability. Cattell (1943) concludes, from his survey of the literature, that inability to do tests quickly is one of the main differentia between older and younger adults, and recommends that tests for adults of mixed age should usually be unspeeded.

The problem is a complex one since the influence of speed varies not only with the age of the subjects and type of test material, but also with the instructions given or the methods of recording speed and power, accuracy or level. As Davidson and Carroll (1945) point out, most time-limit tests emphasize both aspects, and actually measure a mixture of the two components in varying proportions.

McFarland (1928) gives a useful critical review of the early literature. He points out that many investigators have failed to measure speed and power independently, but concludes that they are fairly closely correlated in the performance of mental tests. Himmelweit (1946) also reviews the many rather contradictory researches on speed and accuracy, and shows that they accord reasonably well with the generalization that speed and accuracy are highly correlated among tests of complex mental functions, but may be negatively correlated among motor or manipulative tests. Intermediate relationships are found for simpler mental tests or for mental + manipulative (e.g. mechanical) tests. The separation is increased when, as in many motor performances, subjects are aware of any errors they make. One would suggest in addition that correlations rise when skills are highly practised. The learner is apt to be either quick or accurate, but the experienced worker is usually quick and accurate, or slow and inaccurate. Thus handwriting speed and quality always correlate positively in the primary school, though not highly (cf. Burt, 1917, 1939; Gates, 1924).

In Himmelweit's own experiments, common factors of average variance 35 per cent. were found among quickness scores, also among accuracy scores, on tests of addition, cancellation, underlining words hidden in pied material, and the practical Track Tracer test, even when intelligence as measured by Progressive Matrices was held constant. In the absence of other reference tests it is difficult to specify the nature of these factors. The investigation was mainly concerned with showing that dysthymic mental patients (anxiety cases, etc.) are slower and more accurate than hysteric patients.

Proofs of the Speed Factor in Mental Tests. Davidson and Carroll's (1945) investigation, at the college student level, gave convincing results. The Army Alpha and other verbal and numerical tests were scored for the time taken to try all items once, and for items correct without time limit, as well as by the ordinary time-limit method. Nineteen measures, apart from time-limit ones, were analysed and six factors were claimed. But several of these were inter-correlated, and it appears more justifiable merely to examine the second and third (bipolar) factors, before rotation. These clearly differentiate speed scores from level scores, and verbal tests from numerical tests. Their variance is small compared with that of the first—general—factor, but both approximate to 10 per cent. It is unfortunate that no non-verbal tests were given under the same conditions, but we have no reason to suppose that speed-level scores on these would not have been similarly differentiated.

Similarly Slater (1938) gave untimed CAV (Thorndike) tests to 14-year children and arrived at speed scores by timing each correct answer and calculating the average rate of work. Some non-verbal *g* tests were also given. By tetrad analysis he demonstrated the presence of a *v* group factor in the verbal power scores, and a speed group factor in the speed scores. All the other inter-correlations could be accounted for by *g*. The *g*-saturations of the speed scores were very low. An ingenious application by Tate (1948) of analysis of variance to the (individually-timed) speed of answering graded Arithmetic, Number Series, Sentence Completion and Spatial Relations problems, showed a highly consistent speed factor both in the different materials, and at different difficulty levels. The correlations of speed with level scores were all around zero.

Yet another technique of measurement has been developed by Furneaux (1948). Cyclic tests are used, consisting of batches of items of similar difficulty, each batch being more difficult than the preceding one. These are given with time limit, and accuracy scores are obtained from the percentage of correct responses in the batches attempted, speed scores from total items attempted. The correlation between speed and accuracy under these circumstances is about ·5. Possibly, however, these scores are more akin to Guilford's measures of 'carefulness' than to Slater's and Tate's power and preferred-rate-of-work scores.

Discrepant Investigations. The high correlations between tests given with and without time limits do not disprove the existence of a speed factor, for the time-limit score is usually very largely a power one. Bernstein's (1924) early study is often cited, where numerous tests were done by 11–13 year boys under conditions of leisure or of haste. No distinctive group factors emerged, and both sets correlated equally well with teachers' assessments of intelligence. Moreover, the differences between scores on the two sets failed to correlate with (rather unreliable) estimates of the boys' slowness at work. But these negative results are probably attributable to the fact that even the 'leisure' tests were done with a time limit. In other words the conditions of the experiment and methods of measurement were inadequate to bring out the difference that Davidson and Carroll found. Similarly in Sutherland's (1934) experiments with group verbal, performance, and other tests, the conditions were imperfectly controlled. He partialled out (held constant) power scores obtained without time limit, and did find some residual correlations among time-limit scores, but was unable to prove that these yielded a statistically significant speed factor. He did, however, show that such a factor was likely to be more prominent in simpler cognitive tests than in tests of higher mental functions.

Speed in Tests Other than Intelligence Tests. It will be recalled that rate has been established as a partially distinct factor in reading, at least at the adult level (p. 45). Kelley's (1928) analyses of tests given to 13-year and 9-year groups similarly postulated a separate speed factor in reading and arithmetic speed tests, over and above their general, verbal and numerical content. Whether this is the same as speed at intelligence tests has not been studied. As Sutherland and Himmelweit indicate, a distinct speed factor is most readily demonstrable in simple cognitive or in motor tests. Hargreaves (1927), Holzinger (1934–5) and Woodrow (1938) have used such tests as speed of writing figures or words, copying prose, coding (substitution), counting clusters of dots, and simple addition sums, which show considerable overlap beyond g. Hargreaves found that this factor entered largely into so-called fluency tests. While there is insufficient evidence to justify identifying fluency, in the sense of wealth of associations, with speed, it seems quite possible that Thurstone's W might turn out to be mainly the speed aspect of V. Presumably P and Q, the perceptual speed factors, are also closely related to mental speed.

There is no clear distinction between speed factors and the ease *vs.* difficulty factors discussed above. Thus an investigation by DuBois (1932) showed much higher correlations between easy Arithmetic, Analogies, Directions and Vocabulary tests than between these and power tests. This result might be interpreted as evidence for an ease rather than a speed group factor. Yet another link is suggested by M. D. Eysenck's (1945) work with senile patients, where a group factor was found among tests of oral and writing speed and in digit span or rote memory tests. This has not been duplicated in more normal groups of subjects.

One might expect cognitive and manual dexterity tests to yield separate factors, apart from the slight dependence of both types of test on *g*. But Holzinger showed that there was a common element in his mental speed tests and in tapping, dotting, writing, and tracing a simple maze, as well as specialized factors within each type. In other words there was a general speed factor which could be sub-divided. It is by no means clear where the dividing line comes, whether for example speed of copying prose is more 'mental' or 'motor'. The Division of Occupational Analysis also reports a very general speed factor with loadings for almost all the time limit tests, which is however most prominent in manual tests that do not demand great accuracy.

Conclusions. These findings raise extremely difficult problems for intelligence and other psychological testing although, in view of the high correlation of most time-limit with power scores, they do not justify the criticisms often made of tests for children. (We have admitted that such criticisms are more legitimate in respect of adult tests.) Allowing that level and speed can be distinguished under certain conditions, should we regard them as additional sub-factors, constituting as it were another dimension to our Fig. 2? Or should we regard level scores as the most appropriate measure of any general or group factor, speed being a distinctive factor? If so, is speed general to a great variety of tests or largely specific, or can it be reduced to certain other better established factors, *W*, *P*, *M*, or to ease *vs.* difficulty?

In the writer's view, the solution should depend more on practical considerations than on factor analysis alone, although further intensive investigation of practice, difficulty, carefulness, speed and other factors is urgently needed. For the time being we shall obviously continue chiefly to use time-limit tests, for the sake of administrative convenience. Provided that the limits are generous these should yield reasonable approximations to power scores for the main factors—g, v, n, k, etc. But the important thing is to follow up power, speed and mixed (time-limit) scores, and find which yield the best validities. Thus in $11+$ selection, the grammar schools presumably require a modicum of speed-at-work in addition to power. We ought therefore to find out the optimum weighting, and it might then well turn out that our present tests,

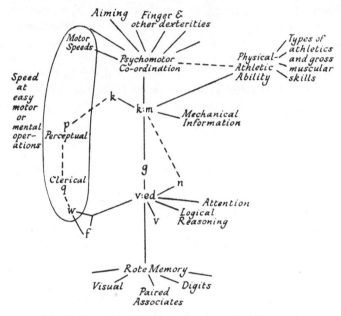

Fig. 4. Diagram of Intellectual and Practical Factors in
Psychological Tests

with slightly increased limits, would reproduce this weighting as accurately as a cumbersome system of separate speed and power measures. Similarly in the vocational field, where the speed and accuracy of simple cognitive, or of manipulative, operations are more readily measurable, follow-up will show the appropriate combination for any job. And when a fairly wide experience has been gained in this way, it will be easier to decide the best means of picturing speed, accuracy, and other components of human abilities.

Conclusions Regarding the Structure of the Main Factors in Psychological Tests. It would be more confusing than helpful to try to portray all the factors mentioned in this book in a single diagram. Hence educational and occupational abilities are shown separately in Figs. 3 and 7. The sensory, perceptual, aesthetic and other factors described in Chapter VIII are also isolated, in Fig. 5. Here however in Fig. 4 we can bring together the findings of this and the two preceding chapters, and forestall those of Chapters IX and X. Personality and physical factors are omitted, though their influence (e.g. on fluency, or on athletic abilities) should not be forgotten. It is not possible to show factors attributable to the form of the test, wrong answer factors, or alterations brought about by practice. But the speed factor is indicated by an enclosed area on the left of the diagram. Some of the links that seem to occur only in selected groups such as high-grade or low-grade subjects, are shown by dotted lines.

CHAPTER VIII

SENSATION, PERCEPTION, IMAGERY, AND AESTHETIC ABILITIES

Abstract. There is little or no empirical evidence for the numerous types of perception, attention, imagery, reaction time, etc., which are so popular in German psychology. A small sensory discrimination factor may be recognized, whose visual branch includes distinctive colour vision sensitivities. The auditory branch (which enters only to a small extent into musical and speech abilities) may also be sub-divided. Numerous visual perception factors have been distinguished by Thurstone and others, though their significance in educational, vocational, or abnormal psychology is not known. Imagery types (visual, auditory, motor) can be distinguished by appropriate techniques. Musical discrimination is well substantiated, and it may be linked with aesthetic factors in the visual arts and in literature.

Types of Perception, Reaction, etc. When the early experimental psychologists, particularly those in Germany, observed individual differences in people's responses to sensory and other stimuli, they were apt to classify them into 'types'. Thus muscular and sensory types were distinguished in simple reaction time, synthetic and analytic types of perception of tachistoscopic material, broad but shallow *vs.* narrow and concentrated types of attention, and so forth. Little or no attempt was made to determine their consistency, e.g. whether people who were synthetic with one set of material were synthetic with other sets. As early as 1904, Spearman questioned this point. Reaction time types soon multiplied and were seen to represent little more than quickness *vs.* slowness. McQueen (1917) found that people who were able to 'distribute their attention' between one pair of tests were not superior in distributing it between other pairs. But German psychologists ignored such results, together with the more objective approach offered by Spearman's techniques. Even in the 1920s and '30s their work was characterized by a plethora

G

of unsubstantiated and unco-ordinated typologies (cf. Vernon's summaries, 1933ab). Very few distinctive factors have emerged from British and American investigations in this field, though admittedly such investigations have been few in number, and much remains to be discovered.

Sensory Factors. In his early study of forty-three schoolboys, Burt (1909) noted higher correlations between four tests of sensory discrimination (two-point threshold, lifted weights, pitch, length of lines) than could be attributed to *g*. He suggested that such discrimination constitutes a wide, though shallow, factor, since each measure of acuity has a large specific component; also that visual and auditory perception might yield distinct sub-factors. Little further work has been done, possibly because most of the tests have to be applied individually and are too time-consuming with large numbers. However, Carey (1915–16) confirmed the existence of an auditory group factor, but found no visual, tactile, or general sensory factor beyond *g*. Burt (1927) points out that his factor would not provide any justification for the popular notion of perceptive *vs.* reflective types. Such types, if they exist at all, are likely to be more a matter of temperament and interest than of abilities.

Differentiation between the senses has also been attempted by means of memory tests, based on the recognition of previously presented visual, auditory or other stimuli. Carey found a rote memory factor, beyond *g*, in visual and auditory material, but only very slight grouping according to sense modality. Walters (1935) found distinctive abilities for visual + auditory recognition, and for gustatory + olfactory. Tactile recognition partook of both factors.

Factor analysis has been applied in the sensory field to colour sensitivities by Burt (1946), Pickford (1949) and Jones (1948); and to smells by M. D. Eysenck (1944) and Hsü (1946). Though it does differentiate types of colour vision, it seems unable to decide between theories of the Helmholtz and Hering varieties. Other difficulties are discussed by Cohen (1949). Recently fourteen tests of visual acuity were analysed among 792 U.S. Army recruits (Personnel Research Section, 1948). The main factors appeared to be: retinal resolution, brightness discrimination, perception of letters, and perception of shapes.

Imagery Factors. Carey also studied types of imagery, but found the current objective tests to be quite useless. He was able to derive fairly reliable measures of visual and auditory imagery from introspections, even among schoolchildren, but was unable to prove any differentiation between these modalities, or any overlap either with visual and auditory discrimination or memory (apart from g). A more promising method was developed by Burt in 1912. He got several persons to assess the vividness of their own images of a hundred different experiences. There was fair agreement between all the ratings, showing that certain experiences can be imaged more readily than others by everybody. But some subjects tended to give higher ratings to their own visual images and low to their auditory and motor images, whereas others assessed their auditory images or their motor images relatively highly. By inter-correlating the ratings of twelve subjects, Burt (1938) was thus able to show that the group factors corresponding to these imagery types carried $18 \cdot 2$ per cent. of variance, as compared with $46 \cdot 7$ per cent. of variance attributable to the general order of vividness. Burt (1940a) has shown also that this technique of 'correlation between persons' reveals the same group factors as the more usual correlations between tests. Further investigation along these lines would be profitable. It is possible that visual and verbal types might be found more fundamental, and that important links might be established with aesthetic, practical and intellectual abilities. Clearly visual imagery has something to do with k. Another research suggesting an imagery factor is that of Ormiston (1939), but her tests are not fully described and no correlations are quoted.

Perceptual Factors. By far the most extensive investigation is that of Thurstone (1944), where forty-three sensory and perceptual tests (almost all visual) were given to 170 students, and ten factors identified. Chief of these was Facility and Firmness in Perceptual Closure, or the ability to see a relatively unorganized stimulus as a good configuration. Several k tests showed high loadings on this factor. Flexibility in Manipulating Conflicting Configurations was another factor present in two-hand co-ordination tests and in certain problem-solving and reasoning tests. It sounds as though this was largely g. Susceptibility to Optical Illusions was distinctive, also Reaction Time to light *or* sound, and an Oscillation factor in rate of fluctuation of reversible perspective figures. Two different Speed factors appeared, but they do not seem to be related to the primary ability, P. Form and colour dominance tests failed to yield a consistent factor, and measures derived from the Rorschach Inkblot test gave a factor among themselves (perhaps in the nature of richness of association), but showed little overlapping with any other perceptual factors. This is in marked contrast to the claims of Oeser (1932) and of numerous German psychologists that preference for form or for colour constitutes an important type which connects up with Rorschach types, with Jaensch's eidetic types, and with physique and temperament (cf. Vernon 1933b). Thurstone suggested that administrators, leaders, good and poor readers and other groups obtain distinctive profiles or patterns of scores on his perceptual factors. No further confirmation of this has been published, and in view of the negative results of much other research, we are entitled to doubt whether they have any significant bearing on educational or vocational abilities, or on personality. They are more likely, perhaps, to be differentially affected in different types of mental illness. In a later article, Thurstone (1948) reports a closure factor in auditory tests, and proposes to investigate whether this is the same as his first visual factor.

M. D. Vernon (1947) studied the perception of a variety of materials presented tachistoscopically, and showed by their intercorrelations that they fell into two main types. The first involved rapid discrimination of fine details of shapes, while the second depended on assimilation of shapes and comprehension of their meaning. She suggests a correspondence between these and Thurstone's Closure and Flexibility factors respectively. The first also sounds very similar to non-verbal P factor. Actually however the second, not the first, gave moderate correlations with a spatial test and with AH4 Pt. 2—a test of g, k and (probably) P. She points out that there is great specificity in perception, since the performance of testees depends so largely on the particular conditions of the experiment, and on the sets or 'schemata' by means of which they interpret what they see.

One large-scale study was made during the war of a battery of perceptual and motor tests designed for selecting A.T.S. recruits for anti-aircraft work. This included visual acuity, aircraft spotting, two tests of perceptual acuity, pursuit meters, dotting, etc. In a group of about 400 women the overlapping was so small and irregular that a first factorization justifiably attributed it all to g. Re-analysis did however show additional factors with variance $11 \cdot 9$ per cent., the g-variance being $4 \cdot 0$ per cent. These appeared to be a general sensory-motor factor (perhaps the same as Guilford's Psychomotor Co-ordination), and sub-factors for the sensory-perceptual and the co-ordination tests. The statistical significance of these factors was doubtful, and none of them except *g* showed any relationship to proficiency. In the U.S.A.A.F., Guilford and Lacey found a distinctive factor in tests involving estimations of lengths and distances. The Thurstones (1941) also note a narrow factor at 14 years in several tests involving counting the numbers of dots in patterns.

Auditory Factors. Rather more work has been done in the auditory and musical fields. The Seashore and other tests such as Drake's and the Kwalwasser-Dykema series always gives a group factor beyond *g*, but tend to be so poor in reliability that no consistent sub-grouping is found. For example, in Drake's (1939) analysis of four Seashore and four other tests among 163 boys aged around 13, there was a general factor with over 30 per cent. variance, and strong residual overlap between Pitch and Intensity, Pitch and Tonal Movement (Kwalwasser), Tonal Movement and Tonal Memory (Seashore). Manzer and Marowitz's (1935) correlations between the ten Kwalwasser-Dykema tests among 452 students suggest a musical training factor (in Pitch and Rhythm Imagery, Tonal Memory and Tonal Movement), and a sensory factor (in Time, Quality, Rhythm, Pitch and Intensity Discrimination, and in Tonal Memory). Several other researches indicate that elementary auditory capacities such as those measured by the Seashore tests have very little relation either to musical ability or to perception of speech (cf. Howells and Schoolland, 1934). Thus among seventeen tests given by the writer to some seventy students, a Musical Knowledge test and total score on the Oregon Music tests had general musical factor loadings of ·84, whereas the Seashore Pitch and Rhythm tests had loadings of ·28 and ·35. The Seashore Tonal Memory test, however, had a general factor loading of ·65, and the three Seashore tests had a considerable group factor of their own.

In an extensive research, Karlin (1942) gave thirty-two tests, mostly auditory, to 200 high school pupils, and identified eight factors after rotation. Though he claims that auditory abilities are complex and yield no general factor, in fact almost all his correlations were positive. The first (unrotated) factor carried some 15 per cent., and the combined bipolars 26 per cent. of variance.

We would agree that group factors are more prominent than general auditory ability in his very miscellaneous battery. The main factors appeared to be:

Pitch discrimination for complex and pure tones, and quality discrimination.

Loudness discrimination.

Time discrimination (overlapping with loudness, and other tests)

Perception of masked and distorted speech.

The remainder, involving auditory span, various memory tests, etc., were less clear-cut.

Musical Ability. Wing (1941) has investigated a large number of music tests, and quotes a typical set of correlations between the seven best ones, which were selected to form a battery for measuring 'Musical Age'. A general factor (40·8 per cent. variance) was strongest in the most complex test of judging goodness of phrasing and rather weaker in simpler judgments of good rhythm or good intensity. This (or rather the summed score on the whole battery) correlates only to about ·3 with intelligence tests, and is, according to the author, but little affected by musical training. But in two experiments where reliable assessments of musical ability were obtainable, its validity averaged ·80. Bipolar factors, with variances 13·4 and 3·1 per cent., indicating the presence of group factors, separate the tests of *perception* of alterations in melodies and chords from tests of *judgment* of suitable harmony, rhythm, etc. A much less marked distinction is indicated between ability to judge or perceive harmony, and ability with melody or rhythm.

Vidor's (1931) research into musicality is suggestive, though carried out on only thirty-five children and without resort to factorization. She claims the highest correlations (i.e. general musical factor saturations) for creative tests such as completing melodies, or making up melodies to fit rhythms. She finds no evidence of distinctive creative and receptive (perceptual) abilities, but thinks that melodic and rhythmic abilities may differentiate. There is no evidence for the latter in Wing's results, and the present writer obtained almost identical correlations with other tests for the Oregon Rhythm and Melody scores. On the other hand the Harmony score correlations often differed, thus confirming Wing's third factor.

Like Wing, Vidor considers musicality to be independent of training, at least in children up to about 15. A closer integration seems likely to develop later; for in the writer's research, measures of training and musical knowledge correlate very highly with Oregon musical judgment scores, and with any other tests based on musical (as distinct from auditory) material. The writer also has some evidence to support the popular view of a connection between mathematical and musical abilities, though he knows of no published proof.

Aesthetic Discrimination. The correlation-between-persons technique has proved useful in the visual and literary arts. Burt (1933) collected fifty reproductions of miscellaneous paintings, and on getting these arranged in order of appreciation by artists and artistically naïve adults and children, found a strong tendency to uniformity. Hence a person's approximation to the standard order can be used as a measure of his artistic discrimination. Eysenck (1940) showed that the same factor extends from paintings of landscapes, portraits, etc., to other visual material such as pictures of clocks, embroidery and vases, and abstract curves and polygons, and even to odours. As with imagery, subsidiary type factors can be established, some individuals for example tending to rate formal, classical art more highly than colourful, impressionistic or representational art, some the reverse. These, however, might be regarded as attitudes or tastes, which fall outside the scope of this book, whereas the general factor is more akin to an aesthetic ability. Guilford and Holley (1949) suggest that an individual's communality may be regarded as measuring his 'objectivity' of judgment, whereas his specificity shows the subjective element in his tastes.

Dewar (1938) found positive though low correlations among children between a modification of Burt's test, and other art judgment tests such as McAdory's, Meier-Seashore's and Bulley's, and teachers' judgments of the children's artistic ability. This confirms the existence of a general factor, but suggests that in children discrimination is rather unreliable, being much affected by specific factors derived from the method of testing, the material used (e.g. paintings, furniture, etc.), and types of taste. Like musical ability, it correlates with intelligence, but not highly.

Similar tests consisting of literary passages were developed by Williams, Winter and Woods (1938), and applied to groups of girls aged 11–17, totalling 256. Here a general literary discrimination factor showed a rather high correlation with a verbal intelligence test, i.e. with $g + v$. In fact its variance was reduced from some 53 per cent. to 16 per cent. by holding intelligence constant. The literary factor also showed some overlap with tests of artistic and musical discrimination, but it is not indicated whether this might be accounted for by g, or whether there is a general aesthetic capacity for all types of art, plus more specialized

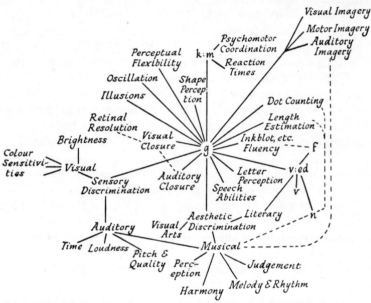

Fig. 5. Diagram of Sensory, Perceptual, Imagery and Aesthetic Discrimination Factors

factors in the different arts. The former might well be true of children, though Eysenck's results suggest the latter among relatively sophisticated adults.

Conclusions. It is particularly difficult to express the findings of the present chapter diagrammatically, because of the lack of any comprehensive investigations which might show the relations between sensory, perceptual and aesthetic, and well-established factors. Moreover, exploration of this field has been extremely scrappy, and an indefinite number of other such factors will probably be revealed by further investigation. There is little or no channelling of perceptual-imaginal abilities into a few major branches by cultural influences as there is in the intellectual field. No attempt has been made, therefore, in Fig. 5 to indicate the size of g-loadings by distances from the centre, nor the amount of overlapping by contiguity. Nevertheless, the diagram serves to put almost all the factors mentioned in this chapter into some sort of order. Note that no general perceptual or imagery ability (akin to general educational or practical ability) is claimed; also that, although all auditory and musical functions are probably linked, there is no proven connection between visuo-perceptual, visual imagery, and visual art factors.

CHAPTER IX

PSYCHOMOTOR AND PHYSICAL ABILITIES

Abstract. There is sufficient overlapping among manual and sensory-motor tests, particularly in unselected groups, to justify the conception of a psychomotor factor over and above g and $k{:}m$, together with group factors for special types of performance. But their variance is so small that their limits and essential content are not known, and they may be much affected by age, sex, practice, etc. Overlapping is greater among the more complex tests, also in low-grade subjects, but this may be due to their greater dependence on mental factors.

The existence of a general physical-athletic factor is well substantiated, together with clear-cut group factors in different types of athletic performance. G and $k{:}m$ enter to a small extent, and there seems to be a linkage between gross and fine muscle co-ordinations.

Specificity of Psychomotor Abilities. Early work on sensory-motor and manual tests (usefully summarized by Weiss Long and Pear, 1932) revealed very low correlations among such tests, and between them and intelligence or vocational proficiency. Since they usually have to be given individually, it has seldom been possible to test large groups, and all correlations tend to be unreliable and lacking in statistical significance. At the same time there is not complete specificity; most of the correlations are positive, though some may be negligible and even negative, especially in high-grade or restricted groups.

In general the overlapping is greater among more complex tests. For example, Farmer's (1927, 1929, 1936) battery of 'aesthetokinetic' tests, namely, Choice Reaction, Dotting Machine and Pursuit Meter, has consistently yielded a group factor, beyond g, the average inter-correlation being about ·25. This battery gives small correlations with several trade skills, and with freedom from accidents. Farmer's work suggests too that accident proneness is a fairly broad factor. For example, those who undergo many accidents in their jobs tend to do the same at home.

R. H. Seashore (1930, 1940) has developed and standardized a reliable battery of six tests, known as the Stanford Motor Skills Unit, namely:

Spool Packing, speed of bimanual co-ordination.

Koerth Pursuit Rotor, accuracy in following a moving target at high speed.

Motor Rhythm, precision in repeating an auditory rhythm on a tapping key.

Serial Discrimination, quickness in making discriminatory finger responses to number signals.

Tapping speed, on a telegraph key.

Speed Rotor, speed of rotatory arm wrist and finger movement in turning a hand drill.

Though he denies the existence of a general motor ability, Seashore's own figures and those of Walker and Adams (1934) yield a mean correlation of over ·3, even among students. He states that the degree of specificity is as great among children down to six years as among adults. McNemar (1936) gave five tests (two from Seashore's battery) to 182 junior high school boys, and found a stronger general factor when some of them had been practised. The mean correlations were ·266 before and ·392 after practice. In low-grade groups such as the defective boys tested by Attenborough and Farber (1934) and the senile adults tested by M. D. Eysenck (1945), the mean correlation between quite simple tests (pegboard, tapping, nuts and bolts, etc., among the former, and ergograph, steadiness and aiming among the latter) average close to ·4; that is, they show some 40 per cent. of common variance.

Group Factors. Tests of closely similar functions tend to yield higher inter-correlations, thus suggesting that it would be more legitimate to talk of dexterities rather than of dexterity or of a general psychomotor ability. However, there is little agreement so far as to which group factors are the most consistent and distinctive.

Earle and Gaw (1930) compared tests depending mainly on speed and others depending more on precision of finger, hand and arm movements, and found an average inter-correlation of ·36 among the former, ·29 among the latter, but only ·13 between the two types of test. They confirm Burt and Moore's (1912) finding that boys tend to be superior on straightforward speed and strength tests, girls on tests that appear to involve 'neat-fingered-ness'. Thus this grouping may be related to sex differences.

Buxton (1938) gave nine steadiness, tapping and packing tests to seventy-six boys and obtained very low average inter-correlations. But factorial analysis suggested the presence of narrow group factors in closely related skills. More extensive was Seashore, Buxton and McCollom's (1940) investigation of nineteen tests among fifty students, which yielded the following groups:

Simple reaction times.
Tapping, oscillatory movements in one plane.
Stylus tapping, between two or more plates.
Postural sway.
Serial discriminatory reactions.
Pursuit co-ordination.
Motor rhythm.

The grouping appeared to be functional rather than anatomical, for alterations in the particular muscles or senses employed reduced the correlations less than did changes in the patterns of behaviour. Dudek and Seashore (1948) quote similar results. The investigation by Allport and Vernon (1933) of expressive movements likewise indicated the existence of fairly general patterns of action in numerous simple tasks (drawing, walking, etc.). For example, there was an areal or expansive tendency, a contrast between centripetal and centrifugal movements, and a factor of strength or emphasis. These types of movement appeared to be related to underlying personality traits. In addition the natural or normal speed adopted in forty-five varied tasks was recorded, and though there was a slight tendency to positive inter-correlation throughout there were more marked group factors of verbal speed (reading, counting, also handwriting), drawing speed (on paper, on blackboard, with foot), and rhythmic or motor speed (tapping or contraction of various muscles). The Division of Occupational Analysis finds two factors among apparatus tests which are identified as F (finger dexterity) and M (manual dexterity). The Minnesota Placing and Turning tests and a new pegboard test are good measures of M, while F emerges in fine assembly work. In addition there is a hand-eye co-ordination or aiming factor in drawing and writing tests (cf. p. 134), and a speed factor in manual and other tests (cf. p. 84). The correlations on which these factors are based have not been published, hence the variances cannot be assessed. Guilford and Lacey (1947) and Melton (1947) find a broad Psychomotor Co-ordination factor in a complex serial reaction time test, pursuit, aiming, and finger dexterity tests, and various smaller factors among pairs of tests. Other factors described by these authors (*S*1, *S*3, cf. p. 75) combined abilities at certain apparatus tests and at paper-and-pencil tests.

Dependence of Psychomotor Abilities on Higher Factors. According to the hierarchical viewpoint, psychomotor factors branch off from the major *k:m* or practical group factor, and several researches do show loadings of sensory-motor tests with higher factors, at least in heterogeneous groups.

Van der Lugt (1948) makes the interesting suggestion that the correlations of manual tests with intelligence are non-linear, being moderately high among very dull children, and zero or even negative among very bright ones. This is borne out by Attenborough and Farber (1934), who obtained coefficients averaging ·52 between dexterity and tapping tests and Stanford-Binet and Otis Primary tests among eighty boys whose I.Q.s ranged from 45 to 105 (median 70). Again M. D. Eysenck (1945) found a mean correlation of ·26 between the Matrix test and Steadiness, Tapping, Dynamometer and Ergograph tests among seventy-five senile patients.

Investigations in the Services. Few psychomotor tests were used on a large scale in the British Services. However, Table IX gives a group-factor analysis of thirteen tests applied to 500 naval recruits—a moderately, but not highly, selected group. Test 102 involves judging the tension of stretched strings. Test 104 consists in picking up ball-bearings with tweezers, spoon and fingers. The others have been described elsewhere (Vernon, 1947b). The Table shows the two major factors and their sub-divisions into verbal numerical, informational, spatial, and manual dexterity minor factors.[1] Here the *g* and *k:m* variance of the two psychomotor tests amounts only to 3·1 per cent., their minor factor content to 7·3 per cent.

Three apparatus tests were regularly applied in the R.A.F.— SMA3, a hand-eye co-ordination test, and a finger dexterity test

---

[1] It should be pointed out that the extraction of as many as eight factors from 500 cases is open to criticism, and that minor factor loadings derived from only two tests each are indeterminate.

(cf. Vernon and Parry, 1949). An analysis of these and nineteen other tests among 785 rather highly selected aircrew candidates gave an average *g*-variance of 4·7 per cent., *k:m* or perceptual factor variance of 6·0 per cent., and an additional psychomotor factor of 16·2 per cent.

Other Studies. Teegarden (1942) quotes correlations for large and heterogeneous groups of young adults between the Kent-Shakow Formboard (simple speed problems and complex problems scored separately), Minnesota Spatial Relations Formboard,

TABLE IX. GROUP-FACTOR ANALYSIS OF MECHANICAL AND OTHER TESTS AMONG 500 ORDINARY SEAMEN

Test	g	v: ed	v	n	k: m	Inf.	Spat.	Dext.	h²
0 Progressive Matrices	·71					·14			·52
1 Abstraction	·79	·17	·30						·74
71 Dictation	·49	·54	·30						·62
3a Arithmetic	·33	·69		·34	—·09	—·14			·73
3b Mathematics	·76	·32		·34	·08				·80
2 Bennett Mechanical	·55				·40	·29			·55
100 Mechanical Information	·26	·09			·45	·64			·69
101 Electrical Information	·50	·14			·31	·65			·79
4 Squares Spatial	·51				·23		·40		·47
97 Memory for Designs	·54				·40		·40		·61
103 Wirebending	·15				·65				·45
102 Tension	·07				·15			·27	·10
104 Ball-lifting	·11				·15			·27	·11
Variance per cent.	25·1	7·2		3·2	8·9		10·9		55·3

Minnesota tests of placing blocks in holes and turning them over, and Cincinnati Pliers Dexterity (a modification of Johnson's Tweezer and Pinboard test). The tests are too few to analyse, but they suggest a small *g* and a larger *k:m* saturation throughout, with an additional manual group factor in all but the complex Kent-Shakow, which is most prominent in the Pliers test.

Earle and Macrae (1929) included nine dexterity and speed tests in a research with sixty-six boys and found a mean correlation of only ·16 with their adaptation of the Stenquist Mechanical Assembly test. But in another group of 125, three dexterity and speed tests correlated ·22 with Stenquist and gave similar coefficients, ranging up to ·36, with the (paper-and-pencil) Form Relations test and Group Test Thirty-four, and with several standard performance tests. A somewhat discrepant result was obtained by Shuttleworth (1942) among 109 13-year technical school boys, who took sixteen tests used in the Birmingham vocational experiments. The Ball-lifting test (SP Test 104) gave a correlation of ·24 with his general factor but on the bipolar factor separating $k:m$ from $v:ed$ tests, neither this dexterity test nor Memory for Designs and Squares spatial tests, showed any mechanical loading. The selectivity of the group may perhaps be responsible.

Cox's Investigations. Perhaps the most illuminating work in this field is that of Cox (1928, 1934), though based chiefly on small groups of schoolboys and on the inconvenient (yet highly delicate) tetrad difference technique of factorization. In his earlier experiments he intentionally eliminated any element of manual dexterity by using paper-and-pencil tests with pictures of mechanical models. He was able to establish overlapping in such tests, beyond g, which he attributed to m factor, that is the capacity for comprehending and employing mechanical relationships and principles. Later he studied tests of assembling and stripping, and showed the same factor to be present in these, particularly in the less routine assembly processes. When routine assembly and stripping and other dexterity tests such as pinboard and eyeboard were compared, there was consistent evidence of small residual overlapping, with g and m held constant, which he attributed to a 'routine manual factor'. Additional minor group factors were indicated among sets of closely similarly dexterity tests. Each test of course, also involved a specific factor, and this specific variance was much greater in the dexterity tests than was their g, m, manual or other factor content.

Minnesota Investigation. Some of the inter-correlations obtained in the Minnesota study of mechanical ability are shown in Table X. Though they were not subjected to group factor or multiple factor analysis by Paterson and Elliot, they indicate the presence of a prominent general factor, presumably a mixture of g and $k:m$. Clearly there is also a $v:ed$ group factor in the Academic Grades and Otis I.Q., possibly entering into the Paper Formboard and Information tests. Packing Blocks and Card Sorting show a dexterity factor which overlaps into the first five mechanical and spatial tests, though not into the informational and interests tests. Wittenborn (1945) analysed these and other Minnesota figures by the centroid method, and his results tend to confirm these suggestions. He claims in addition a Maturational factor in dynamometer tests, height and weight; a Strength factor, mainly in dynamometer tests, and possibly a Steadiness factor, and Perceptual Speed.

TABLE X.   SELECTED CORRELATIONS FROM THE MINNESOTA INVESTIGATION OF MECHANICAL ABILITY

	1	2	3	4	5	6	7	8	9	10	11
1. Quality of Shop Work	·55										
2. Minnesota Assembly Test	·55										
3. Minnesota Spatial Relations Formboard	·53	·56									
4. Paper Formboard	·52	·49	·63								
5. Stenquist Picture Test	·31	·40	·39	·30							
6. Mechanical Information	·42	·35	·40	·57	·34						
7. Mechanical Interests	·64	·42	·46	·39	·28	·47					
8. Home Mechanical Operations	·30	·40	·22	·24	·19	·35	·30				
9. Otis I.Q.	·21	·06	·18	·53	·18	·67	·23	·10			
10. Academic Grades	·42	·13	·26	·40	·28	·54	·25	·12	·57		
11. Packing Blocks	·26	·30	·34	·14	·21	—·04	·12	·00	—·06	·12	
12. Card Sorting	·19	·13	·23	·14	·24	·00	·09	—·12	·05	·09	·052

Harrell's Investigation.   Centroid analyses with rotation of axes naturally obscure any g or $k:m$ content of manual tests. Thus Harrell (1940) obtained the following five independent factors from his application of thirty-two tests (fifteen of them manual) to ninety-one cotton-mill operatives:

(1) A verbal factor in Completion, Opposites and Analogies tests and schooling. Doubtless this is largely g.

(2) A spatial factor in paper-and-pencil tests, including Cube Counting and Minnesota Formboard.

(3) An age and experience factor entering into some of the mechanical tests, but correlating with poor performance on some of the manual speed tests.

(4) A manual dexterity factor especially prominent in Pinboard, Dotting, Assembling and Stripping Nuts and Bolts, and Packing Blocks. Half of the dexterity tests gave appreciable loadings, and few showed significant loadings with the other four factors.

(5) A factor which Harrell suggests is perceptual. But as it has loadings on Routine Assembling and Stripping, Mechanical Assembly and Stenquist Picture tests, one would have thought that it approximates more to a mechanical factor than to non-verbal P.

Studies of the MacQuarrie Test. A number of investigations which throw some light on manual and higher general or group factors have been made with the MacQuarrie battery of paper-and-pencil tests of so-called mechanical aptitude. Bingham (1937) quotes correlations for employees of the Scovill Manufacturing Company between the battery as a whole and verbal and performance tests, which suggest, according to a group-factor analysis by the writer, that it has a g-loading of at least ·6 and a smaller k-loading. Jorgensen (1934) has also found it to have high g-content. Harrell (1940) included it in the research just mentioned. The Copying, Location, Block-Counting and Pursuit tests were chiefly covered by his first two factors ($g + k$), while the Tracing, Tapping and Dotting tests depended on the first and fourth ($g + $ manual). Goodman (1947) and Chapman (1948) factorized the inter-correlations among 329 radio assembly workers, and likewise established a spatial (or $g + k$) factor, and a manual factor in the three latter tests. There were indications of a perceptual or visual inspection group factor in some of the tests. This is borne out by Murphy's (1936) analysis of eighteen tests among 143 14-year boys, which included Copying, Tracing and Tapping from MacQuarrie. Copying fell in a cluster with his spatial tests, but the other two formed a distinct group factor with Substitution and Checking tests from Army Beta, that is with tests akin to P.

Conclusion. Although psychomotor abilities do not seem to be so devoid of structure as early experiments suggested, it is nevertheless true that they are predominantly specific. Thus the notion

H

of dexterity or handiness as a general factor in manual occupations, which can be measured by one or two pegboard, nut and bolt
or similar tests, should be discouraged. The diagram in Fig. 4
attempts to portray the main results reviewed above.

Physical Abilities. Jones and Seashore (1944) point out that
greater generality is usually found among gross than among fine
muscular capacities, and that there is much more justification for a
general athletic than for a general motor factor. Several analyses
of physical measures and athletic tests have been published in the
Research Quarterly of the American Association for Health and
Physical Education (Wendler, 1938; Hall and Wittenborn, 1942;
Brace, 1946, etc.).[1] These are said to reveal factors of Strength,
Speed, Agility, etc. Such trait-names, however, are apt to mislead
(cf. Appendix, p. 134), and it would be better to describe the
factors in terms of the performances they cover. McCloy (1940)
claims that strength, speed of movement and dead weight factors
consistently emerge in such studies. He quotes correlations between six athletic measures, four dynamometer tests, and weight,
among 163 junior high school girls. All correlations are positive
and (except those for weight) fairly large, hence a group-factor
analysis appears more appropriate than his rotated centroid
analysis. Such an analysis by the writer indicates:

(1) A general physical factor in all measures except weight, with
some 42 per cent. variance.
(2) A 'strength' factor in dynamometer tests, weight, and shot-
putting and ball-throwing.
(3) A group factor in two jumping events and one running,
weight being negatively loaded. The variance of Nos. 2
and 3 amounts to some 26 per cent.

A similar research by Highmore (1949) carried out with male
physical training students gave a general factor with $32 \cdot 0$ per cent.
variance, and group factors with $11 \cdot 7$ per cent. for:

(1) Running events.
(2) Putting, throwing and kicking.
(3) Standing and running, broad and high jumps.

A study of nine athletic tests applied to 450 Army recruits was
made during the war. When *g*, age, height and weight were held

[1] Other references are listed, and reviewed, by Highmore (1949).

constant, a general physical factor accounted for 27.4 per cent. of variance, and another 16·4 per cent. was covered by group factors which include:

(1) Running 100 yards, running 1 mile, walking 5 miles, Army Agility test.

(2) Long jump, high jump, obstacle race.

(3) Two types of chinning or pull-up tests.

As in the case of psychomotor abilities, physical ones show some impregnation with g and $k{:}m$, though their group-factor content is much larger. The mean g-loading of the above nine measures was only ·11 (variance 1.2 per cent.). However, in another investigation of 578 Army recruits, thirteen tests or measures were analysed. After the extraction of a large g and a $v{:}ed$ factor, there were small residual correlations, shown in Table XI. These clearly indicate

TABLE XI. CORRELATIONS BETWEEN MECHANICAL AND PHYSICAL TESTS AFTER EXTRACTION OF *G* AND *V:ED*

Test	g loading	Squ.	Mech.	Ass.	Med. Cat.	Youth	Agility
4 Squares Spatial	·67						
2 Bennett Mechanical	·73	·12					
8 Mechanical Assembly	·36	·25	·24				
Medical Category	·34	·06	·03	·16			
Youth (age reversed)	·24	·03	·01	·07	·20		
16 Agility	·31	—·01	·04	·02	·20	·14	
10 Morse Aptitude	·58	—·02	·00	—·04	·03	·16	·06

mechanical and physical group factors. The latter extends into the Morse Aptitude test and suggests a link between physical and auditory abilities. In addition most of the physical measures correlate slightly with the spatial-mechanical, particularly with the manipulative assembly test. The same figures have been analysed by Banks (1949), with similar results. Overlapping between physical and mechanical abilities is shown also by the discovery (cf. Vernon and Parry, 1949) that the Army Assembly test is usually more valid in predicting proficiency at jobs requiring physical effort, in Infantry, R.A.C. and R.E., than in predicting mechanical skill and trainability.

We would expect to find a closer association between all these factors among low-grade adults or children than among high-grade. No investigation of physical tests along with manual, mechanical and intelligence tests appears to have been carried out with feeble-minded subjects, but a study of African recruits is relevant. Thirteen tests given to between 308 and 631 men are listed in Table XII. Most of these are simplified adaptations of British ones; the Fourth Corner is a performance test along the lines of individual Matrices. Three factors were extracted, but the third failed to yield any logical grouping, probably because of the varying numbers of cases, and the two listed in the Table gave a good fit. The first, general, factor hardly represents *g*, in the sense of educing relations, since it gives such large loadings to the simple formboards and dexterity tests. Probably it corresponds to a general adaptability to the unfamiliar testing situation. Mechanical Comprehension gets the poorest loading, perhaps because it is the

TABLE XII. FACTORIZATION OF TESTS GIVEN TO AFRICAN
RECRUITS

Test	Unrotated I	Factors II
Arithmetic	·57	·34
Progressive Matrices (revised)	·66	·29
Fourth Corner Test	·66	·23
Block Design	·68	·18
Cube Construction	·68	·08
Mechanical Comprehension	·27	·07
Formboard, circular insets	·69	·02
Formboard, square insets	·56	—·03
Mechanical assembly	·77	—·07
Screwboard Dexterity	·64	—·20
Reversible Blocks Dexterity	·56	—·21
Pegboard Dexterity	·41	—·30
Agility	·40	—·42

most un-African and the least reliable test. The second factor clearly divides the tests into the primarily cognitive, including verbal, pictorial and performance, and the primarily manipulative and physical. The Formboards partake of both group factors and so show the lowest loadings. The cognitive factor is quite close to British *g*, while the opposite pole is a mixture of our manual dexterity and physical factors. This study raises several interesting speculations. Should we regard *k:m*, not as a 'descendant' of *g*, but as arising in the first place from man's physical abilities which later link up with his mental abilities? Or is there an important racial, or cultural, difference? Further comparative investigations would be very fruitful.

CHAPTER X

PERFORMANCE TESTS AND MECHANICAL ABILITIES

Abstract. Investigations of performance and mechanical tests tend to yield very diverse results owing to the effects of background, age, training, etc. Much work has been done in the Services, as well as among children. This shows that *g* usually plays a large part, except in the more unreliable performance tests and in mechanical assembly tests. In general, performance tests measure the same $g + k$ factors as paper-and-pencil spatial tests, while mechanical tests measure these factors and a mechanical information or experience group factor. Thus, apart from their greater attractiveness, practical or manipulative tests show little or no advantage over paper-and-pencil tests. Additional minor group factors are indicated among special types of performance tests, and within the field of mechanical information.

What Do Performance Tests Measure? Tests such as Formboards, Picture Completion, Porteus Mazes, Kohs Blocks, and Cube Construction have been widely used for some thirty years in clinics and in vocational guidance (cf. Gaw, 1925), to measure a more 'practical' type of intelligence than the mainly verbal Binet or group tests. It has often been assumed that they give some indication of aptitude for mechanical or manual jobs, or for technical as contrasted with academic education. McFarlane (1925) found some overlapping, beyond that due to *g*, among boys but not girls in a number of practical tests including Cube Construction, the assembly of a wheelbarrow out of wooden pieces, and Healy's puzzle box where the testee has to puzzle out an elaborate system of latches and fastenings to open the box. Spearman, however, considered that performance tests are merely rather unreliable *g* tests, and Cattell (1936) reiterated this view. Kohs (1923) put forward his Block Design test purely as a measure of *general* intelligence. El Koussy's (1935) survey of the literature (up to but not including Alexander's work) also showed that the weight of evidence was against any single or clear-cut practical factor in all performance tests, at least among children. Neither Pintner-Paterson's, Gaw's, Drever-Collins's, nor Arthur's standard batteries of tests appear to have been analysed thoroughly, presumably because of the time taken to test sufficient numbers. Kelley (1928) quotes correlations for small groups of 13-year boys and girls between eight of Gaw's tests, but as he chose the ones showing most independence it is not surprising that they failed to yield any logical pattern. Schiller (1934) included three of the poorer Pintner-Paterson tests, also Drawing a Man and the non-verbal Army Beta and Otis Primary group tests in an investigation of twelve tests among 395 nine-year boys and girls. A group-factor analysis by the writer indicates that the Pintner-Paterson total scores and Drawing a Man have g-variance of about 20 per cent. and k-variance of 10 per cent. or less, i.e. very high specificity, the same factors being present in the non-verbal group tests.

Factorial Studies of Performance Tests. Morris (1939) gave the Pinter-Paterson tests and a series of manual tests to a somewhat selected group of fifty-five boys aged $9\frac{1}{2}$. He points out that many of the performance test inter-correlations are so low, sometimes even negative, that they cannot all be measuring the same ability, and claims that the three rotated factors which he extracted correspond to Thurstone's Space, Induction and Perceptual Speed. But his results, which are very unreliable with small numbers, hardly appear to support this identification. Instead they show a general factor with loadings of $\cdot 5$ to $\cdot 6$ for most of the better performance tests and around $\cdot 3$ for the manual tests, and a bipolar factor contrasting most of the tests in these two groups. Teegarden's figures, mentioned above, also show considerable positive correlations between two formboards (the Kent-Shakow Industrial and Minnesota Spatial Relations) and manual dexterity tests in adults. Similarly among Attenborough and Farber's mentally defective boys, there was overlapping of Healy II, Knox Cube, Porteus Mazes, Cube Construction and Dearborn Formboard with Binet and Otis on the one hand, and with Stenquist Assembly and various dexterity tests on the other hand. Vernon's (1937) study of the Moorrees Formboard indicates that its six difficult insets provide a moderate test of g, while its six easy insets measure a rather different ability—probably a kind of manual dexterity.

Thomson (1940) analysed the performance tests used in the Scottish individual test survey of eleven-year-olds and obtained a general factor, present also in Stanford-Binet, together with some indication of a separate group factor in the speeded tests. But as the battery only contained one g or $g + v$ test, a distinct performance factor could not be expected. Burt (1940b), however, showed that additional minor factors were present in the performance tests, one for speeded tests, one for pictorial and a third 'linguistic' factor in tests with elaborate verbal instructions such as Knox Cube, Kohs, Cube Construction and Binet.

Earle and Milner (1929) applied numerous tests to over 300 13–14-year children, and found that they could be classified into three main groups:

(1) Stanford-Binet and Group Test 34—$g + v$ tests with high loadings.
(2) Cube Construction, Dearborn Formboard, Form Relations and Memory for Designs—performance and paper-and-pencil tests—also Stenquist Assembly. These were partly dependent on g, but showed additional overlap suggesting a spatial-practical-mechanical group factor.
(3) Other performance tests including Cube Imitation, Substitution, Picture Completion II and Porteus Mazes—g tests with low saturations and no other common factors. The mean correlations within and between these groups are shown in Table XIII.

TABLE XIII. EARLE AND MILNER'S CORRELATIONS BETWEEN DIFFERENT TYPES OF TESTS

	1	2	3
1	(·80)	·38	·38
2	·38	(·46)	·28
3	·38	·28	(·33)

That the g-loading of performance tests changes with age is suggested by Arthur's (1930) correlations of ·81 at six years and ·26 at 14 years between her battery and Stanford-Binet. We would suggest however, that this is merely due to most of her tests approaching their ceiling among older children, and to the increasing verbality of the Stanford-Binet. More appropriate performance tests do continue to provide a moderate measure of intelligence in adolescents and adults. Even in an extremely high-grade group of 255 Civil Service candidates, the writer found a g-saturation of about ·60 for the Kohs-Misselbrook Block test. Balinsky's (1941) results indicating considerable general factor saturations for the Wechsler-Bellevue performance tests from 9 to 60 years, and doubtful alterations with age, have already been mentioned (p. 29).

Alexander's F and the k-Factor. Alexander's investigation (p. 18) proved that some performance tests do measure a factor beyond g. In his adult group, Picture Completion and Formboard tests actually obtained larger loadings on his F (practical) factor than did the three tests chosen for his performance scale, and Porteus Mazes much the same loadings. The three younger groups took three of the pictorial tests which Cox devised for measuring m (p. 101). In the youngest groups they appeared to act mainly as g tests, but among the older youths they approximated quite closely to the F tests. Possibly because of their complicated instructions they also showed small verbal loadings. These results, and others quoted below, suggest that F is identical with the spatial factor k, and that Cox's m is largely composed of k also.

The g-content of performance tests such as Alexander's is a matter of considerable importance in attempting to differentiate 'academic' and 'practical' types of children at 11+. Burt (1947) suggests that the correlation between reliable intelligence and performance tests is about ·6, making differentiation very difficult. Alexander (1947) claims that it is nearer ·3, though a table published in the Instruction Book of his battery, listing verbal and performance test I.Q.s, yields a correlation of ·54, as Dempster (1948) points out. Alexander considers too that F is quite distinct from the k factor in paper-and-pencil spatial tests. He relies mainly on the evidence of Drew's (1947) factorial investigations, whose accuracy has been called into question by Slater (1947). To the writer, the main fallacy in Drew's work is his identification of F with Passalong scores. This is the least reliable test in Alexander's battery, and when Kohs Blocks and Cube Construction are also considered, the identity of F with k is obvious. Thus in Drew's 11–12+ groups of 353 boys, the correlations appear to be accounted for by:

(1) g.
(2) a verbal group factor in the Moray House test, Spearman's v test and teachers' verbal ability assessments.

(3) a spatial factor in the Alexander tests and Spearman's *k* test, possibly also in a non-verbal *g* test and teachers' assessments of practical ability.

Drew's results for eighty-eight technical school boys (16+) are more complex because the boys were clearly selected for *g* and *v:ed*, and because of the unreliability of the coefficients. But the writer's re-analysis yields:

(1) a *k* factor in the Alexander tests, a formboard, a spatial test and a non-verbal *g* test. This enters too into Technical Drawing and Shopwork marks.

(2) a verbal factor in Simplex and the *v* tests, and in marks for English and Science.

(3) A separate scholastic or *X* factor in all four sets of marks.

Emmett (1949) also re-analysed some of Drew's figures, and found a common factor in Alexander's battery, a *k* test and a non-verbal *g* test. Leff (1949) included the Alexander scale in an analysis of verbal, mechanical, spatial and non-verbal *g* tests among 250 twelve-year boys. The *v*, *m* and *k* tests gave distinctive group factors, and the Alexander tests fell in the same cluster as the *k* ones. There was no trace of a performance factor distinct from paper-and-pencil abilities. Dempster (1948) reports similar results with ninety-one 11-year boys, though he quotes no figures. Price (1940) worked with only eighty-five University students, but his results are similar. He gave three verbal and non-verbal *g* tests, three spatial tests, Kohs Blocks, Passalong, Dearborn Formboard, Cylinder Construction and Woolley's (Blindfold) Formboard. After extracting a general factor, a bipolar factor was found which separated the *g* tests, Passalong and Woolley from the spatial and the other performance tests. Presumably then Passalong and Woolley are the poorest measures of the spatial factor in high-grade adults. The residuals, which are statistically insignificant, do provide a very faint trace of a distinction between paper-and-pencil and manipulative tests.

The only relevant evidence collected in the Services was in a group of 500 air mechanics, who took the Trist-Misselbrook revision of Kohs Blocks. This obtained almost identical loadings on three unrotated factors to those of the Squares spatial group test.

Conclusion. Before proceeding to mechanical tests it would be well to summarize the position. Many of the commonly used performance tests are unreliable, or embody large specific factors, hence it is unsafe to use any battery or scale as a measure of *g*. The correlation of such a battery with Binet or group verbal tests is further reduced by the considerable *v*-element in such tests. Nevertheless, it is likely that *g* is the major common factor in all except the simplest manipulative performance tests, hence it is impossible to differentiate effectively any large proportion of children, at 11+, into academic and practical types. Most of the more thorough performance tests, Kohs Blocks and Cube Construction in particular, bring in a fair amount of the *k* factor which is measured by spatial group tests, and which is closely linked with the *m* or mechanical factor. Though there is little direct evidence, it is probable that some of the simpler ones depend too on a manual dexterity factor or factors. If large enough numbers of subjects are tested with a varied battery, minor group factors begin to emerge among different types of test—pictorial, speeded, etc. But there are no grounds for assuming a broad performance or practical factor distinct from *g*, *k*, *m* and dexterity. Hence, apart from the dexterity element and the greater attractiveness of performance tests to testees, there is no reason why psychologists should not substitute the more reliable and convenient paper-and-pencil mechanical and spatial tests for performance tests.

Mechanical Tests. Murphy (1936) suggested that tests claiming to measure mechanical ability are so variegated that the existence of a distinctive common factor is doubtful. On analysing a battery of eighteen tests (cf. p. 103), she found that a spatial relations factor and a hand-eye co-ordination factor would account for all their inter-correlations. While this may be true of the Mac-Quarrie tests, it is unfair to tests that do involve comprehension or assembling of actual mechanisms, none of which was included by Murphy. We would agree that a large portion of what is commonly called mechanical ability actually consists of *k*; this may be deduced from the Minnesota study and Alexander's, Earle's, Milner's and Macrae's work. Slater (1940) too analysed the Cox and Vincent models tests in his study of spatial tests among apprentices, and found no separate *m* component. Again it is interesting that the sex difference in *k* holds also for mechanical tests. Indeed Williams's research, which included Cox's Designs, revised Bennett Comprehension and Vincent Models, is the only one to show any clear differentiation.

Mechanical Information Constitutes a Distinctive Factor.
In several investigations in the Services, Test 2 Mechanical
Comprehension and Test 4 Squares Spatial obtained much the
same factorial composition (cf. Table V). But when additional
spatial and mechanical comprehension or information tests were
analysed, as in Table IX, a separation emerged between these two
types. Table VII similarly indicates partially distinct k and
mechanical information group factors. The different factor loadings of Mec-B, a picture test based on *comprehension* of the work-
ings of machines and Mec-C, a straightforward *information* test,

TABLE XIV. ALTERNATIVE GROUPINGS OF THIRTEEN
TESTS ANALYSED AMONG 283 R.A.F. FITTERS

Gen-A Verbal
Arithmetic

G-5 R.A.F. Matrices

Group Test 80 Spatial
K-6 Spatial

Vincent Models
Finger Dexterity
Mec-A Bennett Mechanical

SP 103 Wirebending

Mec-B Mechanical Diagrams
Mec-C Mechanical Information
117M Mechanical Information
117E Electrical Information

are noticeable. Guilford (1948ab) claims indeed that the only
distinctive element in any mechanical tests, apart from spatial,
dexterity and other factors, is one of information. The difference
between k and information is further underlined by the rather
disappointing results obtained with k tests in selecting mechanics
in the British Services, and the comparatively good results obtained with information tests (Vernon, 1947b). This may of course
be due partly to the inverse effects of age on the two types of test
(cf. p. 33).

Analyses of Mechanical Tests. The complexity of overlapping between g, k, m, and dexterity, and the extent to which the
predilection of the factorist may affect the grouping, is neatly
illustrated by a research in the R.A.F. by Wheeler (1948). The
tests listed in Table XIV were given to 283 airframe fitters, that is

a group with some previous mechanical training. Several factorial techniques were applied and the tests fell equally well into the four groups or the three groups shown here. In the four-group solution, G-5 Matrices goes with the k tests, information tests are distinct, and Bennett Mechanical Comprehension + two manipulative tests yield a separate mechanical factor. But the alternative analysis groups the k tests (excluding G-5) with mechanical comprehension, and contrasts them with information + Wire-bending; while G-5 goes with the $g + v$ tests. In this study the general factor (a mixture of g and k:m) covered about 28 per cent., and the combined group factors 20 to 22 per cent. of variance.

The American naval classification battery of twelve tests was factorized by Peterson (1943) to yield three factors called Verbal, Mechanical-Spatial and Quantitative Reasoning. This solution was unconvincing, and a re-analysis by the writer gave a more logical picture which is entirely congruent with British results. In addition to a prominent g, a verbal group factor appears in Reading Comprehension, Opposites, Analogies, Completion and Arithmetic, and a k:m factor in the remaining seven tests. Two minor group factors are needed, one in the four mechanical and electrical information measures, and one in Block Counting, Mechanical Comprehension and Surface Development (k) tests.

Mechanical Information Group Factors. A sub-grouping in the information field was suggested by the writer's analysis of six tests among 136 naval radio and electrical mechanics. A prominent general factor of electrical-mechanical knowledge accounted for $43\frac{1}{2}$ per cent. of variance in Bennett's Mechanical Comprehension test, Tests 117 E and M of everyday electrical and mechanical information, an oral test of trade electrical knowledge, a test of knowledge of radio symbols, and Test 3b Mathematics. Though there was no differentiation between electrics and mechanics, a bipolar factor with 5 per cent. variance contrasted the mathematically more advanced Test 3b and Radio Symbols with the more practical or applied information in the oral trade test, 117M and Bennett. A similar study of eight comprehension tests was carried out in the U.S.A.A.F. by Davis (1947). His main bipolar factors contrasted the more verbal tests (Technical Vocabulary, Electricity and Knowledge of Tools) with a test of Practical Experience in Applying Mechanical Devices, and with tests in Principles of Mechanics and Mechanical Movements. If we were to measure more specialized knowledge of different branches of engineering, we should doubtless find further group factors separating, in the same manner as the secondary school or university subjects mentioned in Chapter IV.

Manipulative Tests. Assembly or other manipulative mechanical tests tend to give very high correlations with the $k:m$ complex. In five analyses which included Bennett and Squares paper-and-pencil tests, and Army Assembly, Meccano Assembly or Wirebending, the mean loadings on $k:m$ of the former were ·35 and of the latter, practical, tests ·76. Their respective mean g-loadings were ·59 and ·25. It seems likely therefore that, just as the F of performance tests is covered by k, so assembly tests involve no factor which is not measurable by paper-and-pencil tests of k and information. We would allow that assembly tests, like some performance tests, may bring in a small dexterity component. The Minnesota figures (Table X) suggest that if there is any additional mechanical manipulative factor among boys, it is quite small. Thurstone (1948) is engaged on an extensive research into the structure of mechanical ability, and his findings on this point will be awaited with interest.

One relevant analysis was made among 130 Army recruits under training as driver mechanics. Table XV shows the unrotated

TABLE XV. CENTROID AND GROUP FACTORS AMONG MECHANICAL TESTS APPLIED TO ARMY DRIVER MECHANICS

Test	Centroid Factors (unrotated)			General g+k:m	Group Factors		
	I	II	III				
2 Bennett Mechanical	·654	·154	·318	·662	·339		
4 Squares Spatial	·539	·258	·089	·521	·339		
Meccano Assembly	·876	·141	—·266	·924		·333	
Wiring Dexterity	·551	·291	—·155	·531		·333	
Mechanical Information	·724	—·280	·116	·631			·450
Mechanical Interests	·232	—·298	—·053	·136			·351
Course Marks	·795	—·256	—·085	·707			·471
Variance per cent.	42·8	6·1	3·2	39·5	14·3		

Thurstone factors, and the group factors extracted by Burt's technique. The Wiring test is a complex manual test of joining wires to terminals. Mechanical interests were measured by a test of the Strong type. The general factor is, of course, a mixture of g

and k:m, but there appear to be minor group factors, of doubtful significance, differentiating paper-and-pencil tests, manipulative tests, and measures of interest and information (the latter including the assessments of proficiency at the end of the course).

The finding that paper-and-pencil tests will (provided allowance is made for their higher g-loading) cover almost the same ground as practical performance or mechanical tests is of great importance to vocational psychologists. Practical tests naturally possess greater 'face' validity and may be justifiable on the grounds of their attractiveness to candidates and acceptability to employers. Yet it is a waste of time and money to use them if their statistical validity is not superior. In the investigation just described, the two manipulative tests combined correlate ·674 with the driver mechanics' course results, and the four pencil-and-paper tests correlate ·693.

Many psychologists, including the writer, like performance, assembly, or other practical tests not so much because of the predictive value of their scores, as because the testee's method of tackling the problems, his interest and concentration, etc., appear to give valuable qualitative clues (cf. e.g. Oakley and Macrae, 1937). Here we have the same situation as with the qualitative tests that clinical psychologists apply to neuropsychiatric patients (cf. p. 57). There may well be 'something in it', but if so, the qualities indicated by the tests, over and above the actual test score, should be shown to constitute reliable and consistent group factors. And so far no one has done this.

Effects of Training. It must be recognized that the patterning of k:m abilities depends to a considerable extent on the experience and training of the testees. An analysis of post-war regular entry naval air mechanics, all of whom had some trade experience, included the standard naval Tests 1–4 and 74, four Recruiting Centre tests, and an earlier Recruiting Centre battery of intelligence, arithmetic and dictation tests. Table XVI shows clear mathematical and dictation group factors, but there is no true k:m factor at all. Instead a technical education factor combines mathematics and the comprehension + spatial tests.

In another experiment parallel analyses were made of nine tests given to groups of 240 15-year and 18-year naval artificers. The younger group was just starting, the older group had nearly completed, its engineering training. In Fig. 6 the first bipolar factor

TABLE XVI.   ROTATED CENTROID FACTORS AMONG TESTS APPLIED TO 312 NAVAL AIR MECHANICS. (Loadings less than ·10 omitted).

Test	g	Tech. Educ.	Arith.	Dict.	h²
SP Test 1, Abstraction	·76				·58
RD Test, Abstraction	·78				·61
Recruiting Centre Verbal Intelligence	·43				·19
SP Test 4, Squares Spatial	·42	·11			·20
SP2, Bennett Mechanical Comprehension	·47	·41		—·11	·42
RA Test, Mechanical Comprehension and Information	·45	·40			·37
SP3a, Arithmetic	·29	—·22	·59	·15	·50
SP3b, Mathematics	·59	·37	·53		·77
Recruiting Centre Arithmetic	·56	·24	·56		·70
RB Test, Mathematics	·63	·14	·59		·76
SP Test 74, Dictation	·42			·57	·50
Recruiting Centre Dictation	·24			·60	·42
RC Test, Spelling	·50			·68	·73
Variance per cent.	27·8	4·7	10·1	9·3	51·9

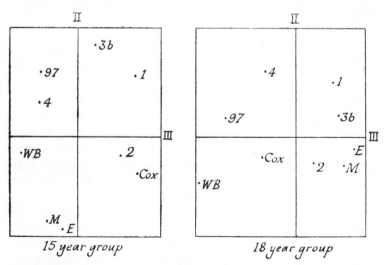

Key to the Tests

1—Abstraction.   Cox—Cox Mechanical Models.   4—Squares Spatial.
2—Bennett Mechanical.   M—Mechanical Information.   97—Memory for Designs.
36—Mathematics.   E—Electrical Information.   WB—Wirebending.

Fig. 6. Graphs of Factor Loadings in 15-year and 18-year Artificer Apprentices

for the younger group chiefly contrasts educational tests like 3b with technical information tests M and E. In the older group this factor has almost vanished and the main distinction, running from R to L instead of from top to bottom, is between technical education including mathematics *and* information on the one hand, and practical ability, chiefly represented by Wirebending, on the other. The technical education factor is presumably the same as that of Table XVI. The spatial tests (4 and 97), Abstraction Test 1 and Mechanical Comprehension Test 2 stay in much the same positions in the two graphs; but 3b, M and E move towards one another, and Wirebending moves outwards—in other words manipulative skill becomes more distinctive. Cox Models is a comprehension test at the younger age, but apparently becomes a more practical one later. Fig. 6 omits the first factor loadings of the tests, since they were closely similar in the two age groups. There was no evidence of greater differentiation of abilities, or lowered influence of g with age (cf. p. 30).

Another instance of alterations in structure with experience and/or with level of ability is offered by the analysis of tests given to African recruits (p. 106). The results were congruent with those obtained in this country, but showed closer integration of mechanical, manual and physical abilities on the one hand, and of intellectual (g) and educational abilities on the other hand. Further differences have been found in this country between men and women.

Analyses Among Women. Six main analyses were carried out on A.T.S. tests, three with representative populations of women recruits, one with a lower grade group of cooks, and two with high-grade groups of motor mechanics and special operators. In the two latter the results were quite similar to those of men, except for the restriction in variance of g, due to high selectivity. Table XVII shows the group-factor analysis loadings for special operators. Note that Spelling (SP 14) and Educational Standard have especially low g-saturations, and that Tests 2 and 4, but not Matrices, measure a $k{:}m$ factor. Among the motor mechanics the most interesting finding was the poor mechanical loading of a Models test. The $k{:}m$-saturations were: Matrices $\cdot12$, Bennett $\cdot44$, Squares $\cdot47$, Assembly $\cdot75$, Meccano Assembly $\cdot64$, Vincent Models $\cdot17$.

Much greater difficulty was experienced in arriving at acceptable factorial solutions among normal women (cf. Table XVII) and cooks. Not only did the Clerical and Spelling tests appear to obtain unduly high *g*-loadings, but Bennett Test 2 had extremely low *g* and *k:m*; presumably it measures a very largely specific factor in women. Further the Matrices test could not be differentiated from the *k:m* tests. Note the similarity of this result with a non-verbal *g* test to the results obtained by Slater among 11–13 year children, and to those of Mellone and McFarlane (pp. 68, 107). Either we must admit then that tests such as Matrices do depend largely on *k:m* in women—and this is the solution adopted in Table XVII—or that the *k:m* factor has hardly

TABLE XVII.   GROUP-FACTOR ANALYSES AMONG 200 REPRESENTATIVE A.T.S. RECRUITS AND 200 SPECIAL OPERATORS

Test	Normal Group				Special Operators			
	g	v:ed	k:m	h²	g	v:ed	k:m	h²
Progressive Matrices	·75		·32	·67	·68		·00	·46
2 Bennett Mechanical	·41		·29	·26	·43		·31	·28
4 Squares Spatial	·53		·51	·55	·38		·50	·39
24 Meccano Assembly	·43		·55	·49	—		—	—
14 Spelling	·64	·51		·67	·16	·74		·58
23 Arithmetic	·68	·34		·58	·49	·51		·50
12 Clerical	·81	·26		·72	·38	·52		·41
17, 25 Verbal	·66	·53		·71	·52	·42		·44
Educational Standard	·57	·45		·53	·23	·51		·32
Variance Per cent.	38·8	10·2	8·4	57·4	18·9	18·9	4·3	42·2

differentiated in Test 2 and only partially in Test 4 Squares and 24 Assembly. The second view would not only mean that spatial-mechanical tests measure hardly anything but *g*, but also that the *v:ed* tests would obtain smaller *g*-loadings than in men and larger *v:ed* loadings. A factorial investigation by Banks (1949) of large groups of Army and A.T.S. recruits confirms the first solution. Probably the main reason for the difference between men and average women is that the SP non-verbal tests give an even less adequate sampling of women's practical abilities than they do of men's. Had there been tests of, say, domestic and social abilities to constitute a contrasting pole with the *v:ed* tests, a more acceptable patterning of abilities might have been found.

Conclusions. The evidence of this and the preceding chapter indicates that we can hardly expect to discover a structure within

I

the $k:m$ complex as definite as that existing in the verbal-numerical field, since so much depends on the experience, training and background of the testees, and on the extent to which they are selected. Psychologists recognize nowadays that muscular development in the infant is neither differentiation of specific skills from generalized mass movements, nor the integration of elementary reflexes into complex habits, but a combination of both. Similarly we may expect group factors in mechanical ability to differentiate when specialized functions are practised, and to reintegrate into fresh patterns. Since considerable growth of $k:m$ occurs in the average male adolescent (cf. Vernon and Parry, 1949), it is probably accompanied by alterations of structure, depending on the skills trained in his employment or hobbies. And as any group of subjects large enough to yield significant factors is likely to be extremely heterogeneous in experience and training, such factors cannot be very clear-cut and cannot reveal much information about the abilities of any particular individual. Vernon and Parry (1949) point out also that k and m tests are considerably more useful in predicting trainability for mechanical jobs at 13–15 years, and among women, than among male adults. This too would be expected if $k:m$ tends to differentiate and to become more complex in structure in men after 15.

We should not expect investigations of the kind summarized above to throw much light on the problem of whether or not mechanical aptitude is innate. It would be foolish to deny the possibility when other aptitudes such as musical clearly possess an innate component. But we should recognize that most of what the layman implies by mechanical aptitude is attributable to g, to training and experience, and to temperamental and interest factors. So far there is no evidence that any person is untrainable in any practical job through lack of aptitude, provided he has sufficient g, persistence and interest, and is not suffering from nervous or muscular disease.

CHAPTER XI

OCCUPATIONAL ABILITIES

Abstract. A prominent general factor of aptitude for all jobs appears to be compounded of g, $v:ed$, and a drive component closely related to X. Beyond this, job abilities group into the more bookish and the more practical, and possibly other major types. But the scope of these group factors is probably small compared with that of minor group or specific factors. Hence transfer of ability from one specialized type of work to another is limited. Also the overlapping between factors established among tests and job factors is disappointing, so that vocational guidance (as distinct from selection) cannot hope to advance very far merely by trying to predict aptitude for general types of work from scores on a battery of tests.

Trainability—General or Specific. It is much more difficult to map out the main factors in vocational than in educational abilities, for the obvious reason that people do not work at several jobs simultaneously as they do at several subjects of study. Moreover, the persons in any single job tend to be more selected, either for intelligence or trade experience, than school pupils. However, several lines of investigation have been partially explored.

During the war it was possible to observe the trainability of men and women from different civilian occupations in different Service jobs. The importance of previous direct experience, i.e. of small group or specific job factors, was evident among drivers, telegraphists, clerks, and many types of tradesmen (cf. Vernon and Parry, 1949). For example, the correlation between previous driving experience and success at Army driving was higher than that of any battery of psychological tests. It is fair to state also that transfer effects were very limited, i.e. that experience in other superficially similar jobs was often of little or no value, though unfortunately no really reliable quantitative data are available. Thus machinists and fitters' and turners' mates did not do any better as naval ordnance, or engine room mechanics than did men from non-engineering occupations such as retail tradesmen, and no type of mechanical background appeared to assist radio or electrical mechanics. Much more influential—though this is difficult to prove—was a kind of general factor comprising intelligence and educational level and personality traits such as keenness, drive, seriousness of purpose. For example, clerks and policemen who tended to be high in such a factor did well at almost any job to which they were allocated, and usually surpassed men with a more practical background. Again it often happened that recruits who failed in one Service job had to be reallocated, and it was usually found necessary to move them to a job requiring lower general ability and application. If they were transferred to another job at the same level, in which they claimed some interest or experience, only too often they failed again. The layman's notion that there exists a niche or special type of work ideally suited to the specialized aptitudes of each individual appeared to be much less true than the view that all types of work and all employees fall along a single high-grade to low-grade continuum. The success of women workers at skilled engineering jobs during the war further supports this view, which has also been advocated recently by Philpott (1947). Admittedly the criterion of success was in most instances one of rapid trainability, and different results might have followed had ultimate proficiency been measurable. But so far as our rather patchy and impressionistic evidence goes, the situation seems to be very similar to that in education: namely that there is a strong general ability factor compounded partly of g (or $g + v:ed$), partly of a temperamental or interest factor akin to X, and that beyond this group factors or general types of vocational abilities are disappointingly small and minor group or specific factors relatively prominent. Though the industriousness or purposiveness factor is obviously complex and is, for example, affected by the recruit's morale or attitude to Service life, yet it is certainly closely related to our X factor. Personnel Selection Officers found that school and work record provided a most useful indicator, and in at least two experiments (Lummis, 1946; Vernon and Parry, 1949, p. 141) direct correlations were obtained between measures of educational 'drive' and proficiency in the Services.

Common Factors in Job Analyses. A second approach is that of Coombs and Satter (1949), who had fifty-four jobs in a large paper mill assessed by job analysis experts for the skills, knowledge, etc., required. The twenty jobs were then taken which showed *fewest* common elements, namely thirty-five to seventy-four out of a possible 104 elements, and correlations were derived from the numbers of elements and factorized. After rotation a clear-cut general + group factor pattern was obtained. The general factor, covering 43·4 per cent. of variance, represented common features or requirements in all types of job. Four 'families' of jobs, with combined variance 17·0 per cent., included:

A. Self-responsible jobs, e.g. employment interviewer, librarian supervisor.
B. Routine entry occupations, e.g. messenger, receptionist, nurse, shop clerk.
C. Skilled manual, e.g. multigraph, multilith and key punch operators.
D. Clerical.

The method might fruitfully be extended to a wider range of jobs, and would no doubt yield additional types. The authors point out that the size of the general factor largely depends on the skill and objectivity with which the assessments are made. But as especial care was taken in this study to avoid subjectivity, and as only the most independent jobs were factorized, its large variance (relative to the group factors) confirms the conclusions of the preceding paragraph.

Analyses of Training Marks. Obviously it would be better to analyse the actual skills of groups of workers, and useful evidence was collected in the Services when trainees were marked or rated for several different sections or aspects of an occupation. The major differentiation between *v:ed* and *k:m* types of work recurred as constantly as it does in the fields of education and of psychological tests. Thus among naval. Army and A.T.S. signallers and telegraphists, ability at theory or bookwork is partially distinct from ability at Morse. Similarly, informational attainments among clerks contrast with typewriting and stenography marks, technical acquirements among R.N.V.R. officer cadets with personality qualities, and so on. Table XVIII shows three (unrotated) factors extracted from eight sets of marks awarded to 250 naval engine room mechanics. A fairly prominent general factor runs through all the marks, but the bipolars indicate two group factors:

(1) Written general paper and electricity—predominantly theoretical subjects.
(2) Sheet metal work and fitting.

The remaining four subjects all give different factor patterns.

TABLE XVIII. CENTROID FACTORS IN THE COURSE MARKS OF ENGINE ROOM MECHANIC TRAINEES

Subject	I	II	III	h²
Written theory paper	·32	—·31	—·40	·36
Electrical Equipment and Wiring	·56	—·56	—·07	·63
Sheet Metal Work	·63	·34	·08	·53
Precision fitting	·66	·39	—·05	·59
Garage	·77	—·09	—·01	·62
Engines	·74	—·10	·47	·77
Oxy-acetylene welding	·49	·08	·27	·32
Centre Lathe	·40	·25	—·31	·32
Variance Per cent.	34·9	9·7	7·1	51·7

Sets of marks awarded to trainees in seven other branches such as signallers, telegraphists, R.N.V.R. officer cadets, and instructors showed much the same degree of overlapping, i.e. the same factor variances. Naval visual signalmen, for example, yielded distinctive group factors for theory or bookwork, for Morse receiving and transmitting, and for visual signalling. With leading torpedomen and electrical mechanics there was somewhat greater specificity, only 38 per cent. of variance being covered, probably because the duties in which they are examined are unusually diversified. Among electrical mechanics there were small group factors representing:

(1) Mining and Workshop.
(2) Gyro Compass and Whitehead (Torpedo).
(3) Schoolwork, Preliminary Electricity and Low Power Electrical Equipment.

Analysis of Objective Measures of Workshop Ability. Now all training marks, even when awarded by independent examiners, are liable to be influenced by the examiners' opinions of the trainees as individuals, their industriousness, alertness, etc. When objectively marked capacities are compared the generality is considerably reduced. A detailed study was made of twenty-seven sets of marks awarded to naval electrical mechanics during the six months' workshop training and theory course, most of them being based on standard test pieces in fitting, turning, etc. While seven sets of theory examination marks gave unrotated factors with variances 46·1, 8·1 and 4·1 (total 58·4 per cent.), the average result for three analyses of objective practical marks was 28·6, 10·6, 4·7 (total 44·1 per cent.). If the bipolar factors were converted into group factors, we should probably find that the group factors, corresponding to different types of job, are more prominent than general workshop ability. A specimen analysis of fitting jobs is shown in Table XIX. The second factor differentiates the first month's practice jobs from the second month's jobs and tests.

TABLE XIX. CENTROID FACTORS IN WORKSHOP PROFICIENCY
MEASURES AMONG 122 NAVAL ELECTRICAL MECHANICS

Marks	I	II	III	h²
Job No. 5478	·55	·19	·15	·36
,, ,, 5848	·80	·37	·08	·78
,, ,, 5001	·59	·42	—·21	·57
,, ,, 5050	·62	·13	—·20	·44
,, ,, 5867	·47	—·36	·35	·48
,, ,, 5838	·54	—·20	·49	·57
Practical Test 1	·46	—·26	—·28	·35
,, ,, 2	·54	—·28	—·38	·52
Variance per cent.	33·8	8·4	8·8	50·9

The third differentiates Nos. 5478 and 5848, which involve angles other than right angles, from Nos. 5001 and 5050 which involve right angles only. No. 5848 which brings in the greatest number of different angles has the highest general factor loading and communality. The third factor also separates the second month's precision jobs from the tests which were done under examination conditions without any advice from instructors. Thus different conditions of work as well as different types of job affect the correlations. Turning, shaping, thread-cutting, and other operations similarly yielded partially distinct factors in other analyses. The contrast between theory and workshop analyses is even more striking when it is pointed out that the trainees were extremely highly selected for intelligence, mathematical and electrical knowledge, whereas they were unselected (apart from good Test 2 and 4 scores) on the practical side, and were drawn from a great variety of—mostly non-mechanical—occupations.

The conclusion follows, then, that though a general ability at, or aptitude for, mechanical work does exist, quite apart from g, it is of small extent when objectively assessed, and factors specific to the particular type of operation or machine are more important. Each test job, occupying the trainees several days, may be aptly compared to a single mathematical test item, in reliability and in overlapping with other jobs or items. Hence, a very extensive sampling of jobs over months would be needed to yield a reliable objective criterion of workshop ability, although doubtless an experienced instructor could arrive at a fairly reliable—yet more subjective—estimate in a briefer time.

The only comparable study in the literature is that of the Minnesota investigators, who unfortunately do not report the overlapping between the various trade operations learned by their subjects. They do, however, mention that the correlation between the first ten weeks (fifty hours) of the boys' shopwork and the next twenty weeks was only ·42, which agrees well with our figures.

Test Factors and Job Factors. How far test factors and job factors overlap it is difficult to say in the absence of investigations where proficiencies at several types of work are compared with numerous psychological tests. One such study was conducted by Wheeler (1948) among R.A.F. airframe fitters. Analysis of course marks alone yielded a general factor with 50 per cent. and two bipolars with 15·5 per cent. of variance. The latter differentiated the marks awarded under examination conditions from those given during the course, also the more practical from the more theoretical marks. So far this duplicates our results quoted above for engine room and electrical mechanics. When the marks were analysed with thirteen psychological tests (cf. Table XIV) the most 'practical' tests 117M, Wirebending and Dexterity grouped with the course marks against the other ten tests; and a second bipolar contrasted the theory marks and $g + v{:}ed$ tests with the practical marks and $k{:}m$ tests.

Numerous follow-up studies (cf. Vernon and Parry, 1949) have similarly shown better validity for $v{:}ed$ tests in work of a clerical, verbal or theoretical nature; $k{:}m$ tests have obtained *relatively* higher validities in work of a practical nature, though $v{:}ed$ tests have been useful there also. At the same time, however good the battery of tests, validity is very far from perfect, indicating the presence of the additional X factor or factors in jobs. Thus the structure of job abilities appears to parallel closely that of educational abilities, and may be roughly represented as in Fig. 7. G, X and $v{:}ed$ together make up general occupational ability; this may be partially split into verbal, mechanical-practical and possibly other types (e.g. managerial, dealing with people, etc.), which themselves sub-divide indefinitely. As in education again the general factor and small group or specific factors cover much more variance than the major types.

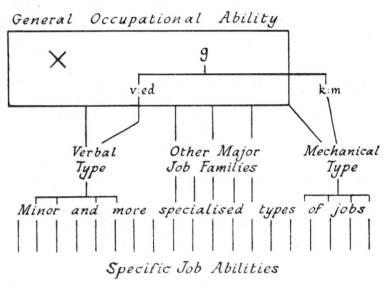

Fig. 7. Diagram illustrating the Structure of Occupational Abilities

We have no sure information as to whether jobs group in accordance with the other main test factors described in preceding chapters. Nevertheless, it is obvious that some jobs require much stronger physique than other, so that our physical factor may link up with these. In spite of the low validity and specificity of manual dexterity tests, they do often yield moderate correlations with machine operating and assembly jobs. The Division of Occupational Analysis claims that its non-verbal perceptual factor is especially relevant to visual inspection jobs in industry, but provides no evidence of validity for this, nor for the three psychomotor, factors. It is interesting, none the less, that the Matrices test and Group Test 70 (although apparently little dependent upon P) gave far their best validities during the war with visual signalling, radar and certain A.A. jobs involving visual perception. The relevance of the verbal perceptual factor, Q, to clerical jobs is well established. No close relation between the spatial factor and jobs that appear to involve k has been established, though it does link with mechanical ability in adolescents, and with some kind of practical efficiency in adults (cf. Vernon, 1947b). The mechanical information factor is much more highly correlated with success at mechanical jobs in general, also specialized trade knowledge tests with specialized trade skills.

Conclusions for Vocational Guidance and Selection. It would seem that we cannot hope to cover much more ground in the prediction of vocational suitability by means of spatial, perceptual, manual, or by rote memory, attention and other types of test than we do already with g, $v:ed$ and $k:m$ tests. Certainly it is worthwhile exploring the relevance of the established test factors for groups of jobs. But it appears unlikely that vocational guidance can ever be reduced to the application of a battery of tests for measuring all the main ability factors, and expecting an individual's pattern of factor scores to tell us what jobs he is suited to, though this is the aim of the Division of Occupational Analysis and of many American psychologists. In order to tap minor job group factors, we should almost certainly have to resort to more elaborate, expensive and time-consuming work-sample tests. These have their place in vocational selection but are hardly practicable for guidance. Psychologists giving guidance are justified in making the fullest possible use of g, $v:ed$ and $k:m$ tests, but thereafter their success is likely to depend chiefly on the extent to which they can gauge each candidate's previous relevant experience, and evaluate both his more general motivation or X, and his more specific attitudes to the jobs under consideration.

GENERAL + GROUP FACTOR *VS.* MULTIPLE FACTOR THEORIES

D IVERGENCES between the methods and conclusions of British and American investigators in the field of factor analysis are much less acute now than they were ten years ago. But there is still sufficient difference in their views on mental structure to make it essential to show why general + group-factor solutions are considered superior in this book.

Factorial Techniques. It should be pointed out first that Thurstone's centroid technique, being perhaps the simplest to apply, is very widely used in Britain. The main difference is that we either do not rotate the resulting factors, but use them to indicate what group factors are present before starting a true group-factor analysis, or else we rotate in such a way as to maximize rather than minimize a general factor. Conversely in America, Holzinger has always favoured group-factor techniques, and R. B. Cattell (1946) regards the hierarchical picture of abilities as superior to the multiple factor. There are a few minor differences of technique. Some British workers prefer Burt's original Simple Summation to the Centroid method, though the latter has a neater device for reflecting signs when extracting bipolar factors. Usually also we guess the communalities for insertion in the diagonal cells and repeat the analysis several times until the guesses approximate to the correct values, instead of—like Thurstone and his followers —inserting the highest correlation in each column at each stage. Thurstone's short-cut is liable to exaggerate the communalities, and therefore the size and number of the later factors (cf. Burt, 1938). But Burt's more accurate successive approximation technique is hardly practicable when the number of tests is large, say fifteen or more, or the number of factors is large.

Number of Statistically Significant Factors. A more important difference between the methods commonly used by factorists in the two countries is that British writers often stop at two factors (or g + two group factors) and seldom exceed four, whereas Americans seldom extract less than five and often exceed twelve. Both agree that factors should satisfy a criterion of statistical significance, but American criteria seem to us so lax that many of the later factors they obtain from smallish populations must be considerably distorted by chance errors. Spearman (1939) strongly criticized Thurstone's original primary factor study on these grounds. Unfortunately centroid analysis (unlike Maximum Likelihood, Principal Components and some other techniques) is mathematically, a rather rough and approximate technique, hence its exact sampling errors are unknown. It seems probable that the chi-squared tests advocated by Burt (1940) are unduly strict, and that the checks popularly used in America, namely, Tucker's and Coombs's, are too lax. But Burt and Banks's (1947) most recent formula for the Standard Error of single loadings,[1] and McNemar's (1942a) logically derived formula for the significance of residuals, have both been checked empirically and, in the writer's experience, yield much the same results. Guilford and Lacey's criterion is the simplest,[2] and though much more rough, it too agrees in showing that most British factorists have in the past been too cautious, most American ones too indulgent.

Disagreement Regarding G. There is thus no essential disagreement on mathematical points, and provided that group-and-multiple-factor analyses account equally well for the original correlations by means of the same limited number of factors, they are equally legitimate. Moreover, many American factorists do, like British ones, find a g-factor nowadays, as was shown in Chapter II. But it still remains true that British writers make g as large as possible, and posit group factors only when the residuals necessitate them, whereas Americans either introduce g as a second order factor, or, if a primary one is unavoidable, tend to minimize it. Again British workers recognize larger or more comprehensive group factors together with sub-factors 'descended'

---

[1] S.E. of a loading, $r = \dfrac{(1-r^2)\sqrt{n}}{\sqrt{N(n-s-1)}}$ where n = number of tests, and s = the number of the factor. The writer would suggest that about half the loadings should exceed twice this S.E. for a factor as a whole to be regarded as significant.

[2] Namely, that the product of the two highest loadings in a factor, regardless of sign, should exceed the S.E. of zero r. Unfortunately Guilford often fails to adhere to his own rule, hence several of the factors claimed in his U.S.A.A.F. researches are certainly not significant.

from them, whereas American primary factors more often all possess much the same status and variance. Not only do such primary factors seem, from our standpoint, to carry some of the variance that would be better attributed to g, but also one or more of them (usually a Reasoning factor) may consist wholly of g.

The main arguments are as follows.

(1) **Size of G in Unselected Populations.** G is so much larger than all other factors put together in unselected populations of adults or children that it is psychologically foolish as well as mathematically difficult to belittle it. It may legitimately be asked why representative populations should be taken as a standard, rather than selected ones such as college students, among whom it is often quite difficult to establish a g. The writer would agree that analyses of selected groups like Thurstone's and Guilford's are useful for bringing up group factors which might otherwise be obscured. But Thurstone (1945) himself acknowledges that selection, though not affecting the main factor pattern, does distort the sizes of the loadings. And he points out that when selection is complex (based on several variables) artificial factors may be introduced. In most investigations of college students selection is based on a great variety of socio-economic, educational and other influences which are unlikely to be correlated with any factor other than g. Hence the g-variance only is reduced and no great harm is done. But Guilford's pilots were mostly doubly selected, by the U.S.A.A.F. Qualifying Examination and by the Aircrew Aptitude battery, that is to say by tests which are themselves more closely correlated with some of the tests to be factorized than with others. And this is likely to have played havoc with the obtained correlations and the resulting factor patterns. True Dudek (1948) has tried to show that the same factors do emerge in a group selected by the Qualifying Examination, and in a group of women pilots, as in an unselected group of candidates. But in fact he gets parallel results only for five of the most commonly accepted factors; the smaller factors differ considerably in these three populations. Moreover, none of these groups had been doubly selected as had many of those in which Guilford's more dubious Reasoning, Integration and Spatial factors occurred.

(2) **Greater Stability of G and the Major Group Factors.** Burt has claimed that group-factor solutions are more invariant or stable than primary factor ones, that is less liable to vary in differ-

ent populations or with alterations in the battery of tests. While this might be difficult to prove, it is clear that g, the major group factors and some of the minor ones almost always turn up in much the same form in any reasonably representative group. In contrast American writers have described at least a hundred ability factors of one kind or another, which are only partially reconcilable with Thurstone's, though it is true that Thurstone's own results show greater uniformity. Balinsky's (1941) investigation of the Wechsler-Bellevue scale is interesting in this respect. In all his age groups there was a clear differentiation between verbal and performance tests, but no other consistent factors were found in several successive groups. The Division of Occupational Analysis also found considerable variations in their nine studies, but the most stable factors were V, N and S. Surely then it is more logical to stress the major general and group factors which almost always turn up and whose statistical significance is indubitable, and to admit that the minor ones are so dependent on the particular set of tests and the heterogeneity and background of the particular populations tested that they do not merit the designation 'primary'.

(3) **Quickness of Group and Multiple-Factor Techniques: Relative Subjectivity.**   Group-factor analysis is very much quicker.   Given the correlations between twenty tests the present writer can usually perform the analysis in a day, where a controid analysis with rotation would take him a week. Banks (1948) makes a similar observation in re-analysing some of Cattell's personality data. Even when a preliminary centroid analysis is made in order to indicate objectively what group factors are present, the time saved on successive approximation to communalities and on rotation is very considerable. It must be admitted, however, as a counter-argument, that there is rather a large element of subjective choice in most group factor analyses, even when they are guided by centroid results.[1] One naturally tends to aim at factor patterns which are consonant with those obtained for the same tests in previous studies, and may therefore fail to realize that some of these preconceptions are wrong. Thurstone would claim that rotation to simple structure is objective, i.e. that there is one best

---

[1] When every test depends on g and one group factor only, and when there are at least three such group factors, then group factor analysis can be done completely objectively by Burt's formula (1940a, p. 482), or by Holzinger's bifactor method. But such a simple pattern is rather rare.

solution to each factorial problem which maximizes the number of insignificant loadings. Indeed some factorists such as Cattell actually carry out their rotations without knowing which test is which. But it is obvious that the majority are less strong-minded, and that their rotations are made in the light of their judgment of the content of the factorized tests. Centroid analysis may therefore be as subjective as group factor.

(4) **Divisibility of Primary Factors.** As would be expected on the hierarchical theory, more detailed investigation of particular primary factors frequently splits them up into smaller components. Examples are provided by Davis's and Langsam's studies of reading ability, Guilford's of the spatial factor, Taylor's and Carroll's studies of V and W, etc. True, Thurstone himself is careful not to claim that his factors are ultimate mental elements, but if the term *primary* is used, it is curious that they should be so unstable. When Simple Structure is aimed at, there is no ready means of indicating that some factors are more comprehensive than others, or can include others. Oblique and second order factors could indeed cover this situation, but no American factorist has yet systematically analysed a varied battery of tests into several higher order factors and sub-factors, along the lines of the group-factor analyses in Tables V and IX.

Unless some such plan is adopted it is difficult to see where factorization is to stop. Guilford's work indicates that almost any specific factor (in Spearman's sense) can be turned into a primary factor, given sufficient ingenuity in test construction. The view was put forward in Chapter III that highly specialized factors, which have no appreciable significance for everyday life, are not worth isolating. If this is agreed, it necessitates some distinction between the more fundamental factors, which are preferably extracted first, and the narrower ones. In other words, factorists should aim not merely to reduce large numbers of variables to a few components that account for their inter-correlations, but also to reduce them to the fewest components which will cover most variance.

(5) **No Test Measures a Single Factor.** In spite of many efforts, no psychologist has been able to devise a test which is truly 'univocal', i.e. which measures only a single primary factor (apart from error variance). Guilford and Michael (1948) admit that in order to measure a person's factor score, it is usually necessary to

add 'suppressor variables', that is to subtract weighted scores on other tests in order to eliminate the unwanted g or other content. Why not admit then that all tests do involve g, instead of artificially removing it by means of rotation?

(6) **Hierarchy a Statistical Artefact?**   One argument in the opposite direction is that the notion of hierarchy arises merely because centroid analysis yields a general factor and a series of bipolar factors sub-dividing the tests into smaller groups.   This might be answered by pointing out that group-factor analysis preceded multiple factor in psychology. Moreover, in most analyses, g differs considerably from the first centroid factor, and group factors do not necessarily correspond to the bipolars; any one group factor often combines parts of the variance of the first factor and of two or more bipolars.   Finally, we have admitted (p. 25f) that the strict hierarchy of Fig. 1 is an over-simplification.

(7) **Psychological Soundness of Procedures Deriving from the Opposed Theories.**   Perhaps the most important objection to a 'neo-faculty' viewpoint is that it tends to encourage undesirable practices in educational and vocational guidance. Although factorists themselves are well aware of the dangers of the 'naming fallacy', the users of their tests are not. If testers are told that a test is a good measure of the verbal factor, or the memory factor, etc., they jump to the conclusion only too easily that such a test will predict ability for any job, or type of education, which seems to them to involve verbal ability, or memory.   The Division of Occupational Analysis's General Aptitude Test Battery provides a flagrant instance.   Personnel officers will naturally suppose that candidates for jobs apparently requiring hand-eye co-ordination should score well on the hand-eye co-ordination factor.   But in actual fact the score for this factor is based purely on two tests of drawing lines and making dots accurately, and there is no evidence whatever as to the validity of these tests for any job.   Previous research would suggest that it is extremely low.   We do not question the great utility of batteries of differential aptitude tests such as this one, or Guilford and Zimmerman's (1948) and others. But they should not be published without objective evidence of their correlations with job success; and if, as is usually the case, the factorial structure of the tests is complex and their loadings with practically important factors over and above g and $v{:}ed$ or $k{:}m$ is small, this should be made clear.

This point is much more obvious to the vocational or educational psychologist who accepts the hierarchical theory. Moreover, this theory considerably simplifies his or her task. Instead of having to apply a very lengthy battery such as the G.A.T.B. to all candidates for guidance, in order to determine their profiles on ten factors, he realizes that a short battery of $v:ed$ and $k:m$ tests, which can be given and scored in one hour, will take him a very long way.[1] It will cover most of the ground in educational or vocational prediction that can ever be covered by tests. He can, however, proceed to give tests of further minor factors (perceptual, manual, etc.) or tests of a more work-sample type referring to particular jobs, in order to achieve a gain in accuracy of some 5 to 10 per cent., if this appears to be needed in any individual case. Again, the hierarchical viewpoint justifies the use, for many purposes, of the I.Q. or of comparable measures of adult intelligence, that is of g or $g + v$ tests alone.[2] To the multiple factorist the I.Q. is meaningless compound, and Thurstone, Guilford and others strongly advocate the substitution of tests of half a dozen, or a dozen or more, factors. But in spite of their criticisms, the I.Q. is found as useful and convenient by American practising psychologists as by British ones. Even if they do not realize it, such psychologists are thereby committed to a hierarchical rather than a multiple-factor viewpoint. And they are less likely to be led astray by their present procedures than they would be by ambitious schemes for differential testing of all the main factors.

[1] Note that the combined score on such a battery will provide a measure of g, without the need of any tests of g alone. Similarly it follows from the hierarchical theory that scores on tests of minor group factors will add up to give a measure of the major group factor from which they derive.

[2] Similarly it justifies the use of general reading attainment tests instead of separate tests for different reading factors which Davis and others advocate.

FACTOR ANALYSIS FROM 1950 TO 1959

Since this book was written there has been a tremendous volume of factorial research, which has greatly extended the range and diversity of alleged factors of the mind. Yet it could hardly be claimed that any very fundamental advances have occurred which would have necessitated rewriting all the preceding chapters. Much work has been carried out in countries other than the United States and Britain—for example in France (Bernyer, Reuchlin, Bonnardel), Sweden (Elmgren, Henrysson), Finland (Ahmavaara), Egypt (El Koussy); and international conferences on factorial techniques and results were held in Uppsala (1953) and Paris (1956).

Statistical Methods. Several textbooks dealing with statistical aspects of factor analysis deserve mention. Shortly before his death, Thomson (1954) published a brief but illuminating interpretation of the subject in geometrical terms. Adcock (1956) has provided a short survey of the aims and techniques of analysis for non-mathematical students. Fruchter's book (1954–b) covers working methods and main results; it summarizes several illustrative analyses and includes a very extensive bibliography. Cattell's book (1952) is particularly useful for its detailed guidance on rotational technique, and on the various 'group' methods of analysis. These latter reduce the labour of successive extraction of one centroid factor after another by pinning down main clusters of tests beforehand; then all the designated factors are extracted simultaneously.

The wider availability, in universities and other institutions, of electronic computers has greatly increased the ease of inter-correlating, and of extracting numerous factors from, large numbers of tests (cf. Cattell, 1954), and made it possible to employ statistically more efficient methods such as Lawley's Maximum Likelihood (cf. Maxwell, 1959a). However computers cannot readily adjust the communalities after each factor, as in the ordinary centroid technique, which is still the most popular. Some workers insert 1·00 in the diagonal cells, thus in effect arriving at principal axes rather than centroid factors. But when the number of tests is large this makes little difference to the loadings.

C. Wrigley (1957) points out the virtual insolubility of the problem of correct communalities, since these will vary with the number of factors the investigator judges to be present; and he makes a case for employing the multiple correlations (squared) of each test with the remainder of the battery. This quantity—which is easily obtained by machine—clearly represents the total overlapping or common variance among the tests, and thus provides an estimate of the true communality.

There has been much discussion, also, of ways to reduce the subjectivity involved in rotating axes, since even if Thurstone's principle of Simple Structure is followed there is considerable room for personal choice. Wrigley suggested an objective technique for orthogonal rotations—the quartimax (Neuhaus and Wrigley, 1954). In essence this maximizes the variance in each row of factor loadings, thus automatically yielding as many zero loadings as possible, and one, or only a few, high loadings for each test.[1] The present writer would support Burt's contention that the sign pattern of the unrotated bipolar factors indicates objectively what factors are present; nevertheless it is certainly helpful to have a quartimax solution as further evidence. Moreover the latter does not, like most Simple Structure solutions, rule out a general factor plus group factors of varying breadth.

Eysenck (1950) criticizes Thurstone's and Cattell's claim that rotation to Simple Structure will *ipso facto* lead to 'psychologically meaningful' factors, and proposes another approach to the rotation problem which he calls Criterion Analysis. If a battery of tests is designed to cover a hypothesized factor—say 'neuroticism'—and the extent to which each test differentiates between normal and neurotic groups is known, then the centroid factors in a normal population can be rotated so that one of these parallels as closely as possible the normal-neurotic differences. In other words, tests which show the highest validity against an objective, external criterion should also yield the highest saturations on a factor internal

[1] Kaiser's modification, the Varimax technique, which maximizes variances within columns (factors) instead of rows (tests) seems more promising in rotating personality or attitude, as distinct from ability, factors.

to the battery. Presumably this comes to much the same thing as including, for example, age or sex differences as variables *within* a battery, and rotating one of the factors to pass through each of these variables; though Eysenck rejects this simpler procedure. However, the most recent trend among statisticians (summarized by Maxwell, 1959a) is to urge the factorist to hypothesize beforehand just what factors are present. If he can specify which tests should show zero loadings on each factor, the factorial and rotational solutions will be completely determined.

In addition to the technical contributions from European authors, listed in the first paragraph, mention should be made of a long series of articles by Burt in the *British Journal of Statistical Psychology* (1947–57). These cover such topics as the historical development of Spearman's work, the statistical significance of factors (1952), the transformation of centroid to general + group factors by matrix algebra, etc. An article by Bernyer (1958) shows the possibility of arriving at virtually the same final picture of the structure of a battery of tests either using the group factor approach, or by rotation to oblique simple structure and extracting a second-order general factor. Burt's reworking of Sutherland's and Renshaw's analyses of ability tests (Renshaw, 1952) illustrates how the former may yield a simpler and more logical solution than the complex set of 5 first-order and 2–4 second-order factors revealed by the latter. That there are still far too great variations in the factorial procedures of different factorists, and weaknesses of technique, is brought out by McNemar (1951) and Guilford (1952).

The Status of Factors. The most interesting book of the past decade is Oléron's *Les Composantes de L'Intelligence d'Après Les Recherches Factorielles*. It provides a refreshingly impartial and logical survey of the British and the American schools. Oléron contrasts Thurstone's 'realist' with Burt's 'nominalist' view of factors, and believes that there is sufficient stability among the results of different researches to justify according factors a certain reality. At least they are valuable constructs which can form the bases for hypotheses (cf. also Barratt, 1956). Unfortunately, however, the best-established factors, such as Thurstone's, represent the external qualities or materials of the tests—verbal, numerical, spatial, etc.—rather than central mental functions. It may be that statistical analysis alone is incapable of yielding these more fundamental functional components of mind. He therefore commends Meili's work (pp. 58–9)[1] though it was conducted on too small a scale to be more than suggestive. And he thinks that this, together with analyses of Gestalt-like closure factors (pp. 89–90), studies of mental pathology such as Halstead's (p. 60), and Guilford's investigations of high-grade intellectual qualities (see below), will be the most productive of future advances.

Oléron shows that g cannot be accorded the status of a fundamental and unique aptitude, as Spearman believed, if only because its presence or absence depends so largely on the heterogeneity of the tested population. At the same time it is not merely a kind of average of the particular battery of tests employed, since it is clearly more marked in tests of more complex intellectual functions than in simpler cognitive processes. It corresponds pretty closely to what we mean by 'intelligence', provided we admit—with Guilford—that this differentiates into a wide range of abilities at higher levels. He criticises Burt's and the present writer's notion of a hierarchy of group factors, particularly their comparison with a genealogical tree which suggests that minor group factors in a sense 'descend from' major ones, and major ones from g[2]. Admittedly it may be misleading to think of v and k as 'growing out of' g. But Burt does not imply this; rather, he holds that abilities are organized in a series of levels, ranging from the simplest sensory and motor capacities to the most general relational ones, and this conception—he argues—is supported by evolutionary and neurological evidence. It is not merely a statistical artifact arising from the initial extraction of a general and bipolar factors (cf. Moursy, 1952). To the present writer, the value of the hierarchical picture and his diagrams Nos. 2–5 and 7 is as much logical or technological (i.e. useful in selection and guidance) as psychological. That is—in classifying or counselling individuals one may first think of them as being high or low in relation to any educational, vocational or cognitive task, and then sub-classify according to the

[1] Page numbers refer to earlier chapters in this book.
[2] In particular Oléron criticizes the writer's suggestion (pp. 27–8) that a comprehensive coverage of abilities would analyze into g 40%, major and minor group factors 20%, narrow group factors, specificity and unreliability 40%, on the grounds that the apparent importance of g is exaggerated since it alone enters into all the tests. But this is quite legitimate: in any one typical test (as well as in the battery as a whole) the average g variance is estimated as 40%, and the variance attributable to its own particular group factor as 20%. Maybe the 20% is an under-estimate, but the writer regards it as reasonable, always provided that the tested population represents the whole range of ability.

verbal-practical and other group factors. The same categorization applies, of course, to tests. But Oléron would maintain that factors can and should be of psychological significance, whether or not they possess demonstrable technological value.

The Differentiation of G. The problem of whether g differentiates with increasing age (pp. 29–31) has been further investigated. Peel and Graham (1951–2) were able to retest at $10\frac{1}{2}$ a group of children who had taken a battery of printed and of performance tests at 9. If anything the general factor variance increased with age. However, Curtis (1949) has brought out the importance of the difficulty-level of the tests; when tests became easier—as in Peel's older group—their generality tends to rise. Kenny (1958) points out that changes in the reliability of the tests are not relevant; they may alter the overall size of factor loadings, but should not affect factorial structure. He argues, also, that it is insufficient to consider merely the absolute level of g-saturations, or the relative proportion of g to group-factor variance: rather we should study changes in the angular disposition of vectors representing mental tests in common factor space. In his own study of 9, $11\frac{1}{2}$ and 14-year pupils, he paid particular attention to securing tests which would be evenly discriminative and which would measure uniform abilities over their whole range of difficulty. Making allowance, also, for any changes in the heterogeneity of his samples, he was unable to find any evidence of differentiation.

Nevertheless, it is probable that we are still oversimplifying the issue in that no test is likely to depend on what are really the same abilities at different age levels. In Vocabulary, for example, a much richer kind of thinking is required for defining 'Courage' than for defining 'Orange'. In spite of such psychological differentiation, the correlations of Vocabulary with other tests, *i.e.* the factorial structure, might remain stable, so long as the selectivity of the population is held constant.

Higher Intellectual Capacities. Further criticisms of the factorial picture of the mind were put forward by Hearnshaw in 1951. Particularly he disputed the notion that we have now reached a complete or final map of human abilities (though this is specifically disclaimed on p. 10). The writer entirely concurs with Hearnshaw's definition of intellect as 'a cluster of high-grade skills concerned with problem solving', and with his belief that our present intelligence tests ignore a number of important intellectual qualities, which might be recognized as additional group factors if properly investigated. Among these he lists:

1. Temporal integration—the capacity to relate events over a period of time, to think with reference to the past and the future. This is markedly lacking in lower animals, is readily disorganized by brain damage, schizophrenia and old age, and it may be weak in maladjusted or psychopathic individuals who fail to acquire long-term goals. In a later paper (1956) Hearnshaw describes several experimental tests involving generalization over a series of successively presented data—as it were, temporal progressive matrices—and indicates that these are not highly loaded with g or v.

2. Concept formation, or capacity for reaching new generalizations, which is covered at present only by a few poorly constructed and poorly standardized clinical tests. Lovell (1955) subsequently showed that such tests as the Wisconsin, Vinacke's and Trist-Semeonoff's could be adapted for group application and that—together with non-verbal classification or similarities tests—they yielded a conceptualization or categorization factor over and above g, v and k. Not only is this ability particularly liable to deteriorate with ageing and lack of intellectual stimulation, but in another research (Butt, 1957) it seemed to be strongly linked with secondary school achievement.

A further contribution in this area is that of Beard (1957) who applied the factorial approach to Piaget's theories of concept development. She adapted over 90 tests from Piaget's writings and applied these individually to sixty 6 or 7-year olds, along with the Terman-Merrill test. Tetrachoric inter-correlations for a small population are, of course, too unreliable to yield a very definite factorial picture. However, a large general factor appeared which was almost identical with Mental Age, showing that all types of concept development depend more on individual differences in intelligence than, as Piaget suggests, on chronological age. Over and above this there was some tendency for particular types of test—concepts of the world, of space and time, number, mechanical-scientific, etc., to yield small group factors.

3. Judgment or 'wisdom'—the ability to structure the details of a problem situation according to their significance in the light of the individual's organized past experience, e.g. the skill of the clinician. Possibly this quality is a general ability, possibly specific

to each field of interest such as medicine, politics, business, artistic appreciation, etc. Its importance is certainly recognized by the layman, and although it is specifically excluded in intelligence tests, attempts have recently been made to incorporate it in educational attainments tests (cf. Bloom, 1956). A rather different interpretation of the nature of judgment has been put forward by Guilford, to whose outstanding work we now turn.

Over the past decade, Guilford and his colleagues at the University of Southern California have issued a long series of reports on 'The Aptitudes of High-level Personnel'. While starting from the list of factors claimed in the USAAF studies (pp. 21–2), he has been particularly concerned with the variety and structure of higher intellectual abilities, claiming—with good justification—that these are far too diverse and complex to be represented by a single intelligence or *g*. Each research begins with a careful theoretical analysis of some domain of intellect—*e.g.* reasoning, judgment, planning, creativity—guided by previous factorial results and leading to the postulation of a set of hypothetical components or distinctive abilities. Several tests are then constructed to cover each of these components, and are applied to a high-grade population, such as air officer cadets, along with a battery of 'reference tests' of familiar factorial composition. A dozen or more factors are extracted and rotated orthogonally and, after isolating the familiar Verbal, Visualization, Number, etc., the new factors serve to confirm, modify, or contradict the initial hypotheses. By this cumulative procedure their nature becomes progressively clarified and—in theory at least—all domains are eventually covered.

Guilford's composite map or chart of intellect now includes some fifty factors, plus almost as many blank spaces that he hopes to fill later, and these are grouped under five main headings representing different kinds of mental operations.[1]

I. Recognition factors (including Verbal Comprehension, Spatial Orientation and various types of Eduction, Planning and Foresight).

II. Convergent thinking factors, which issue in a predetermined result (including Eduction of Correlates, Deduction, Numerical Facility, etc.).

[1] The chart given in 'The Structure of Intellect' (1956) has been considerably modified in a later article (1959), and will doubtless be modified further.

III. Divergent thinking (Originality, Fluency and Flexibility factors).

IV. Evaluation and judgment (also Sensitivity to Problems, Perceptual Speed, Estimation of Lengths, etc.).

 V. Memory factors (Visual, Auditory, Memory Span, Meaningful Memory, etc.).

Each of these headings is cross-classified, first by content or material, and secondly by the products or type of thing cognized, discovered, evaluated or remembered. The three categories of content are:

Figural (non-verbal).

Structural or symbolic (e.g. letters or numbers).

Conceptual or semantic (verbal).

Since all the tests employed have been group paper-and-pencil ones, we do not know whether practical performance tests might not involve a fourth category. Guilford himself suggests that there should be a further 'behavioural' category, to include varieties of what is often called 'social intelligence'.

We will illustrate one complete section of his scheme by the following chart of I. Cognition Factors.

Product	Figural	Structural	Conceptual
Units	Figural closure Auditory figural recognition	Cognizing symbolic units	Verbal comprehension
Classes	Figure classification	Symbolic classification	Verbal classification
Relations	Eduction of figural relations (*e.g.* Progressive Matrices)	Eduction of structural relations	Eduction of conceptual relations (e.g. Analogies)
Systems	Spatial orientation	Eduction of structural patterns	General reasoning
Transformations	Visualization		
Implications	Perceptual foresight		Conceptual foresight

For detailed descriptions of each factor and of the tests that chiefly compose them, the reader must refer to Guilford's original reports and articles (Guilford, 1956, 1959; Guilford *et al.*, 1950–59; Green, Guilford *et al.*, 1953, Hertzka, Guilford *et al.*, 1954; Wilson, Guilford *et al.*, 1953). Despite one's admiration for the breadth and ingenuity of Guilford's work, one must confess to grave doubts regarding its ultimate validity. The following weaknesses should be pointed out.

1. There is no good proof of the independence of anything like such a large number of factors, even in highly-selected groups. Most of the separate researches cover only some half-dozen of the new factors at a time, and if even a dozen could be studied simultaneously (together with reference factors), it is probable that several would coalesce or mutually modify one another. Again, if broad verbal, spatial and numerical (i.e. 'material' factors) were first removed, one might hope that the three columns would usually coalesce into one. Guilford does not deny that there may be second-order factors running through sets of several of his listed factors, but he has not yet published any study of these because they are liable to vary so markedly with the selectivity of the tested population.

2. No other laboratory or research institution seems to have been convinced of the validity of Guilford's scheme, nor (with few exceptions) to have used his factors as a basis for fresh exprimentation. And although the consistency of findings from one research by Guilford to another is quite striking, investigations by others seldom provide much confirmation. Several large-scale studies such as those of Adkins and Lyerly on reasoning (1952) Botzum (1951) and Pemberton (1952a) on closure, Rimoldi (1951) and Corter (1952) have yielded results which can be only partially reconciled with one another or with Guilford's classifications. A less elaborate scheme based on fewer, more distinctive, factors might gain wider acceptance, show greater stability from one research to another and greater practical utility; though Guilford would no doubt answer that it would give a less complete picture of the complexities of intellect.

3. There is a serious dearth of external validatory evidence to show that the new factors give additional information about thinking in everyday life. Certainly this is difficult to come by, but one would hope for proof that each new factor could contribute

to the selection of people with thinking capacities needed for particular jobs or courses of study (cf. p. 27). A small-scale research by Hills (1955) into the relations between college mathematics grades and 9 tests highly loaded on 9 of the factors led to the disappointing conclusion that 'there is no particular ability or set of abilities or traits which is universally associated with success in mathematics'. Certain tests appeared to be predictive of some courses at one institution, but not of similar courses given by other instructors, or in other institutions. Single tests are not, of course, the same as factor measurements. But until some external or 'real-life' meaning can be attached to more of the factors, the criticism can hardly be refuted that they represent not so much thinking abilities as abilities to do the various kinds of psychological tests. This suspicion is strengthened by our later discussion of 'formal' factors.

One notable exception to these strictures is provided by Guilford's factor of Originality, though even here a rather broader factor, including parts of his flexibility and fluency factors, would seem more useful. The measurement of Originality represents a *volte face* from the tendency, among American psychologists, to rely exclusively on multiple-choice (i.e. 'convergent') aptitude and attainment tests. Thus a common factor is found among creative-response tests like the following (though it is not known how much of this could be resolved into $g + v$, or possibly concept-formation, in less homogeneous groups):

1. Consequences. E.g. if everyone in the world suddenly doubled in height, write down as many changes as possible which would be likely to occur.

2. Unusual uses. Think of as many unusual uses as possible for a newspaper (e.g. lighting a fire), for a brick, etc.

Scoring based on numbers of responses turns these into Ideational Fluency tests, according to Guilford better measures of Originality are obtained by scoring for uncommonness or unusualness of the responses.

3. Writing titles for plots of short stories. Here the scoring is based on ratings for cleverness of responses.

4. Unusual anagrams.

5. Original responses to Rorschach inkblots or T.A.T.

An interesting feature of Guilford's factor is that it yielded slight negative loadings for certain multiple-choice tests of other factors which were scored for rather arbitrary and conventional responses. In a later research with Coast Guard cadets (Guilford, 1955), it correlated $-·08$ with Reading Comprehension, $-·15$ with Engineering Drawing grades, and $-·22$ with Cruise ratings. Such results by no means prove that multiple-choice tests as such are antithetical to originality, as some critics of new-type examinations believe. But at least they suggest that creativity is a measurable quality which is unlikely to find scope in the conventional type of test. Conceivably it does find expression in the essay-type examination, which is much more widely employed in the European than in the American educational system; but its recognition by the particular examiner who marks such work is notoriously chancy.

Further researches by Barron (1955) and Drevdahl (1956) have provided some external confirmation of validity, namely promising positive correlations between tests such as those mentioned above and ratings for creativity. Moreover they revealed a psychologically plausible picture of the personality of the 'creative' individual. He tends to be non-conformist, self-sufficient, introverted, radical and intolerant—in other words the sort of person who may fail to make a very favourable impression on peers, teachers or employers. With some further development, therefore, originality tests should yield a particularly valuable supplement to conventional tests and personal assessments in the selection of students or employees who are likely to be capable of future creative work. Guilford *et al.* have also published an extensive investigation into the relations between 12 thinking factors (including Originality) and 24 personality variables, measured by inventories. Though most of the coefficients were very small, they generally gave a psychologically plausible picture. Originality was associated with interests in aesthetic expression, in meditative and original thinking, and negatively with need for discipline and orderliness. Guilford's picture is not entirely congruent with Barron's, but this may be because his personality tests hardly covered the social traits mentioned above.

Unintentional Factors. A good deal more evidence on practice, difficulty, speed and other factors (Chap. VII) has accumulated in recent years; and it seems possible that these unwanted or unsuspected influences on test scores may often play a larger part than functional differences in the production of factors. For example, the differentiation that many factorists, from Thurstone onwards, have drawn between *I* or inductive reasoning and *D* or deductive reasoning may arise, not so much because they involve distinguishable intellectual processes as because most *I* tests involve non-verbal, numerical or symbolic material, whereas most *D* tests consist of meaningful verbal problems. May it not be that the vast number of factors claimed by Guilford, and the lack of agreement among other factorists, are partly due to various irrelevant aspects of test performance?

The writer has discussed this problem at length elsewhere (Vernon, 1958), with particular reference to the testing of educational attainments. In this area the effects of form of response are best illustrated by the phenomena of examination-, or test-, sophistication. Where essay-examinations are used, the ability of students to write fluently, legibly, with correct usage and spelling and to make a good impression on the examiners, affects their marks in any subject, thus constituting an additional common factor. Similarly, where students are sophisticated to new-type tests and examinations, they become more adept in recognizing unsuspected clues, in reading the questions before the passages or 'item-stems' to which they refer, in apportioning their time and guessing wisely, etc. This likewise enhances correlations between tests of different subjects or different functions. But as the test-facility factor is very different from the essay-facility factor, correlations between essay and new-type examinations in the same subject are always far from perfect.

Many American achievement tests or prognostic tests at high school and college level take the form of complex reading comprehension tests; *i.e.* a passage is quoted and a series of new-type questions require the examinee to answer facts about it, or make inferences from it. It is natural therefore that correlations between such tests in different subjects (science, social studies, literature, etc.) tend to be very high—almost as high as their reliabilities—and that the tests are therefore rather inefficient instruments in differentiating abilities along different lines, e.g. in showing whether a student is likely to do relatively better in science or arts courses (cf. pp. 168–70). Moreover, while educational testers are greatly interested in differentiating such mental functions as critical thinking, ability to apply knowledge, judgment, etc., this is found to be very difficult because of the high correlations between tests designed to elicit them. Derrick (1953), for example, constructed series of questions which were classified by competent judges as involving chiefly ascertainment of facts, inferences from, or judgments of, reading passages. But he was unable to discover any factors corresponding to these functions, nor according to the length of the passages. Actually his correlations do indicate some differentiation between the very long passage studied at leisure and the medium or short passages, also between the factual and other questions. Moreover the factual *vs.* inferential + judgmental factor might well have been more obvious had the different kinds of questions been based on different passages. Thus in another research by Howard (1943) into a General Science test, the questions involving more complex inferences clearly involved a rather different factor from questions requiring simpler processes.

However, the influence of the form of the test item as such should not be over-stressed. In a recent research by the writer, in which students answered vocabulary and reading tests either in their own written phrases, or by multiple-choice, no clear differentiation by form of response emerged. At the same time definite evidence was obtained of a comprehension factor, in both forms of item, over and above mere knowledge of words (thus contradicting Thurstone's analysis of Davis's reading tests, pp. 45–6). The results suggested also that when students study the comprehension passages before seeing the questions and answer later from memory, the test measures a somewhat different—and educationally more valuable—ability. Similarly Kline (1956) factorized a number of tests of attainment in algebra, and obtained almost identical factor-content for parallel creative-response and multiple-choice tests. However an interesting factor called 'algebraic-manipulative-skill' emerged in all the more elementary tests, each of which consisted of a single process such as 'Simplify . . .' problems, or 'Solve . . .' problems; and this factor was absent in tests involving more varied 'sets' or operations in successive questions.

Another extraneous influence on test scores may arise when answers are recorded on a different sheet from the question paper, as is commonly the case in modern machine-scored tests. Some evidence was obtained in an investigation in the British Army (cf. p. 69) that this constitutes a handicap to duller adults—presumably also to young children—and that it introduces an irrelevant factor related to Clerical Ability or the *P* factor.

Guilford himself draws attention to the possible influence on factors of the type of test score chosen (cf. the Fluency and Originality scores in the Unusual Uses test, p. 145); and mentions the effects of learning during the test. When confronted with an unfamiliar test (such as many of those devised to elicit Guilford's new factors), testees approach it with various preconceptions based on past experience which may interfere with their adaptation to the test requirements. In some instances, practice in doing one test has been shown to have positive or negative transfer effects to other tests (de Weerdt, 1927). Thus the mere order in which a large battery of tests is given may well affect the factorial content of particular tests. In an unpublished research at the British Admiralty by E. Elliott, the same battery of five verbal, number, spatial and mechanical tests was applied in five different orders to groups of some 250 recruits each. Both the mean scores on certain tests and their correlations with other tests were found to vary significantly with position in the series, though it was difficult to see much 'sense' in these variations.

Cronbach (1950) has drawn attention to what he calls 'response sets', particularly in personality and attitude tests. When testees are required to choose between, say, Like, Indifferent, Dislike, or between Strongly Agree, Agree, Doubtful, Disagree and Strongly Disagree responses, some are more apt than others to give a predominance of positive or acquiscent responses, and some give more extreme, fewer intermediate, responses than others. Certain ability tests also permit these variations in personal 'style' of response (cf. Gaier *et al.*, 1953); and in most multiple-choice tests with time limits, some testees are more rash in guessing than others (cf. p. 80). Richardson (1956) has shown that scores based on wrong responses may be more valid in relation to later scholastic performance than scores based on rights, presumably because they embody Guilford's Carefulness factor. Fruchter (1953) analysed the rights and wrongs scores on 24 experimental tests, and though he obtained much the same factors from both sets, he noted considerable changes in the loadings of particular tests. In a time-limit test, right scores tend to measure speed of work, whereas a weighted or a wrong score gives a better measure of power. Such research provides an opportunity to adjust the scoring of some tests so as to maximize the factors in which the investigator is interested.

An interesting series of studies of psychomotor skills by Fleishman and Hempel (1954, 1955) has shown how factorial content may alter with increasing practice. The testees underwent a long series of trials on discrimination reaction or complex co-ordination tests, and successive sets of scores were analysed along with other reference tests. At the earlier stages of practice the psychomotor tests tend to show considerable loadings with cognitive factors (mechanical, spatial, visualization, etc.)—that is, the subjects tackle them in the light of previous experience—whereas at later stages other motor factors become relatively more important, or a factor specific to the test in question emerges. This helps to explain why neither success during the early stages of learning a trade skill, nor tests which correlate well with these early stages (e.g. paper-and-pencil tests), may be highly predictive of ultimate proficiency. Although no fresh evidence has come to hand, it seems likely that similar effects of learning could be demonstrated in tests of unfamiliar intellectual skills.

There have been several contributions to the problem of speed and difficulty factors (cf. pp. 79–85). Much as fluency factors seem to veer over into verbal, so Perceptual Speed tends to link with Spatial Relations and Visualization factors. Zimmerman (1954) showed that a difficult form of Visualization of Maneuvers (*sic*) test was chiefly loaded on the Visualization factor, a very easy form on P factor. However, he was unable to confirm a further hypothesis that still more difficult items would tend to test R or Reasoning factor. Similarly Fleishman (1957) devised a visual discrimination test whose difficulty could be increased by altering the angle between the display panel and the response panel. Performance at the easiest angles only was loaded with Perceptual Speed, as determined by other reference tests.

Carroll (1950) has pointed out that a spurious ease *vs.* difficulty factor can arise in factorizing the items within a test, even if inter-correlated by the tetrachoric technique, unless item performance is corrected for chance success. Applying this correction to Guilford's study of the Seashore pitch test (p. 79), he claims that the difficulty factors disappeared and a single factor accounted for all the item inter-correlations. Gourlay (1951) and Dingman

(1958) provide support for Carroll. The latter applied 9 tests at specified difficulty levels, and inter-correlated raw scores and scores corrected for guessing, by 4 techniques. On factorizing these 8 correlation matrices separately, he obtained the same test-content factors in all analyses; and the hypothesized difficulty factor appeared only rather irregularly. But it was most obvious in the product-moment correlations between raw scores, least so in the tetrachoric correlations between corrected scores.

Another investigation (which is of especial technical interest for its application of Lawley's Maximum Likelihood method to large numbers of variables) was conducted by Lord (1956). Here too level or power tests, moderately speeded and highly speeded tests were given under each of three headings— Verbal, Spatial and Arithmetical Reasoning, together with speeded N, P and W tests. In addition to the expected content factors, there were four distinct (though oblique) speed factors corresponding to N, P, verbal speed and spatial speed, though no separate arithmetical reasoning speed. A second-order or more general speed factor ran through all four. Easy tests given at speed, therefore, do measure somewhat different abilities from more difficult ones. Moreover Lord included academic grades in his analysis and was able to show that these are better predicted by level tests + a certain weighting of speed than by intermediate, moderately speeded tests (cf. the present writer's argument on pp. 84–5).

Porebski (1954), from a study of power and speed tests of reasoning, number and spatial abilities, concluded that the speed-power distinction is of greater importance than test-content distinctions. But this result naturally followed from choosing very strongly contrasted tests; his power tests required several hours of voluntary work and must therefore have depended considerably on the testees' persistence. A more comprehensive study, yielding a rather novel conception of the effects of speed and difficulty on mental factors, was undertaken by Mangan (1959). He gave 38 ability tests under varied conditions requiring speed and/or accuracy, or persistence, to two hundred 12-year boys. $G + v$, n, P and possibly a W factor emerged, as expected, but in addition most tests were loaded on a persistence factor, or on a bipolar factor contrasting speed with accuracy at simple tasks. Howie (1956) likewise found that speed *vs.* accuracy operated in cognitive tests as an 'individual trait'. Mangan's results suggest—as indicated in Fig. 8—that content or functional factors (g, V, N, S, reasoning etc.) cannot ever be measured, as it were, in isolation, but are always conditioned by the 'work-attitude' that the test instructions and timing impose. No doubt such attitudes are themselves complex, and often specific to the particular test; but persistence and speed-accuracy show a fair degree of generality, the former affecting all results on difficult power tests given with ample or unlimited time, the latter entering when the material is easy and time restricted. Their influence has not been generally recognized because most investigators have confined most of their tests to much the same timing and difficulty level, so that the work-attitude component was fairly constant throughout; indeed it has often become confounded with g. Alternatively, some new factor or factors may have been claimed which arose primarily from speed-difficulty differences. Rather similar conclusions have been reached by Furneaux, using a very different approach (cf. Eysenck, 1953). He argues that performance in ability tests depends on three independent components—intellectual efficiency, speed and persistence. Most 'general intelligence' tests involve a haphazard mixture of these components, as also of diverse functions (perceiving, recalling, reasoning, etc.), and of facilities with diverse materials (verbal, spatial, etc.).

DIAGRAM OF CONTENT AND WORK-ATTITUDE FACTORS

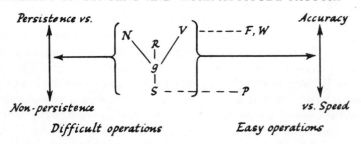

Fig. 8

It would follow, from the work described in this Section, that factorists will have to adjust themselves to a more fluid and dynamic views of factors than was envisaged by earlier workers such as the Thurstones, for whom each factor was a rather stable and definite entity, and on which any one test would be expected to show a stable loading. At the same time the importance of these influences should not be exaggerated; the evidence does not suggest that they greatly affect the major factors emerging from a conventional battery of moderately speeded tests. But item-form effects, interaction and transfer, practice effects, work-attitudes and response sets, etc., may increasingly influence the correlations as batteries get larger, involve more unfamiliar tasks, or more extreme speed or difficulty conditions. Thus there is always the danger that factors may arise, not from important differences in human psychological functioning, but from unsuspected characteristics of the tests, and that these may perpetuate the situation whereby every factorist puts forward different, and ever-lengthening, lists of factors. It seems desirable, therefore, to confine our factorial picture of the mind to the most widely established factors which can be shown to have real-life counterparts or extrinsic validity. This is reinforced by Maxwell's (1959a) reminder that we still cannot satisfactorily assess the Standard Errors of factor loadings. Probably they are quite large and, consequently, factor patterns are highly unstable.

Campbell and Fiske (1959) have recently discussed much the same problem in the personality field and concluded: 'Method or apparatus factors make very large contributions to psychological measurements'. They show the importance of good experimental design in isolating or eliminating such method effects. Two or more traits should be studied simultaneously by two or more methods. For example, returning to our example of Induction and Deduction factors (p. 147), both should be tested by verbal *and* non-verbal tests. We would suggest, too, that in such instances, greater use should be made of introspections by the subjects regarding the nature of the processes they employ in dealing with tests aimed at hypothetically different functions. Factorists are too apt to interpret factors on the basis of their own subjective analyses of the nature of the loaded tests, and to assume that their subjects, even at a very different mental level, tackle these tests by the same mental processes as they do. Barratt (1953) provides a neat example of the use of introspective self-ratings to show that visual imagery is associated with performance in k-saturated tests, but not with performance in non-verbal reasoning tests.

Verbal and Reasoning Factors. Oléron believes that, despite the variations between different factorists, it is possible to agree on a fairly extensive and useful list of factors, and cites French's valuable survey (1951). French attempted to amalgamate the findings of all the published studies of adolescents and adults which followed Thurstone's technique of analysis and rotation. Factors which seem to be essentially identical in half or more of the researches are:

V, N, S, P (including clerical ability) and D (including reasoning factors which are sometimes denoted as R).

Those appearing in nine or more (one eighth) of the published studies are:

Finger Dexterity, Induction, Associative (rote) Memory, Mechanical Experience, Psychomotor Co-ordination, Visualization.

While those which have been reported in four to eight studies are:

Aiming, Attention (Guilford's Integration II), Academic Grades, Flexibility of Closure, Ideational Fluency, Judgment, Length Estimation, Manual Dexterity, Pilot Interest, Planning, Schooling, Spatial Orientation, Speed of Closure, Visual Memory, Word Fluency.

The Educational Testing Service, in America, has collected sets of 3 or 4 tests which seem most representative of each of 15 of the main factors on this list, and issued them in a standard 'kit' for use as reference tests by future workers (French, 1954).

Note that g does not appear on French's list. He suggests that, when a general factor still persists after rotation to simple structure (or reappears as a second-order factor), it is attributable mainly to differences in schooling.

There is no fresh work to report on the V factor as such, though Morgan (1956) provides a useful survey of the literature. Reasoning, however, has been, and still is a source of much controversy. Guilford, as we have seen, allows a General Reasoning factor, but argues that it is concerned with comprehending and structuring problems in preparation for solving them, whereas problem-solving as such involves a variety of convergent and divergent thinking factors (Guilford *et al.*, 1956). But in a great many studies by other factorists, the reasoning factor—as defined largely by mathematical problems tests—certainly has a much broader scope. This corresponds to what Thurstone called R or restrictive reasoning—reasoning to a delimited solution. In some researches, however, R is amalgamated with D—deduction, or reasoning from the general to the specific (as by French); and in others with I—induction or finding the underlying principle. In Zimmerman's (1953) re-analysis of Thurstone's original Primary Mental Abilities correlations, all three factors appear (though I becomes a rather specialised factor in auditory and figure-classification tests). Adkins and Lyerly's (1951) large-scale research was designed to elucidate the nature of reasoning among army personnel, but it seems rather to have added to the confusion. Five out of 16 extracted factors were related to reasoning, namely:

Deduction.

Concept Formation.

Hypothesis Verification (largely based on a Matrices test like Raven's).

Perception of Abstract Similarities (mainly classification and analogies tests) and—

Flexibility of Perceptual Closure (in various non-verbal tests).

There was considerable obliquity among these, and several second-order factors were super-imposed by Matin and Adkins (1954).

When a g is allowed, the picture is simplified since additional reasoning group factors are fairly small. Butt (1957) analysed 23 tests among 200 13 to 14-year boys and girls of around average ability, and obtained a clearcut Induction group factor in Number and Letter Series, Abstraction, Concept Formation and Matrices; also a Deduction factor in Syllogisms, Pedigrees, Reasoning Problems, Coding and Arithmetical Problems. The former showed a strong sex difference in favour of boys and seems, from other researches, to be related to success in science courses, whereas the Deduction factor may be more relevant to language courses. Two studies of 11 to 12-year Australian children by Howie (1950, 1953 revealed one reasoning factor beyond g; but the number of tests was small, and the results differed between the sexes and with the method of scoring, so that the nature of the factor is not very clear: Howie described it as primarily 'a capacity to make and hold a pattern in complex conceptual material'. In an early research carried out under Burt, now described by Wheeler (1958), verbal intelligence was held constant. The main factor in a long series of verbal and practical reasoning problem tests was defined as— organizing data into logically coherent systems. This subdivided into minor group factors—analytic or explicit and synthetic or implicit, referring largely to verbal and spatial-pictorial problems respectively, and these clearly correspond to the so-called deductive and inductive types. An additional factor running through many, but not all, of the tests is called Apprehension of Relations, but its function in reasoning is not made clear.

All these British studies dealt with children, and the greater complexity of American results is no doubt partly due to their derivation from more intellectually mature and selected students.

Integration and Judgment. In Guilford's wartime work several Integration factors were claimed (p. 62), based on tests which demanded the bearing in mind and combination of a number of conditions or rules. One of these appears in the Memory category of his 1956 scheme. A corresponding factor was found in a large-scale study by Lucas and French (1953) of navy cadets, additional to the R or D and other conventional factors. The same research included tests aimed at Planning and Judgment factors, but these failed to emerge with any clarity.

In the course of the USAAF researches, Judgment was defined as 'the ability to make wise choices from a number of alternative solutions to a practical problem . . . (in the light of) practical feasibility, experience or social custom'. It was not, however, confirmed in Hertzka and Guilford's (1954) post-war research into evaluative abilities, though still listed under Guilford's Evaluation category.

Fluency and Flexibility. In the field of Fluency, there is wide agreement that several types can be distinguished, in accordance with Taylor's and Carroll's earlier work (pp. 51–2). Guilford claims four such factors:

1. Word Fluency, in tests based on word structure not meaning (e.g. write as many words as possible ending in -ion).
2. Associational Fluency for words of similar meaning (as in controlled association tests).
3. Ideational Fluency, where little restriction occurs (e.g. names of animals).
4. Expressional Fluency (e.g. producing connected discourse).

It still seems likely that there is something common to all of these (cf. Denton and Taylor, 1955); and both Rogers (1953) and Morgan (1956) show that, when unselected subjects are tested, much the most important determinant of all types of fluency score is $g + v$. In addition, however, Rogers found clearly distinct group factors in (*a*) oral, and (*b*) written fluency tests, together with very small factors suggestive of Guilford's restrictive (1 and 2) and ideational (3) types. Morgan obtained a first factor with 59·5% variance in a battery of 33 verbal and fluency tests; the second, with only 5% variance, divided the fluency from the vocabulary and comprehension tests.

Two other factors in Guilford's divergent thinking group are called Spontaneous Flexibility and Adaptive Flexibility. The former is said to represent freedom from inertia in associative thinking. As suggested above, it is difficult to distinguish from Originality, being based on tests like 'Unusual Uses' (p. 145). The latter is defined as ability to shift mental sets freely or to restructure one's approach; it arises from verbal or non-verbal tests of problems which require unconventional solutions. Wand (1958) found significant overlapping among several tests of intellectual (adaptive) flexibility or resourcefulness (over and above V, S, etc.) and some relation with tests of cognitive rigidity and flexibility of closure; but she did not attempt to arrive at a definitive map of flexibility factors. In his own research on such factors (1957), Guilford included an adaptation of Luchins' well-known water-jars test of rigidity. Actually it was found to yield no loadings on Flexibility, but rather to depend on General Reasoning and, Logical Evaluation. However, in Lovell's investigation (p. 141) three similar tests (though very low in reliability) did show some saturation with his flexibility-in-concept-formation factor. On the other hand, tests of cognitive rigidity of the 'creative effort' type obtained near-zero loadings on the same factor; and this is confirmed by Kleemeier and Dudek's study (1950) in which, for example, number tests requiring frequent switches from addition to subtraction gave the same factor pattern as did single-operation tests.

Obviously Guilford's factors do not go far in covering all the phenomena which have been described under rigidity, perseveration, mental inertia, deterioration, etc. There has been much work in this area during the 1950's, yet we still seem to be no nearer to finding consistent factors, or relationships, among sensory, motor, perceptual, conceptual and attitudinal flexibility tests (cf. Wand, 1958, Chown, 1959). Possibly progress might be more rapid if populations of a wide adult age-range were tested, since declines with age in many sensory-motor and intellectual performances are well established, and these are often described in terms of decreasing flexibility.

Closure Factors. In Thurstone's study of perception (pp. 89–90) two major factors were identified as Speed and Flexibility of Closure. They reappeared in a later monograph (Thurstone, 1951), being defined, respectively, as 'fusing a perceptual field into a single percept', and 'keeping a configuration in mind against distractions'. Thurstone further suggested that the first might be related to Induction, the second to Deductive reasoning. Botzum (1951) and Pemberton (1952a) claim to have found some confirmation for this identification, though it is not very convincing. Actually Pemberton's second-order analysis backs up the writer's suggestion (p. 90) of a link between Speed of Closure and P factor, Flexibility and S factor; and Botzum's main second-order factor combines Space and Flexibility of Closure with Induction and Deduction.

To the present writer, the most interesting characteristic of such factors is not, as Oléron suggests, that they represent truly functional characteristics of mental processes, but that they often show personality correlates. In Pemberton's study, several questionnaire tests of personality were given, and he went on to find (1952b) suggestive personality differences between those who score relatively highly on tests of Flexibility and Speed of Closure, Fluency, Space, etc. There is some evidence, too, that certain tests of perceptual judgment and adaptability and tests of closure can be of value in assessing the personalities of Air Force officers (Crutchfield *et al.*, 1958). However in other researches where ability and personality testa are factorized together (e.g. Denton and Taylor, 1955), they tend to show little overlapping, apart from the generally observed relation between certain types of fluency and extraversion. Guilford suggests that only some 2 to 4% of the variance of creative thinking abilities among high-grade normal adults can be ascribed to non-cognitive traits; though possibly this conclusion should be regarded as a reflection on the artificiality of the tests employed.

Mathematical Abilities. There have been several studies, mostly by British factorists, in the field of mathematics, and J. Wrigley (1958) provides an extensive review of the literature. Barakat (1951) and Wrigley were both able to show a large common element in attainments at different branches of mathematics among 14-year grammar school pupils, which was distinct from the N factor in mechanical arithmetic. For the most part this consists of g, but Wrigley obtained an additional small mathematical factor in six analyses in different schools—622 boys in all. There was a slight tendency in both researches for verbal ability to correlate negatively with mathematical, after removing g; while spatial ability showed a small loading in geometry only. Sayed (1951) compared plane and solid geometry at 6th form level with a variety of spatial and other tests, and claimed to find evidence of a 2-dimensional space factor in the former, 3-dimensional in the latter.

A research by Lee (1955) attempted to study the understanding of elements, concepts and modes of thought basic to mathematical attainment, among 1st to 5th form grammar school pupils. In each age-group there was evidence of two major factors representing recognition of variable or class, and of order or correspondence; and these gave significant correlations with attainment measures. It would be interesting to investigate their relations to Guilford's Eduction factors.

Kline's (1956) study of algebra among American 10th grade pupils differed typically from the British approach in including 38 tests and extracting a dozen factors. However, most of the common variance of the algebra tests was covered by 3 factors:

Deductive Reasoning (much the same as British g)

Verbal ability, entering into algebra tests which involved a good deal of reading, and

A purely algebraic factor in the more routine attainments (cf. p. 148).

As in other researches the N factor was found to be largely irrelevant to algebraic attainments. However, Swineford (1949) points out that N is by no means confined only to arithmetical computation; it often shows small loadings on tests such as Digit Memory, Cancellation, etc., that involve number. She attributes this to a feeling of at-homeness *vs.* inhibitedness when confronted with numbers. This influence of attitude on ability is more marked among girls than boys.

Spatial, Visualization and Mechanical Abilities. A large number of researches on spatial factors are summarized by Anderson *et al.* (1954) and, more briefly, by Fruchter (1954a).

They give the impression of considerable confusion: for American factorists reject the conception of a single, broad, spatial factor, but are by no means unanimous regarding the subdivisions into which it should be broken down. Guilford's distinction between Visualization (visual manipulative ability) and Spatial Relations or Spatial Orientation (comprehending spatial relations relative to the body orientation of the observer) has already been outlined (p. 75); and this is retained in his present scheme. Zimmerman (1953) claims that his re-analysis of Thurstone's PMA resulst supports it, most of the spatial tests like Paper Formboard, Punched holes, etc., being loaded on Visualization, and those with an orientation content like Flags and Hands falling under the S factor.

However, in 1949–51 Thurstone carried out a large-scale study of mechanical aptitude among 350 Technical high school boys and obtained four spatial factors:

S–1: 'Ability to visualize a rigid configuration when it is moved into different positions'.

S–2: 'Ability to visualize a configuration in which there is movement or displacement among the parts'.

S–3: A minor factor in the Lozenges and Cubes tests only.

K: A kinaesthetic factor in the Hands test and another called the Bolts test, in both of which testees tend to use hand movements to guide their responses.

Speed and Flexibility of Closure were also distinguished. There was a good deal of overlapping among all the factors except S–2, which justifies Oléron's suggestion that much of the complexity of American spatial factors would disappear if a g were allowed. The factors most closely related to mechanical inclinations were S–2 and Flexibility of Closure.

Now we may agree with Anderson and other writers that Thurstone's S–2 and Guilford's Visualization are identical. Clearly they constitute the essence of British k. But it seems much more arbitrary to equate S–3 (or S–1 and S–3) to Spatial Relations. Also the status of Thurstone's K is obscure: Michael, Guilford *et al.* (1957) wish to retain it as a left-right discrimination factor, possibly involved in certain psychomotor tests, but not as part of Spatial Orientation.

Zimmerman (1954), as mentioned above, attributes the distinction between Vz and S–R (Spatial Relations), at least in part, to the higher difficulty level of Vz tests. Other suggestions have been put forward. Fruchter (1954) points out that Vz tests are exclusively paper and pencil, though inclusive of mechanical comprehension; while various performance and psychomotor tests show loadings on Spatial Relations. Michael *et al.* (1957) note that the former usually involves manipulation of parts, whereas the latter refers to whole configurations. All these writers seem to agree that the various factors tend to be oblique, and that their differentiation is apt to vary with the kind of population tested. Roff (1952) indeed reports a correlation of 0·75 between visualization and orientation factors; and Lucas and French (1953) were unable to separate them, even at naval cadet level (cf. also French, 1957). Again it is instructive to study the correlations obtained in a research by Michael, Zimmerman and Guilford (1950), which was specifically designed to confirm the distinction. Here the mean correlation, among psychology students, of three Visualization tests was 0·514, and of three Spatial Relations tests 0·376, while the correlation between Visualization and Spatial Relations tests averaged 0·415. This would suggest that separate group factors have only about 5% as much variance as a factor common to both groups.

Some further evidence for the distinction between Thurstone's *S–1* and *S–2* was obtained by Fuchs (1952) in an analysis of spatial items in the American Army General Classification test. There seems to be no confirmation for Sayed's claim for a difference between two- and three-dimensional spatial perception (p. 151). The possibility that performance tests involve factors other than the k in paper and pencil tests (cf. Alexander, p. 110) is raised again by Bernyer's (1958) study of two groups of French apprentices. Using centroid and group-factor techniques he arrives at the following factor-pattern in 16 varied tests:

Reasoning — *g* — *Mechanical experience* — k *(general spatial and practical)* — *Paper and pencil spatial* — *Performance* — *Manual dexterity*

The small performance factor was found chiefly in Block Assembly and Wiggly Blocks tests.

Fleishman and Hempel's studies (p. 150) indicate that Spatial Relations may be important in dealing with an unfamiliar motor task, and become less so with practice. Visualization shows the same trend, though less consistently relevant.

The close relation of visual and kinaesthetic perception was confirmed in a study by Barney (1952) of Lowenfeld's theory of visual and haptic types. The common variance of such varied tests as Kohs Blocks, Gottschaldt Figures, Form Relations and Memory for Designs, and two blindfold performance tests was accounted for by g and a single k factor. Note, incidentally, that the Gottschaldt Hidden Figures, usually taken as a Flexibility of Closure test in American researches, appeared as a $g + k$ test in this, and in Lovell's (1955) investigations.

We have already drawn attention to Barratt's demonstration that self-reported visual imagery plays a part in k tests. Chowdhury (1956) attempted to assess visual and other imagery by a variety of techniques, finding that they yielded highly inconsistent results. Neither visualization nor kinaesthesis, as reported in introspective experiments, correlated with performance on k tests, but the former did show a significant positive relation to mechanical and scientific interests and information.

Manual and Physical Abilities. In the psychomotor field the most important work is that of Fleishman and Hempel. One study (Fleishman, 1954) involved the application of 27 apparatus tests and 11 printed tests of motor abilities to 400 Air Force recruits. The mean communality was 51%, and half of this was attributable to the first, general, factor. In other words, there was much less specificity than is often believed. However, after rotation, ten orthogonal factors were distinguished:

    I. Tapping—speed of wrist-finger movements.

    II. Fine dexterity, e.g. at pin- or peg-boards.

    III. Rate of arm movements, e.g. in target aiming.

    IV. Aiming in printed tests.

    V. Arm-hand steadiness, e.g. in track-tracing and aiming.

    VI. Reaction time, auditory or visual.

    VII. Manual dexterity in moving large blocks with whole hand.

    VIII. Psychomotor speed in printed tests.

IX. Psychomotor co-ordination in complex co-ordination and pursuit tests.

X. Spatial relations, in discrimination reaction time and complex co-ordination.

Notice the almost complete lack of overlap between printed group tests devised to measure dexterity and practical tasks. Another investigation (1956) involved the factorization of 16 apparatus and 7 printed reference tests among U.S. naval air pilots. The precise nature of the nine factors claimed is difficult to follow; but they support the author's contention that motor skills, particularly at complex tasks, are not necessarily highly specific, that there are some broad group factors extending to a variety of tasks, and that some of these are partially sampled by printed spatial tests. Similarly, in an investigation of 8 arm-hand co-ordination and steadiness tests by Seashore *et al.* (1949), three factors were distinguished which together covered as much as two-thirds of the variance.

Vincent (1958) attempted to establish distinctive factors of speed and precision in manual tasks, and gave 13 tests to a group of 15–16 year olds. These included tests of:

(i) Simple finger and wrist movements, e.g. tapping.

(ii) Ordinary speeded dexterity tests, e.g. ball-lifting, peg-board.

(iii) Untimed tasks involving careful co-ordination, e.g. model-building.

There was a strong speed factor, mainly in the first set (corresponding to Fleishman and Hempel's Factor I), and a smaller skill factor in the third group, with $13\frac{1}{2}\%$ variance. But the second group, instead of overlapping the first and third, depended mainly on a separate factor, presumably the same as Cox's 'routine manual factor' (p. 101) or Fleishman's Factor II.

In the field of athletic skills the most interesting study is that by Brogden *et al.* (1952) of 31 measures among officer cadets. The greatest part of the variance was attributed to two second-order factors apparently representing muscular endurance (particularly in running) and 'mobilization' (particularly for throwing or jumping); but there were 10 primary factors covering more specialized types of physical proficiency. One wonders whether a general + group factor approach would not have provided a simpler picture, though admittedly one would expect more differentiation in a young, fit, population than among the heterogeneous recruits studied by the present writer (pp.104–5). Highmore and Taylor (1954) showed that a general factor (variance 38%) and three group factors (totalling 17%) similarly represent the athletic performances of 11-year-old boys.

Perceptual Speed. There is little fresh to report on Perceptual Speed, except that Guilford now classifies it as an Evaluative factor, or rather as a pair of factors under the Figural and Symbolic headings; the latter would cover the conventional clerical test. Similarly French (1957) found a distinction between *P*—defined as speed in perceiving detail, and speed of symbol discrimination.

Bair (1951) claimed that the various published tests of Clerical Aptitude involve a complex mixture of abilities, and applied 17 tests, yielding 36 scores, to high school commercial students. Three quite plausible factors were obtained after rotation:

I. *V*—highest in Otis intelligence and spelling.

II. Speed of checking, including speed of handwriting.

III. 'Perceptual analysis', i.e. accuracy.

Memory and Learning. A useful survey of work on memory factors is provided by Kelley (1954). In his own investigation with 442 pilot trainees, 27 varied memory tests and 13 reference tests yielded three main memory factors:

I. Rote memory for discrete materials (words syllables, numbers), presented either auditorily or visually.

II. Meaningful memory for related materials, verbal or non-verbal.

III. Span memory, for grasping numbers, letters, etc., at a single presentation.

In addition there was some suggestion of visual and auditory memory factors, but no tendency for differentiation by type of recall—recognition, paired associates, etc. The finding of a meaningful memory factor seems to conflict with the view of this book (p. 60). However it overlapped in part with the *V*-factor, and the best tests of the factor were largely mechanical (giving the second of a pair of related nouns, supplying a missing word from a sentence, or the last line of a limerick, etc.). Moreover all the tests involved immediate reproduction, rather than the relatively permanent understanding involved in logical memory. Thus we would persist in regarding the latter as an aspect of $g + v$, rather than as a distinguishable faculty.

Thurstone, in 1951, added to his original M–1—rote memory for paired associates (cf. p. 18)—an M–2 factor—memory for pictures and geometrical designs, and M–3—keeping in mind some perceptual detail. Guilford (1956) lists 7 factors, including Kelley's, but has not yet, himself, explored the area. Probably a much larger number could be distinguished by varying the type of material, and conditions of learning and recall; though whether the abilities to perform psychological memory experiments have any useful everyday life counterparts is more questionable.

The technique of studying learning abilities was advanced by Stake's investigation (1958), even though his results are rather obscure. He criticises previous work on gains resulting from practice, such as Woodrow's (cf. p. 78), on the grounds that only simple cognitive functions were tested, and that gain scores are crude measures, inevitably low in reliability. He himself studied 12 varied learning tasks, some rote, some relational, and fitted hyperbolas to the learning curves. Each performance was then assessed for total errors during learning, for slope (curvature), and for regularity (goodness of fit). However, the first two of these correlated closely for most tasks, suggesting that Stake was measuring total success during learning rather than improvement as such. Thus his generally positive correlations between these measures and I.Q. or school achievement are not surprising. On factorizing all the measures, together with reference tests, the results suggested that there is little overlapping between known psychological factors and learning abilities, and that learning itself depends on a complex of factors; it is not a unitary trait. That there may be rather more generality in broader and more prolonged tasks is suggested by Tilton's investigation (1953). He gave standardized achievement tests in 8 school subjects to 4th grade pupils, and repeated them some 20 months later. The gain scores in different subjects all intercorrelated positively to an average of 0·30 (0·51 when corrected for attenuation); this indicated a strong general factor, though also some patterning, in school learning. Gains also correlated positively with initial achievement.

Progress scores may likewise be of considerable prognostic value, according to recent investigations in the selection of mechanics (Allison, 1954). Recruits were given several short practices at an unfamiliar mechanical task, and their gains in skill were found to be predictive of later occupational proficiency. The bearings of such work on educational and vocational selection would merit much fuller exploration.

Analysis of Individual Intelligence Scales. It is generally agreed that intelligence scales like the Terman-Merrill, Wechsler and WISC, although they yield a reliable total-score I.Q. indicative of a strong general factor, are factorially complex (pp. 72–3). There have been numerous analyses, particularly of the Wechsler scales.

Maxwell (1959b) extracted two factors only from WISC correlations, being mainly concerned to show that the Verbal and Performance I.Q.s are illogical measures to work with in clinical diagnosis because of their close overlapping. He presents simplified regression equations for calculating a general-intelligence standard score and a verbal-performance dichotomy score.

Hammer (1950) and Gault (1954) show that, both among adults and children, the Wechsler scales yield a fairly consistent bifactor pattern consisting of g (30 to 39% variance) and three group factors (6 to 10% variance each). The latter obviously represent verbal, spatial-practical, and memory (or number) ability, particularly in the Digit Memory test. Cohen (1952) similarly investigated neurotic schizophrenic and brain-damaged patients and obtained three corresponding centroid factors (the third being named 'Freedom from Distractibility'), together with a strong second-order factor. Birren (1952) studied elderly patients, and although his rotations and interpretation differed, the results are essentially the same. Saunders (1959) points out that the discovery of only three main types of ability follows largely from factorizing such a small number of sub-tests; and Davis (1956) made an interesting attempt to pin down a wider range of factors by giving additional reference tests. However, these were so poorly chosen, and the testees so heterogeneous (ages 12–17), that the eleven factors extracted confuse rather than clarify the issue. Similarly it is difficult to see the point of extracting and rotating ten factors from McNemar's tetrachoric correlations between Terman-Merrill items applied to 13-year-olds, as Jones (1954) has done. For example, to call a factor Closure or imposing structure on an unorganized field (which is chiefly present in Plan of Search, Induction, and 'The Shadow' Absurdity) takes us nowhere, unless it can be demonstrated that the factor is representative of some more generally known function or ability. Jones (1949) has also refactorized, in somewhat less detail, the correlations for 7-, 9-, 11- and 13-year-olds and shown, as McNemar had admitted, that the composition of the scale tends to differ at different age-levels.

Miscellaneous Applications. Finally, one or two of the many applications of factor analysis to some less conventional aspects of human abilities may be mentioned. Osgood's well-known work on the 'semantic differential' aims to discriminate the meanings of concepts by assigning them to positions on a limited number of continua or adjectival scales. For example, most people have little hesitation in placing the concept LADY towards the right-hand end of the scale:

Rough   *Smooth*

The most inclusive scales were reached by factorizing 50 such adjectival pairs, namely:

I. Evaluative: good-bad, beautiful-ugly, clean-dirty, fair-unfair, etc.

II. Potency: large-small, strong-weak, heavy-light, etc.

III. Activity: fast-slow, active-passive, sharp-dull, etc.

Between them these covered roughly half the variance of all the scales (Osgood and Suci, 1955).

Torgerson and Green (1950) classified 20 markers of a set of English essays, finding a strong general factor and three small group factors, representing different marker-biases. One of these was closely associated with a sex difference in outlook on the 'good' essay. A complementary research by Remondino (1959) into the grouping of 20 essay qualities showed that both experienced and inexperienced markers tend to distinguish:

I. Graphic representation—handwriting and appearance.

II. Language usage—spelling, grammar, word formation, sentence construction.

III. Content and arrangement—wealth and completeness of ideas, organization.

IV. Personal aspects—originality, imagination, maturity.

There is some overlapping among these, i.e. a general factor in addition.

Stolurow and Newman (1959) analysed 23 presumed measures of the readability of reading passages and identified the main under-

M

lying components as (1) word difficulty, (2) sentence length and proportion of simple sentences. Vernon (1951) assessed 50 radio educational broadcasts for 37 qualities, including objective measures such as sentence length, and subjectively-rated ones such as Logical Structure and Good Delivery. Factorization yielded four main dimensions:

I. Interestingness of content.

II. Concrete illustrations and treatment *vs.* abstract style.

III. Conversational, personal and human style *vs.* straight lecture bookish.

IV. Intelligibility—easy vocabulary, sentence length, number of teaching points, of metaphors, logical organization, etc.

The first and fourth of these chiefly determined the effectiveness of the talks as measured by the ability of listeners to reproduce the main points of what they had heard.

Burt (1958) analysed the preference of adult readers for different type-faces in reading material, and obtained factors which distinguished Old from Modern, Continental, British and other accepted varieties of faces.

Educational and Occupational Types. The classification of courses of study, or jobs, cannot readily be undertaken by ordinary factorial techniques (cf. pp. 121–3). The essential problem—known as differential prediction—is one of great current interest and technical complexity. Given a number of 'predictors' (e.g a battery of tests, which inevitably tend to inter-correlate quite highly), and a number of 'criteria' such as success in arts, science or other subjects or in different occupations (which are also likely to inter-correlate), how can we best weight the predictors so as to show the course or job for which any individual is best fitted? Had mental testers and factorists really succeeded in distinguishing and measuring all the main dimensions of human ability, the individual's pattern of scores on such factors would be expected to provide the answer. With this end in view a number of batteries of allegedly pure-factor or differential tests have been issued besides Thurstone's P.M.A. and the U.S.E.S. General Aptitude Test Battery (p. 21). However, the results are uniformly disappointing. Tests of V and R factors (in other words $g + v{:}ed$) usually give the highest correlations with success in every school or university subject. N tests sometimes contribute a little to arithmetical (*not* mathematical) attainment, *S* to scientific and technical, and *P* to commercial courses. *W* and *M* are seldom of any relevance (cf. Shaw, 1949; Holzinger and Crowder, 1955). Table XX, for example, lists the median correlations with school grades among numerous classes of boys (mostly 15- to 18-year) for the Psychological Corporation's Differential Aptitude Tests.[1]

TABLE XX. MEDIAN CORRELATIONS OF DIFFER-
ENTIAL APTITUDE TESTS WITH SCHOOL MARKS.

	English	Maths	Science	Social Studies
Verbal reasoning	·49	·33	·54	·48
Numerical computation	·48	·47	·52	·46
Abstract reasoning	·32	·32	·42	·32
Space	·26	·26	·34	·24
Mechanical comprehansion	·21	·19	·40	·21
Clerical speed and accuracy	·22	·16	·24	·21
Spelling	·44	·28	·36	·36
Sentences (English usage)	·50	·32	·45	·43

The four highest correlations for each of the four school courses are italicized, and it will be seen that uniformity in prediction is far more marked than differentiation.

The most extensive occupational findings are those of Thorndike (1957) and Thorndike and Hagen (1959). In the first of these studies, 20 varied tests were correlated with training course success in 46 Air Force jobs. By means of a kind of principal components analysis it was found that a single regression equation covered 77·7% of the predictable variance in all jobs; in other words, much the same weighting of the battery, representing a sort of *g* factor, was applicable for any type of training. A second equation (as it were a factor orthogonal to the first one) added 6·6%, and clearly helped to differentiate between mechanical and clerical types of job; the next, adding only a further 3·4%, seemed mainly to distinguish high- from low-level technical jobs.

In Thorndike and Hagen's enormous investigation, the Air Force test scores of 10,000 recruits were compared with their civilian jobs some 12 years later, and with certain indices of success (e.g. income). Here the test validities were virtually zero, but there were clearly distinguishable patterns of test scores between men in over a hundred commonly chosen occupations.

---

[1] These are *not* issued as factorially-pure tests.

Twenty-two of these occupations were taken which did not vary widely in occupational level, and multiple discriminant analysis of the test scores was carried out. Since the general tendency we have noted (p. 122) for higher-level occupations to require high all-round test scores was held constant, the most prominent discriminant was found to differentiate the test patterns characteristic of mathematical-scientific jobs (e.g. mechanical engineer, physician) from non-quantitative jobs (e.g. hotel manager, salesman). Subsequent latent roots were very much smaller, but they seem to resemble the factorial classification reached by the writer (Vernon, 1949c) from analysing judged similarities of jobs— namely Verbal *vs.* Active, and Gregarious *vs.* Isolated (his other main dimension, Welfare *vs.* Administrative failed to appear in this particular list of jobs).

Further ingenious techniques of multiple prediction have been worked out by Horst (1959), by means of which, from a battery of tests applied to college freshmen, each student's probable success in any of 32 courses, as well as his overall grades, can be predicted with considerable efficiency, and thus used by counsellers to guide his choice of courses. The calculations involved in applying the correlations obtained from following up earlier batches of students to a new intake would be quite impracticable without the assistance of electronic computers. But the implication that is of main interest for factor theory is that tests of the type usually included in factor batteries, while often useful for predicting general aptitude, are poor discriminators. It is subject-matter tests (e.g. Scientific Vocabulary, Mathematical Concepts, previous specific high school grades) and tests of interests like the Strong or Kuder which provide most of the evidence for differential success. These are, of course, tests which show low, sometimes negative, intercorrelations and which would therefore, in a factor analysis, yield narrow group factors—each perhaps relevant only to one or two of the criteria—rather than broad abilities (cf. p. 27n).

Conclusions. We may claim that most of the conclusions reached in 1950 have been confirmed, though, of course, with some modifications and extensions. However, in the light of recent studies, the following points seem to merit particular emphasis.

Tests designed to measure distinctive mental functions or abilities are not very successful for three main reasons:

1. Because they often involve 'formal', speed-difficulty, practice

or sophistication components, work-attitudes and sets, which produce unwanted factors, or at least distort the factorial picture. For example the P.M.A. battery is particularly unsuitable for differential prediction because its component tests are mostly speeded and this enhances their average inter-correlation.

2. Because of the strong influence of type of material—verbal, number, figural or spatial, symbolic—what Guilford calls content —which has some, but not very much, 'real-life' significance. Thus verbal tests generally tend to be more predictive for Arts courses and clerical jobs, non-verbal for scientific and technical ones. But there has been scarcely any progress in assessing different sorts of mental functions required for different educational, vocational or other purposes.

3. Because the assumption of a *g* factor is almost unavoidable, except when its variance is greatly reduced by studying highly selected groups (cf. p. 131). One would readily admit that it is an unsatisfactory and imprecise assumption. Thus much of what has been termed *g* in published researches should be attributed to No. 1 and/or 2; e.g. to the use of speeded tests with verbal material. It is not, as Spearman hoped, determinate, i.e. objectively definable as the highest common factor in any battery of tests; since such a factor will always be biased by the group factors (wanted or unwanted) in the particular tests employed. Other criticisms such as Kelley's (p. 16) that *g* represents heterogeneity, or French's that it arises from educational, or social class, differences, are beside the point. They apply equally to intelligence as generally conceived by psychologists; yet psychologists—apart from followers of Thurstone and Guilford—are clearly unable to dispense with this concept of intelligence.

We would, however, close with a constructive proposal which, we believe, would go far to reconcile the American and British approaches to factor analysis, and which should greatly simplify the present chaotic picture of innumerable, partly overlapping, partly inconsistent, factors. This is that every factorial investigation should include in its battery sufficient tests (preferably agreed standard ones) to give good all-round measures of *V*, *N*, *S* and *I*,[1] very much as defined by Thurstone, or alternatively of

[1] The writer would favour so-called Inductive tests of reasoning rather than Deductive, since they would then largely cover the variance attributable to figural (non-verbal) and symbolic test material.

British $g + v{:}ed + k{:}m$. It would not be difficult to arrive at a technique for extracting the maximum variance in any battery attributable to these, regardless of their obliquity. That is, it would not matter that in a heterogeneous population they would be highly inter-correlated (concealing a common g), whereas in more selected ones they might be relatively independent or orthogonal. This complex of factors should be extracted first so as to eliminate very largely the influences listed under Nos. 1, 2 and 3) above. Only then should the residual correlations be studied for indications of further common or group factors. We believe that there would be very little significant overlapping left in many correlation matrices, but what was left would have a much better chance of yielding factors that would be psychologically meaningful and stable from one research to another. It should also become accepted practice that such additional factors should not only be statistically significant, but should also be validated against external criteria (as for example P and Originality have been), or studied experimentally or introspectively. On the one hand this would discipline factorial research by making it subject to the canons of what contemporary psychology calls construct-validation (Cronbach and Meehl, 1955). On the other it would encourage the development of tests with low *VNSI* content which would be more useful than those at present available for practical diagnostic purposes.

BIBLIOGRAPHY

Adcock, C. (1948), A Re-analysis of Slater's Spatial Judgment Research. *Occup. Psychol.*, 22, 213–216.

Adcock, C. J. (1954), *Factorial Analysis for Non-Mathematicians.* Melbourne University Press. Pp. 88.

Adkins, D. C. & Lyerly, S.B. (1952), *Factor Analysis of Reasoning Tests.* Chapel Hill, N.C.: University of North Carolina Press. Pp. 122.

Ahmavaara, Y. (1956), *On the Unified Factor Theory of Mind.* Helsinki: Academia Scientiarum Fennica. Pp. 176.

Alexander, W. P. (1935), Intelligence, Concrete and Abstract. *Brit. J. Psychol. Monogr. Suppl.*, 19. Pp. 177.

Alexander, W. P. (1947), Symposium on the Selection of Pupils for Different Types of Secondary Schools: II.—An Administrator's Point of View. *Brit. J. Educ. Psychol.*, 17, 123–130.

Allison, R. B. (1954), *Learning Measures as Predictors of Success in Torpedoman's Mates School.* Princeton, N.J.: Educational Testing Service, ONR Project 151–113. Pp. 25.

Allport, G. W. & Vernon, P. E. (1933), *Studies in Expressive Movement.* New York: Macmillan. Pp. 269.

Anastasi, A. (1930), A Group Factor in Immediate Memory. *Arch. Psychol.*, 120. Pp. 61.

Anastasi, A. (1932), Further Studies on the Memory Factor. *Arch. Psychol.*, 142. Pp. 60.

Anastasi, A. (1936). The Influence of Specific Experience Upon Mental Organization. *Genet. Psychol. Monogr.*, 18, 245–355.

Anastasi, A. (1948), The Nature of Psychological 'Traits', *Psychol. Rev.* 55, 127–138.

Anderson, G. V., Fruchter, B. *et al.* (1954), *Survey of Research on Spatial Factors.* Air Force Personnel Training and Research Center, Research Bulletin. Pp. 59.

Arthur, G. (1930), *A Point Scale of Performance Tests*, Vol. I. New York: Commonwealth Fund. Pp. 82.

Artley, A. S. (1943), The Appraisal of Reading Comprehension. *J. Educ. Psychol.*, 34, 55–60.

Artley, A. S. (1944), A Study of Certain Relationships Existing Between General Reading Comprehension and Reading Comprehension in a Specific Subject Matter Area. *J Educ. Res.*, 37, 464–473.

Attenborough, J. & Farber, M. (1934), The Relation Between Intelligence, Mechanical Ability, and Manual Dexterity in Special School Children. *Brit. J. Educ. Psychol.*, 4, 140–161.

Bair, J. T. (1951), Factor Analysis of Clerical Aptitude Tests. *J. Appl. Psychol.*, 35, 245–249.

Balinsky, B. (1941), An Analysis of the Mental Factors of Various Age Groups from Nine to Sixty. *Genet. Psychol. Monogr.*, 23, 191–234.

Banks, C. (1948), Primary Personality Factors in Women: A Reanalysis. *Brit. J. Psychol. Statist. Sec.*, 1, 204–218.

Banks, C. (1949), Factor Analysis of Assessments for Army Recruits. *Brit. J. Psychol. Statist. Sec.*, 2, 76–89.

Barakat, M. K. (1951), A Factorial Study of Mathematical Abilities. *Brit. J. Statist. Psychol.*, 4, 137–156.

Barney, W. D. (1950), *A Study of Perception and its Relation to the Art Expression of a Group of Adolescents*. Ph.D. Thesis, University of London Library.

Barratt, P. E. (1953), Imagery and Thinking. *Austral. J. Psychol.*, 5, 154–164.

Barratt, P. E. (1956), The Role of Factors in Ability Theory. *Austral. J. Psychol.*, 8, 93–105.

Barron, F. (1955), The Disposition towards Originality. *J. Abn. Soc. Psychol.*, 51, 478–485.

Beard, R. (1957), *An Investigation of Concept Formation among Infant School Children.* Ph.D. Thesis, University of London Library.

Bentley, M. (1948), Factors and Functions in Human Resources. *Amer. J. Psychol.*, 61, 286–291.

Bernstein, E. (1924), Quickness and Intelligence. *Brit. J. Psychol. Monogr. Suppl.*, 7. Pp. 55.

Bernyer, G. (1958), Second Order Factors and the Organization of Cognitive Functions. *Brit. J. Statist. Psychol.*, 11, 19-29.

Bingham, W. V. (1937), *Aptitudes and Aptitude Testing*. New York: Harper. Pp.390.

Birren, J. E. (1952), A Factorial Analysis of the Wechsler-Bellevue Scale given to an Elderly Population. *J. Consult. Psychol.*, 16, 399–405.

Blackwell, A. M. (1940), A Comprehensive Investigation into the Factors Involved in Mathematical Ability of Boys and Girls. *Brit. J. Educ. Psychol.*, 10, 143–153, 212–222.

Blakey, R. (1940), A Re-analysis of a Test of the Theory of Two Factors. *Psychometrika*, 5, 121–136.

Blakey, R. I. (1941), A Factor Analysis of a Non-verbal Reasoning Test. *Educ. Psychol. Measmt.*, 1, 187–198.

Bloom, B. S. (1956), *Taxonomy of Educational Objectives*. New York: Longmans, Green. Pp. 207.

Botzum, W. A. (1951), A Factorial Study of the Reasoning and Closure Factors. *Psychometrika*, 16, 361–386.

Brace, D. K. (1946), Studies in Motor Learning of Gross Bodily Motor Skills. *Res. Quart. Amer. Ass. Hlth. Phys. Educ.*, 17, 242-253.

Bradford, E. J. G. (1946), Selection for Technical Education. *Brit. J. Educ. Psychol.*, 16, 20–31, 69–81.

Brener, R., (1940), An Experimental Investigation of Memory Span. *J. Exper. Psychol.*, 26, 467–482.

Brigham, C. C. (1932), *A Study of Error*. New York: College Entrance Examination Board. Pp. 384.

Brogden, H. *et al.* (1952), *A Factor Analysis of Measures of Physical Proficiency*. Washington, D.C.: Department of the Army, Personnel Research Section, Report 937.

Brown, W. & Stephenson, W. (1933), A Test of the Theory of Two Factors. *Brit. J. Psychol.*, 23, 352–370.

Brown, W. & Thomson, G. H. (1921), *The Essentials of Mental Measurement*. Cambridge: Cambridge University Press. Pp. 216.

Bryan, A. I. (1934), Organization of Memory in Young Children. *Arch. Psychol.*, 162. Pp. 56.

Burt, C. (1909), Experimental Tests of General Intelligence. *Brit. J. Psychol.*, 3, 94–177.

Burt, C. (1917), *The Distribution and Relations of Educational Abilities*. London: King. Pp. 93.

Burt, C. (1927), *The Measurement of Mental Capacities*. Edinburgh: Oliver and Boyd. Pp. 52.

Burt, C. (1938), Factor Analysis by Sub-Matrices. *J. Psychol.*, 6, 339–375.

Burt, C. (1939a), The Relations of Educational Abilities. *Brit. J. Educ. Psychol.*, 9, 45–71.

Burt, C. (1939b), The Latest Revision of the Binet Intelligence Tests. *Eugen. Rev.*, 30, 255–260.

Burt, C. (1940a), *The Factors of the Mind*. London: University of London Press. Pp. 509.

Burt, C. (1940b), Critical Notice of 'An Analysis of Performance Test Scores of a Representative Group of Scottish Children' by Godfrey H. Thomson. *Brit. J. Educ. Psychol.*, 10, 238–244.

Burt, C. (1943), The Education of the Young Adolescent: The Psychological Implications of the Norwood Report. *Brit. J. Educ. Psychol.*, 13, 126–140.

Burt, C. (1944), Mental Abilities and Mental Factors. *Brit. J. Educ. Psychol.*, 14, 85–94.

Burt, C. (1946), The Relation Between Eye-Colour and Defective Colour Vision. *Eugen. Rev.*, 37, 149–156.

Burt, C. (1947), Symposium on the Selection of Pupils for Different Types of Secondary Schools: I.—A General Survey. *Brit. J. Educ. Psychol.*, 17, 57–71.

Burt, C. (1949), Alternative Methods of Factor Analysis and their Relations to Pearson's method of 'Principal Axes'. *Brit. J. Psychol. Statist. Sec.* 2, 98–121.

Burt, C. (1952), Tests of Significance in Factor Analysis. *Brit. J. Statist. Psychol.*, 5, 109–133.

Burt, C. (1959), *A Psychological Study of Typography*. Oxford University Press. Pp. 67.

Burt, C. & Banks, C. (1947), A Factor Analysis of Body Measurements for British Adult Males. *Ann. Eugen.*, 13, 238–256.

Burt, C. & John, E. (1942), A Factorial Analysis of Terman Binet Tests. *Brit. J. Educ. Psychol.*, 12, 117–127, 156–161.

Burt, C. & Moore, R. C. (1912), The Mental Differences Between the Sexes. *J. Exper. Pedagog.* 1, 273–284, 355–388.

Burt, C. *et al.* (1933), *How the Mind Works*. London: Allen and Unwin. Pp. 336.

Butt, A. S. (1957), *The Differentiation of Reasoning Abilities at Adolescence*. Ph.D. Thesis, University of London Library.

Buxton, C. (1938), The Application of Multiple Factorial Methods to the Study of Motor Abilities. *Psychometrika*, 3, 85–93.

Campbell, D. T. & Fiske, D. W. (1959), Convergent and Discriminant Validation by the Multitrait-Multimethod Matrix. *Psychol. Bull.*, 56, 81–105.

Carey, N. (1915–16), Factors in the Mental Processes of School Children. *Brit. J. Psychol.*, 7, 453–490; 8, 70–92, 170–182.

Carlson, H. B. (137), Factor Analysis of Memory Ability. *J. Exper. Psychol.*, 21, 477–492.

Carroll, J. B. (1941), A Factor Analysis of Verbal Abilities. *Psychometrika*, 6, 279–307.

Carroll, J. B. (1950), Factor Analysis: Problems and Results. *Amer. Psychologist*, 5, 369.

Carter, H. D. (1928), The Organization of Mechanical Intelligence. *J. Genet. Psychol.*, 35, 270–285.

Cattell, R. B. (1936), *A Guide to Mental Testing*. London: University of London Press. Pp. 312.

Cattell, R. B. (1943), The Measurement of Adult Intelligence. *Psychol. Bull.*, 40, 153–193.

Cattell, R. B. (1946), *Description and Measurement of Personality*. London: Harrap. Pp. 602.

Cattell, R. B. (1952), *Factor Analysis*. New York: Harper. Pp. 462.

Cattell, R. B. (1954), Growing Points in Factor Analysis. *Austral. J. Psychol.*, 6, 105–140.

Chapman, R. L. (1948), The MacQuarrie Test for Mechanical Ability. *Psychometrika*, 13, 175–179.

Chowdhury, K. R. (1956), *An Experimental Study of Imagery and Its Relation to Abilities and Interests*. Ph.D. Thesis, University of London Library.

Chown, S. M. (1959), Rigidity—A Flexible Concept. *Psychol. Bull.*, 56, 195–223.

Clark, M. P. (1944), Changes in Primary Mental Abilities with Age *Arch. Psychol.*, 291. Pp. 30.

Cohen, J. (1949), Color Vision and Factor Analysis. *Psychol. Rev.*, 56, 224–233.

Cohen, J. (1952), Factors Underlying Wechsler-Bellevue Responses of Three Neuropsychiatric Groups. *J. Abn. Soc. Psychol.*, 47, 359–365.

Comrey, A. L. (1949), A Factorial Study of Achievement in West Point Courses. *Educ. Psychol. Measmt.*, 9, 193–209.

Coombs, C. H. (1941), A Factorial Study of Number Ability. *Psychometrika*, 6, 161–189.

Coombs, C. H. & Satter, G. A. (1949), A Factorial Approach to Job Families. *Psychometrika*, 14, 33–42.

Corter, H. M. (1952), Factor Analysis of some Reasoning Tests. *Psychol. Monogr.* Vol. 66, No. 340. Pp. 31.

Cox, J. W. (1928), *Mechanical Aptitude*. London: Methuen. Pp. 209.

Cox, J. W. (1934), *Manual Skill: Its Organization and Development*. Cambridge: Cambridge University Press. Pp. 247.

Cronbach, L. J. (1950), Further Evidence on Response Sets and Test Design. *Educ. Psychol. Measmt.*, 10, 3–31.

Cronbach, L. J. & Meehl, P. E. (1955), Construct Validity in Psychological Tests. *Psychol. Bull.*, 52, 281–302.

Crutchfield, R. S. *et al.* (1958), *Perceptual Performance and the Effective Person*. Lackland Air Force Base, Tex.: Wright Air Development Center, Personnel Laboratory. Pp. 94.

Cureton, E. E. (1947), The Verbal Relations Factor and Vocabulary. *Amer. Psychologist*, 2, 286–287.

Curran, D. & Guttman, E. (1945), *Psychological Medicine* (2nd edit.). Edinburgh: Livingstone. Pp. 246.

Curtis, H. A. (1949), A Study of the Relative Effects of Age and of Test Difficulty upon Factor Patterns. *Genet. Psychol. Monogr* 40, 99–148.

Davidson, W. M. & Carroll, J. B. (1945), Speed and Level Components in Time-Limit Scores: A Factor Analysis. *Educ. Psychol. Measmt.*, 5, 411–428.

Davis, F. B. (1944), Fundamental Factors of Comprehension in Reading. *Psychometrika*, 9, 185–197.

Davis, F. B. (1947), *The A.A.F. Qualifying Examination*. Army Air Forces Aviat. Psychol. Prog. Res. Rep., No. 6. Washington, D.C.: U.S. Government Printing Office. Pp. 266.

Davis, P. C. (1956), A Factor Analysis of the Wechsler-Bellevue Scale. *Educ. Psychol. Measmt.*, 16, 127–146.

Dearborn, W. F. & Rothney, J. W. M. (1941), *Predicting the Child's Development*. Cambridge, Mass.: Sci-Art. Pp. 360.

Dempster, J. J. B. (1948), Symposium on the Selection of Pupils for Different Types of Secondary Schools: V.—The Selector's Point of View. *Brit. J. Educ. Psychol.*, 18, 121–133.

Denton, J. C. & Taylor, C. W. (1955), A Factor Analysis of Mental Abilities and Personality Traits. *Psychometrika*, 20, 75·81.

Derrick, C. (1953), *Three Aspects of Reading Comprehension as Measured by Tests of Different Lengths*. Princeton, N.J.: Educational Testing Service, Research Bulletin, 53–58. Pp. 176.

Dewar, H. (1938), A Comparison of Tests of Artistic Appreciation. *Brit. J. Educ. Psychol.*, 8, 29–49.

De Weerdt, E. H. (1927), The Transfer Effect of Practice in

Related Functions upon a Group Intelligence Test. *School & Soc.*, 25, 438–440.

Dingman, H. F. (1958), The Relation between Coefficients of Correlation and Difficulty Factors. *Brit. J. Statist. Psychol.*, 11, 13–17.

Doppelt, J. E. (1949), The Organization of Mental Abilities in The Age Range Thirteen to Seventeen. *Amer. Psychologist*, 4, 242.

Doppelt, J. E. (1950), *The Organization of Mental Abilities in the Age Range 13 to 17.* New York, Columbia University, Teachers College Contributions to Education, No. 962. Pp.86.

Drake, R. M. (1939), Factorial Analysis of Music Tests by the Spearman Tetrad-Difference Technique. *J. Musicol.*, 1, 6–10.

Drevdahl, J. E. (1956), Factors of Importance for Creativity. *J. Clin. Psychol.*, 12, 21–26.

Drew, L. J. (1947), An Investigation into the Measurement of Technical Ability. *Occup. Psychol.*, 21, 34–48.

DuBois, P. H. (1932), A Speed Factor in Mental Tests. *Arch. Psychol.*, 141. Pp. 38.

Dudek, F. J. (1948), The Dependence of Factorial Composition of Aptitude Tests Upon Population Differences Among Pilot Trainees. I. The Isolation of Factors. *Educ. Psychol. Measmt.*, 8, 613–633.

Dudek, F. J. & Seashore, R. H. (1948), Factorial Analysis of Arm-Hand Precision Tests. *Amer. Psychologist*, 3, 252.

Dunlop, A. B. (1942), Observations on the Reading Attainment of a Group of Infant School Children in Glasgow. *Brit. J. Educ. Psychol.*, 12, 76–77.

Dvorak, B. J. (1947), The New USES General Aptitude Test Battery. *J. Appl. Psychol.*, 31, 372–376.

Earle, F. M. (1948), *The Duplex Series of Ability Tests for Age Groups 10 to 14.* London: Harrap.

Earle, F. M. & Gaw G. (1930), The Measurement of Manual Dexterities. *Nat. Inst. Industr. Psychol. Rep.* No. 4. Pp. 88.

Earle, F. M. & Macrae, A. (1929), Tests of Mechanical Ability. *Nat. Inst. Industr. Psychol. Rep.*, No. 3. Pp. 42.

Earle, F. M. & Milner, M. *et al.* (1929), The Use of Performance Tests of Intelligence in Vocational Guidance. *Industr. Hlth. Res. Board Rep.*, No. 53. Pp. 70.

El Koussy, A. A. H. (1935), The Visual Perception of Space. *Brit. J. Psychol. Monogr. Suppl.*, 20. Pp. 89.

Elmgren, J. (1952), *School and Psychology*. Stockholm. Pp. 342.

Elmgren, J. (1958), *Some Fundamental Problems in Psychological Factor Analysis*. Acta Universitatis Gothoburgensis, 54, No. 3. Pp. 44.

Emmett, W. G. (1949), Evidence of a Space Factor at 11 + and Earlier. *Brit. J. Psychol. Statist. Sec.*, 2, 3–16.

Eysenck, H. J. (1939), Critical Notice of 'Primary Mental Abilities' by L. L. Thurstone. *Brit. J. Educ. Psychol.*, 9, 270–275.

Eysenck, H. J. (1947), *Dimensions of Personality*. London: Kegan Paul, Trench, Trubner. Pp. 308.

Eysenck, H. J. (1950), Criterion Analysis—An Application of the Hypothetico-Deductive Method to Factor Analysis. *Psychol. Rev.*, 57, 38–53.

Eysenck, H. J. (1953), *Uses and Abuses of Psychology*. London: Penguin Books. Pp. 318.

Eysenck, H. J. & Halstead, H. (1945), The Memory Function. I. A Factorial Study of Fifteen Clinical Tests. *Amer. J. Psychiat.*, 102, 174–179.

Eysenck, M. D. (1944), An Experimental and Statistical Study of Smell Preferences. *J. Exper. Psychol.*, 39, 246–252.

Eysenck, M. D. (1945), An Exploratory Study of Mental Organization in Senility. *J. Neurol. Neurosurg. & Psychiat.*, 8, 15–21.

Farmer, E. (1927), A Group Factor in Sensory-Motor Tests. *Brit. J. Psychol.*, 17, 327–334.

Farmer, E. & Chambers, E. G. (1929), A Study of Personal Qualities in Accident Proneness and Proficiency. *Industr. Hlth. Res. Board Rep.*, No. 55. Pp. 80.

Farmer, E. & Chambers, E. G. (1936), The Prognostic Value of Some Psychological Tests. *Industr. Hlth. Res. Board Rep.*, No. 74, Pp. 41.

Feder, D. D. (1938), Comprehension Maturity Tests—A New Technique in Mental Measurement. *J. Educ. Psychol.*, 29, 597–606.

Ferguson, G. A. (1941). The Factorial Interpretation of Test Difficulty. *Psychometrika*, 6, 323–329.

Fleishman, E. A. (1954), Discriminant Analysis of Psychomotor Abilities. *J. Exper. Psychol.*, 48, 437–454.

Fleishman, E. A. (1957), Factor Structure in Relation to Task Difficulty in Psychomotor Performance. *Educ. Psychol. Measmt.*, 17, 522–532.

Fleishman, E. A. & Hempel, W. E. (1954), Changes in Factor

Structure of a Complex Psychomotor Test as a Function of Practice. *Psychometrika*, 19, 239–252.

Fleishman, E. A. & Hempel, W. E. (1955), The Relation between Abilities and Improvement with Practice in a Visual Discrimination Reaction Task. *J. Exper. Psychol.*, 49, 301–312.

Fleishman, E. A. & Hempel, W. E. (1956). Factorial Analysis of Complex Psychomotor Performance and Related Skills. *J. Appl. Psychol.*, 40, 96–104.

Fleming, C. M. (1948), *Adolescence*. London: Routledge and Kegan Paul. Pp. 262.

French, J. W. (1951), The Description of Aptitude and Achievement Tests in Terms of Rotated Factors. *Psychometr. Monogr.*, 5. Pp. 278.

French, J. W. (1954), *Kit of Selected Tests for Reference Aptitude and Achievement Factors*. Princeton, N.J.: Educational Testing Service.

French, J. W. (1957), The Factorial Invariance of Pure-Factor Tests. *J. Educ. Psychol.*, 48, 93–109.

Fruchter, B. (1948). The Nature of Verbal Fluency. *Educ. Psychol. Measmt.*, 8, 33–47.

Fruchter, B. (1953), Differences in Factor Content of Rights and Wrongs Scores. *Psychometrika*, 18, 257–265.

Fruchter, B. (1954a), Measurement of Spatial Abilities. *Educ. Psychol. Measmt.*, 14, 387–395.

Fruchter, B. (1954b), *Introduction to Factor Analysis*. New York: Van Nostrand. Pp. 280.

Fuchs, E. F. *et al.* (1952), *A Factor Analysis of Spatial Relations Items*. Washington, D.C.: Department of the Army, Personnel Research Section, Report 978.

Furneaux, W. D. (1948), Some Factors Affecting the Design of 'g' with Particular Reference to the Relation of 'Speed' and 'Power'. *Proc. Twelfth Intern. Congr. Psychol.* Edinburgh.

Gaier, E. L., Lee, M. C. & McQuitty, L. L. (1953), Response Patterns in a Test of Logical Inference. *Educ. Psychol. Measmt.*, 13, 550–567.

Gans, R. (1940). A Study of Critical Reading Comprehension in the Intermediate Grades. *Teach. Coll. Contr. Educ.*, No. 811. New York: Teachers College, Columbia University, Bureau of Publications. Pp. 135.

Garrett, H. E. (1946), A Developmental Theory of Intelligence. *Amer. Psychologist*, 1, 372–378.

Gates, A. I. (1921), An Experimental and Statistical Study of Reading and Reading Tests. *J. Educ. Psychol.*, 12, 303–314, 378–391, 445–464.

Gates, A. I. (1924), The Relation of Quality and Speed of Performance: A Formula for Combining the Two in the Case of Handwriting. *J. Educ. Psychol.*, 15, 129–144.

Gault, U. (1954), Factorial Patterns of the Wechsler Intelligence Scales. *Austral. J. Psychol.*, 6, 85–89.

Gaw, F. (1925), Performance Tests of Intelligence. *Industr., Fat. Res. Board Rep.*, No. 31. Pp. 45.

Gewirtz, J. L. (1948), Studies in Word Fluency. *J. Genet. Psychol.*, 72, 165–184.

Goodman, C. H. (1943), A Factorial Analysis of Thurstone's Sixteen Primary Mental Ability Tests. *Psychometrika*, 8, 141–151.

Goodman, C. H. (1947), The MacQuarrie Test for Mechanical Ability. II. Factor Analysis. *J. Appl. Psychol.*, 31, 150–154.

Gourlay, N. (1951), Difficulty Factors Arising from the Use of Tetrachoric Correlations in Factor Analysis. *Brit. J. Statist. Psychol.*, 4, 65–76.

Green, R. F., Guilford, J. P. & Christensen, P. R. (1953), Factor Analytic Study of Reasoning Abilities. *Psychometrika*, 18, 135–160.

Greene, E. B. (1941), *Measurements of Human Behavior*. New York: Odyssey Press. Pp. 777.

Greene, E. B. (1943), An Analysis of Random and Systematic Changes with Practice. *Psychometrika*, 8, 37–52.

Guilford, J. P. (1936), *Psychometric Methods*. New York: McGraw Hill. Pp. 566.

Guilford, J. P. (1940), Human Abilities. *Psychol. Rev.*, 47, 367–394.

Guilford, J. P. (1941), The Difficulty of a Test and Its Factor Composition. *Psychometrika*, 6, 67–77.

Guilford, J. P. (1948a), Some Lessons from Aviation Psychology *Amer. Psychologist*, 3, 3–11.

Guilford, J. P. (1948b), Factor Analysis in a Test Development Program. *Psychol. Rev.*, 55, 79–94.

Guilford, J. P. (1952), When Not to Factor Analyze. *Psychol. Bull.* 49, 26–37.

Guilford, J. P. (1956), The Structure of Intellect. *Psychol. Bull.* 53, 267–293.

Guilford, J. P. (1959), Three Faces of Intellect. *Amer. Psychologist*, 14, 469–479.

Guilford, J. P. & Holley, J. W. (1949), A Factorial Approach to the Analysis of Variance in Esthetic Judgments. *J. Exper. Psychol.*, 39, 208–218.

Guilford, J. P. & Lacey, J. I. (1947), *Printed Classification Tests*. Army Air Forces Aviat. Psychol. Prog. Res. Rep. No. 5. Washington, D.C.: U.S. Government Printing Office. Pp. 919.

Guilford, J. P. & Michael, W. B. (1948), Approaches to Univocal Factor Scores. *Psychometrika*, 13, 1–22.

Guilford, J. P. & Zimmerman, W. S. (1948), The Guilford-Zimmerman Aptitude Survey. *J. Appl. Psychol.*, 32, 24–34.

Guilford, J. P. *et al.* (1950–1957). *Reports from the Psychological Laboratory, University of Southern California*, Nos. 1–20.

Guilford, J. P. *et al.* (1956), The Nature of the General Reasoning Factor. Psychol. Rev., 63, 169–172.

Hall, D. M. & Wittenborn, J. R. (1942), Motor Fitness Tests for Farm Boys. *Res. Quart. Amer. Ass. Hlth. Phys. Educ.*, 13, 432–443.

Hall, W. E. & Robinson, F. P. (1945), An Analytical Approach to the Study of Reading Skills. *J. Educ. Psychol.*, 36, 429–442.

Halstead, W. C. (1945), A Power Factor (P) in General Intelligence: The Effect of Brain Injuries. *J. Psychol.*, 20, 57–64.

Halstead, W. C. (1947), *Brain and Intelligence*. Chicago: University of Chicago Press. Pp. 206.

Hammer, A. G. (1948). *The Factorial Analysis of Mental Test Items with Special Reference to the Terman-Merrill Binet*. Unpublished Thesis: Australian Council for Education Research.

Hammer, A. G. (1950), A Factorial Analysis of the Bellevue Tests. *Austral. J. Psychol.*, 1, 108–114.

Hargreaves, H. L. (1927), The 'Faculty' of Imagination. *Brit. J. Psychol. Monogr. Supp.*, 10. Pp. 74.

Harrell, W. (1940), A Factor Analysis of Mechanical Ability Tests. *Psychometrika*, 5, 17–33.

Harris, C. W. (1948), An Exploration of Language Skill Patterns. *J. Educ. Psychol.*, 39, 321–336.

Hartshorne, H. & May, M.A. (1928), *Studies in Deceit*. New York: Macmillan. Pp. 720.

Hearnshaw, L. S. (1951), Exploring the Intellect. *Brit. J. Psychol.*, 42, 315–321.

Hearnshaw, L. S. (1956), Temporal Integration and Behaviour. *Bull. Brit. Psychol. Soc.*, No. 30, 1–20.

Heese, K. W. (1942), A General Factor in Improvement with Practice. *Psychometrika*, 7, 213–223.

Henrysson, S. (1957), *Applicability of Factor Analysis in the Behavioral Sciences.* Stockholm Studies in Educational Psychology, No. 1. Stockholm: Almquist & Wiksell. Pp. 156.

Hertzka, A. F., Guilford, J. P. *et al.* (1954), A Factor-Analytic Study of Evaluative Abilities. *Educ. Psychol. Measmt.*, 14, 579–597.

Hertzman, M. (1936), The Effects of the Relative Difficulty of Mental Tests on Patterns of Mental Organization. *Arch Psychol.*, 197. Pp. 69.

Highmore, G. (1949), *A Factorial Analysis of Athletic Ability Preparatory to the Formulation of a Series of Prognostic Tests.* Unpublished Thesis. University of London.

Highmore, G. & Taylor, W. R. (1954), A Factorial Analysis of Athletic Ability. *Brit. J. Statist. Psychol.*, 7, 1–8.

Hills, J. R. (1955), The Relationship between Certain Factor-Analyzed Abilities and Success in College Mathematics. *Univ. So. Calif. Rep.* from the Psychol. Lab., No. 15. Pp. 16.

Himmelweit, H. T. (1946), Speed and Accuracy of Work as Related to Temperament. *Brit. J. Psychol.*, 36, 132–144.

Holzinger, K. J. (1934–5), *Preliminary Report on Spearman-Holzinger Unitary Trait Study.* Chicago: Statist. Lab. Dept. Educ. Univ. Chicago. No. 2. Pp. 26. No. 4. Pp. 78.

Holzinger, K. J. (1938), Relationships Between Three Multiple Orthogonal Factors and Four Bifactors. *J. Educ. Psychol.*, 29, 513–519.

Holzinger, K. J. & Crowder, N.A. (1955), *Holzinger-Crowder Uni-Factor Tests.* Yonkers, N.Y.: World Book Co.

Holzinger, K. J. & Harman, H. H. (1937), Relationships Between Factors Obtained from Certain Analyses. *J. Educ. Psychol.*, 28, 321–345.

Holzinger, K. J. & Harman, H. H. (1938), Comparison of Two Factorial Analyses. *Psychometrika*, 3, 45–60.

Holzinger, K. J. & Swineford, F. (1939), A Study in Factor Analysis: The Stability of a Bi-factor Solution. *Univ. Chicago, Suppl. Educ. Monogr.*, No. 48. Pp. 91.

Holzinger, K. J. & Swineford, F. (1946), The Relation of Two Bi-factors to Achievement in Geometry and Other Subjects. *J. Educ. Psychol.*, 37, 257–265.

Horst, P. (1959), *Differential Prediction of Academic Success.* Seattle: University of Washington, ONR–477 (08). Pp. 37.

Howard, F. T. (1943), *Complexity of Mental Processes in Science Testing.* New York, Columbia University, Teachers College Contributions to Education No. 879. Pp. 54.

Howells, T. H. & Schoolland, J. B. (1934), An Experimental Study of Speech Perception. *J. Gen. Psychol.*, 11, 337–347.

Howie, D. (1950), Scholastic Aptitude, Reasoning, Fluency and Concentration. *Austral. J. Psychol.*, 2, 100–113.

Howie, D. (1953), A Reasoning Factor Indicated by General Factor Analysis. *Austral. J. Psychol.*, 5, 28–41.

Howie, D. (1956), Speed and Accuracy. *Austral. J. Psychol.*, 8, 111–118.

Hsü, E. H. (1946), A Factorial Analysis of Olfaction. *Psychometrika*, 11, 31–42.

Hsü, E. H. (1948), Factor Analysis, Differential Bio-Process, and Mental Organization. *J. Gen. Psychol.*, 38, 147–158.

Ingham, J. G. (1949), *An Investigation into the Relationship Between Memory and Intelligence.* Unpublished Thesis. University of London.

Johnson, D. M. & Reynolds, F. (1941), A Factor Analysis of Verbal Ability. *Psychol. Rec.*, 4, 183–195.

Jones, F. N. (1948), A Factor Analysis of Visibility Data. *Amer. J. Psychol.*, 61, 361–369.

Jones, H. E. & Seashore, R. H. (1944), The Development of Physical Abilities. The Development of Fine Motor and Mechanical Abilities. 43rd *Yrbk. Nat. Soc. Stud. Educ.*, 100–145.

Jones, L. V. (1949), A Factor Analysis of the Stanford-Binet at Four Age Levels. *Psychometrika*, 14, 299–331.

Jones, L. V. (1954), Primary Abilities in the Stanford-Binet, Age 13. *J. Genet. Psychol.*, 84, 125–147.

Jorgensen, C. (1934), Analysis of Some Psychological Tests by the Spearman Factor Method. *Brit. J. Educ. Psychol.*, 4, 96–109.

Karlin, J. E. (1942), A Factorial Study of Auditory Function. *Psychometrika*, 7, 251–279.

Kelley, H. P. (1954), *A Factor Analysis of Memory Ability.* Princeton, N.J.: Educational Testing Service, ONR 150–088. Pp. 79.

N*

Kelley, T. L. (1927), *Interpretation of Educational Measurements.* New York: World Book Company. Pp. 353.

Kelley, T. L. (1928), *Crossroads in the Mind of Man.* Stanford, Calif.: Stanford University Press. Pp. 238.

Kenny, P. B. (1958), A Note on the Formal Requirement for Factorial Studies of Differentiation of Abilities with Age. *Aust. J. Educ.,* 121–122.

Kerr, G. (1942), Aptitude Testing for Secondary Courses. *Occup. Psychol.* 16, 73–78.

Kleemeier, R. W. & Dudek, F. J. (1950), A Factorial Investigation of Flexibility. *Educ. Psychol. Measmt.,* 10, 107–119.

Kline, W. E. (1956), *A Synthesis of Two Factor Analysis of Intermediate Algebra.* Princeton, N.J.: Princeton University and Educational Testing Service, Technical Report.

Knight, A. R. (1933), *Intelligence and Intelligence Tests.* London: Methuen. Pp. 98.

Kohs, S. C. (1923), *Intelligence Measurement.* New York. Macmillan. Pp. 312.

Langsam, R. S. (1941), A Factorial Analysis of Reading Ability. *J. Exper. Educ.,* 10, 57–63.

Lee, D. M. (1955), A Study of Specific Abilities and Attainment in Mathematics. *Brit. J. Educ. Psychol.,* 25, 178–189.

Lindsley, D. B. (1943), Preliminary Report of Results from Oscilloscope Operator Tests Experimental Edition. *Office of Scientific Research and Development Report,* No. 1813.

Leff, B. (1949), *Some Aspects of the Measurement of Technical Aptitude in Boys Aged Twelve.* M.A. Thesis, University of London Library.

Lord, F. M. (1956), A Study of Speed Factors in Tests and Academic Grades. *Psychometrika,* 21, 31–50.

Lovell, K. (1955), Intellectual Deterioration in Adolescents and Young Adults. *Brit. J. Psychol.,* 46, 199–210.

Lucas, C. M. & French, J. W. (1953), *A Factor Analysis of Experimental Tests of Integration, Judgment and Planning.* Princeton, N. J.: Educational Testing Service, Research Bulletin 53–16, Pp. 29.

Lummis, C. (1946), The Relation of School Attendance to Employment Records, Army Conduct and Performance in Tests. *Brit. J. Educ. Psychol.,* 16, 13–19.

McClelland, W. (1942), *Selection for Secondary Education. London:* University of London Press. Pp. 264.

McCloy, C. H. (1940), The Measurement of Speed in Motor Performance. *Psychometrika*, 5, 173–182.

McDonough, M. R. (1929), The Empirical Study of Character. *Cath. Univ. Amer. Stud. Psychol. & Psychiat.*, No. 2. Pp. 222.

McFarland, R. A. (1928), The Role of Speed in Mental Ability. *Psychol. Bull.*, 25, 595–612.

McFarlane, M. (1925). A Study of Practical Ability. *Brit. J. Psychol. Monogr. Supp.*, 8. Pp. 75.

McNemar, Q. (1936), Practice and 'General' Motor Ability. *J. Gen. Psychol.* 14, 464–466.

McNemar, Q. (1942a), On the Number of Factors. *Psychometrika*, 7, 9–18.

McNemar, Q. (1942b), *The Revision of the Stanford-Binet Scale.* Boston: Mass.: Houghton Mifflin. Pp. 189.

McNemar, Q. (1951), The Factors in Factoring Behavior. *Psychometrika*, 16, 353–359.

McQueen, E. N. (1917), The Distribution of Attention. *Brit. J. Psychol. Monogr. Supp.*, 5. Pp. 142.

Mangan, G. F. (1959), A Factorial Study of Speed, Power and Related Temperament Variables. *Brit. J. Educ, Psychol.*, 29, 144–154.

Manzer, C. W. & Marowitz, S. (1935), The Performance of a Group of College Students on the Kwalwasser-Dykema Music Tests. *J. Appl. Psychol.*, 19, 331–346.

Matin, L. & Adkins, D. C. (1954), A Second Order Factor Analysis of Reasoning Abilities. *Psychometrika*, 19, 71–78.

Maxwell, A. E. (1959a), Statistical Methods in Factor Analysis. *Psychol. Bull.*, 56, 228–235.

Maxwell, A. E. (1959b), A Factor Analysis of the Wechsler Intelligence Scale for Children. *Brit. J. Educ. Psychol.*, 29, 237–241.

Meili, R. (1946), L'Analyse de l'Intelligence. *Arch. Psychol. Genève.*, 31, 1–64.

Mellone, M. A. (1944), A Factorial Study of Picture Tests for Young Children. *Brit. J. Psychol.*, 35, 9–16.

Melton, A. W. (1947), *Apparatus Tests.* Army Air Forces Aviat. Psychol. Prog. Res. Rep., No. 4. Washington, D.C.: U.S. Government Printing Office. Pp. 1056.

Michael, W. B., Guilford, J. P. *et al.* (1957), The Description of Spatial Visualization Abilities. *Educ. Psychol. Measmt.*, 17, 185–199.

Michael, W. B., Zimmerman, W. S. & Guilford, J. P. (1950), An Investigation of Two Hypotheses Regarding the Nature of the Spatial-Relations and Visualization Factors. *Educ. Psychol. Measmt.*, 10, 187–213.

Morgan, G. A. V. (1956), Verbal Abilities in Primary School Children. *Durham. Res. Rev.*, 7, 97–107.

Morris, C. M. (1939), A Critical Analysis of Certain Performance Tests. *J. Genet. Psychol.*, 54, 85–105.

Moursy, E. M. (1952), The Hierarchical Organization of Cognitive Levels. *Brit. J. Stat. Psychol.*, 5, 151–180.

Murphy, L. W. (1936), The Relation Between Mechanical Ability Tests and Verbal and Non-verbal Intelligence Tests. *J. Psychol.*, 2, 353–366.

Muscio, B. (1922), Motor Capacity with Special Reference to Vocational Guidance. *Brit. J. Psychol.*, 13, 157–184.

Myers, C. S. (1947), A New Analysis of Intelligence. A Critical Notice. *Occup. Psychol.*, 21, 17–23.

Neuhaus, J. O. & Wrigley, C. (1954), The Quartimax Method. *Brit. J. Statist. Psychol.*, 7, 81–91.

Oakley, C. A. & Macrae, A. (1937), *Handbook of Vocational Guidance.* London: University of London Press. Pp. 337.

Oeser, O. A. (1932), Some Experiments on the Abstraction of Form and Colour. *Brit. J. Psychol.*, 22, 200–215, 287–323.

Oldham, H. W. (1937–38), A Psychological Study of Mathematical Ability. *Brit. J. Educ. Psychol.*, 7, 269–286; 8, 16–28.

Oléron, P. (1957), *Les Composantes de L'Intelligence d'après les Recherches Factorielles.* Paris: Presses Universitaires de France. Pp. 517.

Ormiston, M. (1939), The Bearing of General and Special Abilities Upon Scholastic Success at the Beginning and End of a Secondary School Career. *Brit. J. Educ. Psychol.*, 9, 164–173, 213–223.

Osgood, C. E. & Suci, G. J. (1955), Factor Analysis of Meaning. *J. Exper. Psychol.*, 50, 325–338.

Paris Symposium (1956), *L'Analyse Factorielle et les Applications.* Colloques Internationaux du Centre National de la Recherche Scientifique. Pp. 427.

Paterson, D. G. Elliot, R. M. *et al.* (1930), *Minnesota Mechanical*

Ability Tests. Minneapolis: Minnesota University Press. Pp. 586.

Peel, E. A. (1949), Symposium on the Selection of Pupils for Different Types of Secondary Schools. VI. Evidence of a Practical Factor at the Age of Eleven. *Brit. J. Educ. Psychol.*, 19, 1–15.

Peel, E. A. & Graham, D. (1951–2), Differentiation of Abilities in Primary School Children. *Durham Res. Rev.*, 2, 40–48; 3, 31–34.

Pemberton, C. (1952a), The Closure Factors Related to Other Cognitive Processes. *Psychometrika*, 17, 267–288.

Pemberton, C. L. (1952b), The Closure Factors Related to Temperament. *J. Pers.*, 21, 159–175.

Perrin, F. A. C. (1921), An Experimental Study of Motor Ability. *J. Exper. Psychol.*, 4, 24–56.

Personnel Research Section, Adjutant General's Office (1948), *Studies in Visual Acuity*. P.R.S. Report, No. 742. Washington, D.C.: U.S. Government Printing Office. Pp. 161.

Peterson, D. A. (1943), Factor Analysis of the New United States Navy Basic Classification Test Battery. *Office of Scientific Research and Development Report* No. 3004. Washington, D.C.: U.S. Department of Commerce, 1946. Pp. 13.

Philpott, S. J. F. (1947), Man's Adaptability. *Advancement of Science*, 4, 230–242.

Pickford, R. W. (1949), Individual Differences in Colour Vision and Their Measurement. *J. Psychol.*, 27, 153–202.

Porebski, O. (1954), A Psychological and Statistical Study of Speed and Power as Variables of Human Ability. *Occup. Psychol.*, 29, 218–229.

Price, E. J. J. (1940), The Nature of the Practical Factor (*F*). *Brit. J. Psychol.*, 30, 341–351.

Reichard, S. (1944), Mental Organization and Age Level. *Arch. Psychol.*, 295. Pp. 30.

Remondino, C. (1959), A Factorial Analysis of the Evaluation of Scholastic Compositions in the Mother Tongue. *Brit. J. Educ. Psychol.*, 29, 242–251.

Renshaw, T. (1952), Factor Rotation by the Method of Extended Vectors: A Review of Dr. Sutherland's Paper. *Brit. J. Statist. Psychol.*, 5, 7–18.

Reyburn, H. A. & Taylor, J. G. (1941), Some Factors of Intelligence. *Brit. J. Psychol.*, 31, 249–261.

Richardson, S. C. (1956), Some Evidence Relating to the Validity of Selection for Grammar Schools. *Brit. J. Educ. Psychol.*, 26, 13–24.

Rimoldi, H. J. A. (1951), The Central Intellective Factor. *Psychometrika*, 16, 75–101.

Roff, M. (1953), A Factorial Study of Tests in the Perceptual Area. *Psychometr. Monogr.*, 8, Pp. 41.

Rogers, C. A. (1953), The Structure of Verbal Fluency. *Brit. J. Psychol.*, 44, 368–380.

Saunders, D. R. (1959), *On the Dimensionality of the WAIS Battery for Two Groups of Normal Males.* Princeton, N.J.: Educational Testing Service, Research Bulletin, 59–7. Pp. 17.

Sayed, F. B. (1951), *The Cognitive Factors in Geometrical Ability.* Ph.D. Thesis, University of Reading Library.

Schiller, B. (1934), Verbal, Numerical and Spatial Abilities of Young Children. *Arch. Psychol.*, 161. Pp. 69.

Seashore, R. H. (1930), Individual Differences in Motor Skills. *J. Gen. Psychol.*, 3, 38–66.

Seashore, R. H. (1940), An Experimental and Theoretical Analysis of Fine Motor Skills. *Amer. J. Psychol.*, 53, 86–98.

Seashore, R. H., Buxton, C. E. & McCollom, I. N. (1940), Multiple Factorial Analysis of Fine Motor Skills. *Amer. J. Psychol.*, 53, 251–259.

Seashore, R. H., Dudek, F. J. & Holtzman, W. (1949), A Factorial Analysis of Arm-Hand Precision Tests. *J. Appl. Psychol.*, 33, 579–584.

Shaefer, W. C. (1940), The Relation of Test Difficulty and Factorial Composition Determined from Individual and Group Forms of Primary Mental Abilities Tests. *Psychometrika*, 5, 316–317.

Shaw, D. C. (1949), A Study of the Relationships between Thurstone Primary Mental Abilities and High School Achievement. *J. Educ. Psychol.*, 40, 239–249.

Shuttleworth, C. W. (1942), Tests of Technical Aptitude. *Occup. Psychol.*, 16, 175–182.

Sisk, H. L. (1940), A Multiple Factor Analysis of Mental Abilities in the Freshman Engineering Curriculum. *J. Psychol.*, 9, 165–177.

Slater, E. & Slater P., (1944), A Heuristic Theory of Neurosis. *J. Neurol. Neurosurg. & Psychiat.*, 7, 49–55.

Slater, P. (1938), Speed of Work in Intelligence Tests. *Brit. J. Psychol.*, 29, 55–68.

Slater, P. (1940), Some Group Tests of Spatial Judgment or Practical Ability. *Occup. Psychol.*, 14, 40–55.

Slater, P. (1941), Tests for Selecting Secondary and Technical School Children. *Occup. Psychol.*, 15, 10–25.

Slater, P. (1947), Evidence on Selection for Technical Schools. *Occup. Psychol.*, 21, 135–140.

Slater, P. & Bennett, E. (1943), The Development of Spatial Judgment and its Relation to Some Educational Problems. *Occup. Psychol.*, 17, 139–155.

Smith, G. M. (1933), Group Factors in Mental Tests Similar in Material or in Structure. *Arch. Psychol.*, 156. Pp. 56.

Smith, I. M. (1948), Measuring Spatial Ability in School Pupils. *Occup. Psychol.*, 22, 150–159.

Smith, M. & McDougall, W. (1920), Some Experiments in Learning and Retention. *Brit. J. Psychol.*, 10, 199–209.

Spearman, C. (1904), 'General Intelligence', Objectively Determined and Measured. *Amer. J. Psychol.*, 15, 201–293.

Spearman, C. (1927), *The Abilities of Man*. London: Macmillan. Pp. 415.

Spearman, C. (1939), Thurstone's Work Re-worked. *J. Educ. Psychol.*, 30, 1–16.

Staff Division of Occupational Analysis, War Manpower Commission (1945), Factor Analysis of Occupational Aptitude Tests. *Educ. Psychol. Measmt.*, 5, 147–155.

Staff, Test and Research Section, Training, Standards and Curriculum Division, Bureau of Naval Personnel (1945), Psychological Test Construction and Research in the Bureau of Naval Personnel: Development of the Basic Test Battery for Enlisted Personnel. *Psychol. Bull.*, 42, 561–571.

Stake, R. E. (1958), *Learning Parameters, Aptitudes and Achievements*. Princeton, N.J., Psychology Department. Pp. 66.

Stephenson, W. (1931), Tetrad-Differences for Non-Verbal Subtests. Tetrad-Differences for Verbal Subtests. Tetrad-Differences for Verbal Subtests Relative to Non-verbal Subtests. *J. Educ. Psychol.*, 22, 167–185, 255–267, 334–350.

Stephenson, W., Studman, G. L. et al. (1934), Spearman Factors and Psychiatry. *Brit. J. Med. Psychol.*, 14, 101–135.

Stolurow, L. M. & Newman, J. R. (1959), A Factional Analysis of Objective Features of Printed Language Presumably Related to Reading Difficulty. *J. Educ. Res.*, 52, 243–251.

192   *The Structure of Human Abilities*

Sutcliffe, A. & Canham, J. W. (1937), *Experiments in Homework and Physical Education*. London: Murray. Pp. 194.

Sutherland, J. (1941–42), An Investigation into some Aspects of Problem Solving in Arithmetic. *Brit. J. Educ. Psychol.*, 11, 215–222; 12, 35–46.

Sutherland, J. D. (1934), The Speed Factor in Intelligent Reactions. *Brit. J. Psychol.*, 24, 276–294.

Swineford, F. (1947), Growth in the General and Verbal Bifactors from Grade VII to Grade IX. *J. Educ. Psychol.*, 38, 257–272.

Swineford, F. (1949), A Number Factor. *J. Educ. Psychol.*, 40, 157–167.

Tate, M. W. (1948), Individual Differences in Speed of Response in Mental Test Materials of Varying Degrees of Difficulty. *Educ. Psychol. Measmt.*, 8, 353–374.

Taylor, C. W. (1947), A Factorial Study of Fluency in Writing. *Psychometrika*, 12, 239–262.

Teegarden, L. (1942), Manipulative Performance of Young Adult Applicants at a Public Employment Office. *J. Appl. Psychol.*, 26, 633–652, 754–769.

Thomas, F. C. (1935), *Ability and Knowledge*. London: Macmillan. Pp. 338.

Thomson, G. H. (1939), *The Factorial Analysis of Human Ability*. London: University of London Press. Pp. 326.

Thomson, G. H. (1940), *An Analysis of Performance Test Scores of a Representative Group of Scottish Children*. London: University of London Press. Pp. 58.

Thomson, G. H. (1954), *The Geometry of Mental Measurement*. London: University of London Press. Pp. 60.

Thorndike, R. L. (1957), *The Optimum Test Composites to Predict a Set of Criteria*. Air Force Personnel and Training Research Center-TN-57-103.

Thorndike, R. L. & Hagen, E. (1950), *10,000 Careers*. New York: John Wiley. Pp. 346.

Thornton, G. R. (1939), A Factor Analysis of Tests Designed to Measure Persistence. *Psychol. Rev. Monogr.*, 51, No. 229. Pp. 42.

Thurstone, L. L. (1931), Multiple Factor Analysis. *Psychol. Rev.*, 38, 406–427.

Thurstone, L. L. (1938a), Primary Mental Abilities. *Psychometr. Monogr.*, 1. Pp. 121.

Thurstone, L. L. (1938b), The Perceptual Factor. *Psychometrika*, 3, 1–17.

Thurstone, L. L. (1940), Experimental Study of Simple Structure. *Psychometrika*, 5, 153–168.

Thurstone, L. L. (1944), *A Factorial Study of Perception*. Chicago: University of Chicago Press. Pp. 148.

Thurstone, L. L. (1945), The Effects of Selection in Factor Analysis. *Psychometrika*, 10, 165–198.

Thurstone, L. L. (1946), Note on a Reanalysis of Davis' Reading Tests. *Psychometrika*, 11, 185–188.

Thurstone, L. L. (1948), Psychological Implications of Factor Analysis. *Amer. Psychologist*, 3, 402–408.

Thurstone, L. L. (1951), *An Analysis of Mechanical Aptitude*. University of Chicago, Psychometric Laboratory. Pp. 26.

Thurstone, L. L. & T. G. (1941), Factorial Studies of Intelligence. *Psychometr. Monogr.*, 2. Pp. 94.

Thurstone, T. G. (1941), Primary Mental Abilities of Children. *Educ. Psychol. Measmt.*, 1, 105–116.

Thurstone, T. G. (1948), Factorial Studies of Mental Abilities of Children. *Proc. Twelfth Intern. Congr. Psychol.* Edinburgh.

Tilton, J. W. (1953), The Intercorrelation between Measures of School Learning. *J. Psychol.*, 35, 169–179.

Torgerson, W. S. & Green, B. F. (1950). *A Factor Analysis of English Essay Readers*. Princeton, N.J.: Educational Testing Service, Research Bulletin, 50–30. Pp. 12.

Uppsala Symposium (1953), *Uppsala Symposium on Psychological Factor Analysis*. Nordisk Psyckologi's Monogr. Ser., No. 3.

Van der Lugt, M. J. A. (1948), The V.D.L. Psychomotor Scale for the Measurement of Manual Ability. *Amer. Psychologist*, 3, 256.

Vernon, M. D. (1947), Different Types of Perceptual Ability. *Brit. J. Psychol.*, 38, 79–89.

Vernon, P. E. (1933a), The American v. the German Methods of Approach to the Study of Temperament and Personality. *Brit. J. Psychol.*, 24, 156–177.

Vernon, P. E. (1933b), The Rorschach Inkblot Test. II. *Brit. J. Med. Psychol.*, 13, 179–205.

Vernon, P. E. (1937), A Study of the Norms and the Validity of Certain Mental Tests at a Child Guidance Clinic. *Brit. J. Educ. Psychol.*, 7, 72–88, 115–137.

Vernon, P. E. (1938), *The Standardization of a Graded Word Reading Test*. London: University of London Press. Pp. 43.

Vernon, P. E. (1939), Educational Abilities of Training College Students. *Brit. J. Educ. Psychol.*, 9, 233–250.

Vernon, P. E. (1940), *The Measurement of Abilities*. London: University of London Press. Pp. 308.

Vernon, P. E. (1947a), Research on Personnel Selection in the Royal Navy and the British Army. *Amer. Psychologist*, 2, 35–51.

Vernon, P. E. (1947b), Psychological Tests in the Royal Navy, Army and A.T.S. *Occup. Psychol.*, 21, 53–74.

Vernon, P. E. (1947c), The Variations of Intelligence with Occupation, Age and Locality. *Brit. J. Psychol. Statist. Sec.*, 1, 52–63.

Vernon, P. E. (1949a), The Structure of Practical Abilities. *Occup. Psychol.*, 23, 81–96.

Vernon, P. E. (1949b), Recent Developments in the Measurement of Intelligence and Special Abilities. *Brit. Med. Bull.*, 6, 21–23.

Vernon, P. E. (1949c), Classifying Highgrade Occupational Interests. *J. Abn. Soc. Psychol.*, 44, 85–96.

Vernon, P. E. (1951), The Intelligibility of Broadcast Talks. *B.B.C. Quart.*, 5, 206–212.

Vernon, P. E. (1958), *Educational Testing and Test-Form Factors*. Princeton, N.J.: Educational Testing Service, Research Bulletin 58–3. Pp. 77.

Vernon, P. E. & Parry, J. B. (1949), *Personnel Selection in the British Forces*. London: University of London Press. Pp. 324.

Vidor, M. (1931), *Was ist Musikalitat?* München: C. H. Beck. Pp. 57 + 28.

Vincent, D. F. (1955), *Speed and Precision in Manual Skills*. London: National Institute of Industrial Psychology, Report No. 11. Pp. 19.

Walker, R. Y. & Adams, R. D. (1934), Motor Skills: The Validity of Serial Motor Tests for Predicting Typewriting Proficiency. *J. Gen. Psychol.*, 11, 173–186.

Walters, E. (1935), Retentivity in the Special Senses. *Ability and Knowledge*, by F. C. Thomas. Pp. 312–315.

Wand, B. (1958), *Flexibility in Intellectual Performance*. Princeton, N.J.: Educational Testing Service, ONR, 151–113. Pp. 133.

Weiss Long, A. E. & Pear, T. H. (1932), A Classification of Vocational Tests of Dexterity. *Industr. Hlth. Res. Board Rep.*, No. 64. Pp. 60.

Wendler, A. J. (1938), A Critical Analysis of Test Elements Used in Physical Education. *Res. Quart. Amer. Ass. Hlth. Phys. Educ.*, 9, 64–76.

Wheeler, D. (1958), Studies in the Development of Reasoning in School Children. *Brit. J. Stat. Psychol.*, 11, 137–159.

Wheeler, D. K. (1948), *Factors in Mechanical Ability Among Adults*. Unpublished Thesis. University of London.

Wherry, R. J. & Gaylord, R. H. (1944), Factor Patterns of Test Items and Tests as a Function of the Correlation Coefficient: Content, Difficulty and Constant Error Factors. *Psychometrika*, 9, 237–244.

Williams, E. D., Winter, L. & Woods, J. M. (1938), Tests of Literary Appreciation. *Brit. J. Educ. Psychol.*, 8, 265–284.

Williams, H. S. (1948), *Some Aspects of the Measurement and Maturation of Mechanical Aptitude in Boys Aged Twelve to Fourteen*. Unpublished Thesis. University of London.

Wilson, J. H. (1933), Group Factors Among Abilities Involved in a School Certificate Examination. *Brit. J. Educ. Psychol.*, 3, 71–86, 99–108.

Wilson, R. C., Guilford, J. P. & Christensen, P. R. (1953), The Measurement of Individual Differences in Originality. *Psychol. Bull.*, 50, 362–370.

Wing, H. D. (1941), A Factorial Study of Musical Tests. *Brit. J. Psychol.*, 31, 341–355.

Wissler, C. (1901), The Correlation of Mental and Physical Tests. *Psychol. Rev. Monogr.*, 3, 1–63.

Wittenborn, J. R. (1943), Factorial Equations for Tests of Attention. *Psychometrika*, 8, 19–35.

Wittenborn, J. R. (1945), Mechanical Ability, Its Nature and Measurement. I. An Analysis of the Variables Employed in the Preliminary Minnesota Experiment. II. Manual Dexterity. *Educ. Psychol. Measmt.*, 5, 241–260, 395–409.

Wittenborn, J. R. & Larsen, R. P. (1944), A Factorial Study of Achievement in College German. *J. Educ. Psychol.*, 35, 39–48.

Wolf, R. R. (1939), Differential Forecasts of Achievement and their Use in Educational Counselling. *Psychol. Rev. Monogr.*, 51, No. 227. Pp. 53.

Wolfle, D. (1940), Factor Analysis to 1940. *Psychometr. Monogr.*, 3. Pp. 69.

o

Woodrow, H. (1938), The Relation Between Abilities and Improvement with Practice. *J. Educ. Psychol.*, 29, 215–230.

Woodrow, H. (1939a), Factors in Improvement with Practice. *J. Psychol.*, 7, 55–70.

Woodrow, H. (1939b), The Common Factors in Fifty-Two Mental Tests. *Psychometrika*, 4, 99–108.

Wright, R. E. (1939), A Factor Analysis of the Original Stanford-Binet Scale. *Psychometrika*, 4, 209–220.

Wrigley, C. (1957), The Distinction between Common and Specific Variance in Factor Theory. *Brit. J. Stat. Psychol.*, 10, 81–98.

Wrigley, J. (1958), The Factorial Nature of Ability in Elementary Mathematics. *Brit. J. Educ. Psychol.*, 28, 61–78.

Yela, M. (1949), Application of the Concept of Simple Structure To Alexander's Data. *Psychometrika*, 14, 121–135.

Zimmerman, W. S. (1953), A Revised Orthogonal Rotational Solution for Thurstone's Original Primary Mental Abilities Test Battery. *Psychometrika*, 18, 77–93.

Zimmerman, W. S. (1954), The Influence of Item Complexity upon the Factor Composition of a Spatial Composition Test. *Educ. Psychol. Measmt.*, 14, 106–119.

INDEX

Note: psychological tests (apart from those with recognised titles) and factors are usually listed under the names of abilites.

Illustration of the Mathematical Fundamentals of Factor Analysis. It is unfortunate that this approach to the analysis of abilities involves somewhat complicated mathematics, since this frightens or antagonizes many of the teachers, employers, and others who are most prone to discuss abilities unscientifically. Yet the basic principles are very simple, as the following hypothetical examples will show.

TABLE I.—CORRELATION COEFFICIENTS BETWEEN SIX
PSYCHOLOGICAL TESTS

Tests	1	2	3	4	5	6
1. Vocabulary		+·76	+·79	+·45	+·41	+·34
2. Analogies	+·76		+·68	+·44	+·35	+·26
3. Classifications	+·79	+·68		+·49	+·39	+·32
4. Block Design	+·45	+·44	+·49		+·58	+·44
5. Spatial	+·41	+·35	+·39	+·58		+·55
6. Formboard	+·34	+·26	+·32	+·44	+·55	

Table I gives the correlations that might be obtained between six tests applied to a large group of children (Block Design and Formboard being given individually). Inspection suggests that the correlations between the first three and last three are relatively small, i.e. that ability at verbal tests is partially distinct from ability at practical or spatial tests. But the separation is incomplete. All the correlations are positive, showing that all tests have something in common, presumably of the nature of general intelligence. By the appropriate techniques we can find how far each test measures this general ability or factor which we shall call g, and Table II lists the loadings, saturations or correlations with g. Now if this was the only underlying ability, we could reproduce the test intercorrelations simply by taking the products of their g-loadings. For example:

$$r_{35} = r_{3g} \times r_{5g} = ·8 \times ·5 = ·40$$

Such products are listed in Table II, and in Table III each product has been subtracted from the corresponding original correlation to show what overlapping, if any, remains. These are known as *residual correlations*.

TABLE II.—G-LOADINGS OF THE SIX TESTS AND THEIR
PRODUCTS

	G-Loadings	Products					
		1	2	3	4	5	6
1. Vocabulary	·8		·56	·64	·48	·40	·32
2. Analogies	·7	·56		·56	·42	·35	·28
3. Classifications	·8	·64	·56		·48	·40	·32
4. Block Design	·6	·48	·42	·48		·30	·24
5. Spatial	·5	·40	·35	·40	·30		·20
6. Formboard	·4	·32	·28	·32	·24	·20	

TABLE III.—RESIDUAL CORRELATIONS AFTER SUBTRACTING
THE OVERLAPPING ATTRIBUTABLE TO G

	1	2	3	4	5	6
1. Vocabulary		+·20	+·15	+·03	+·01	+·02
2. Analogies	+·20		+·12	+·02	+·00	—·02
3. Classifications	+·15	+·12		+·01	—·01	+·00
4. Block Design	—·03	+·02	+·01		+·28	+·21
5. Spatial	+·01	+·00	—·01	+·28		+·35
6. Formboard	+·02	—·02	+·00	+·20	+·35	

The residuals between the first three and last three tests are not all zero, but are so close to it that they can reasonably be attributed to chance errors in the original correlations. Within each group of three however the residuals are large, showing that distinct verbal and practical-spatial abilities are present. Each set can be analysed separately, and if the following loadings are multiplied out, they exactly reproduce the residual correlations:

	Verbal-factor loading			Spatial factor loading
1. Vocabulary	·5	4. Block Design		·4
2. Analogies	·4	5. Spatial		·7
3. Classifications	·3	6. Formboard		·5

Subsidiary abilities, over and above *g*, are called *group factors*, since they run through a limited group of tests. It is preferable to name them by symbols, such as *v* for verbal, *k* for spatial, rather than giving them ability-names which may readily be misinterpreted. Similarly we use *g* to refer to the objectively established general factor, instead of the subjective and indefinable term intelligence.

The *communality* of any test, i.e. its total factor-content, is shown by the squares of its factor loadings. Table IV lists these loadings, their squares, the communality (h^2), and what is left over from 1.0, i.e. the *specificities*.[1] Thus we can state that the Vocabulary test measures 64 per cent. *g*, 25 per cent. *v*, and the remaining 11 per cent. is specific. The Formboard is a much poorer *g*

TABLE IV.—COMPLETED FACTOR ANALYSIS OF SIX PSYCHO-
LOGICAL TESTS

	Loadings			Squares of Loadings			Communality h^2	Specificity $1—h^2$
	g	v	k	g	v	k		
1. Vocabulary	·8	·5		·64	·25		·89	·11
2. Analogies	·7	·4		·49	·16		·65	·35
3. Classifications	·8	·3		·64	·09		·73	·27
4. Block Design	·6		·4	·36		·16	·52	·48
5. Spatial	·5		·7	·25		·49	·74	·26
6. Formboard	·4		·5	·16		·25	·41	·59
Variance				42·3	8·3	15·0	65·7	34·3

test, only 16 per cent. of what it measures being attributable to the general factor, 25 per cent. to *k*, and 59 per cent. specific. Such figures are known as the *variances* of the factors, and the average variance of each factor is given in the bottom row. These figures represent the importance or size of the factors in this battery of six tests.

[1] Many factorists further subdivide this term into the unreliability or error-variance of the test, and its true specificity. For example if the reliability co-efficient of the Vocabulary test is shown to be ·94, then the error variance is ·06 and the variance of the factor specific to the test alone ·05 (cf. textbooks of psychological statistics such as Guilford, 1936).

Factors Are Not Mental Elements Like Faculties. From this example it should be clear that a factor is a construct which accounts for the objectively determined correlations between tests, in contrast to a faculty which is a hypothetical mental power. We can if we wish go on to theorize about the psychological nature and origin of factors. Better, we can conduct experiments to discover just what performances involve a factor, among which groups of people it emerges, and what conditions affect it. But factors should be regarded primarily as categories for classifying mental or behavioural performances, rather than as entities in the mind or nervous system. Since by means of factor analysis we can reduce a large battery of tests to a few underlying factors there is a certain parallel to the analysis of chemical compounds into their constituent elements. But this analogy should not be pressed too far, for we shall see later that factors are much too fluid, too dependent on the particular groups and particular tests studied, to be compared with elements. For example we might expect, and will indeed find, that the factors in scholastic abilities are dependent on how school subjects are taught. Some teachers emphasize the connections between the various branches of mathematics, or between a country's language and its literature and history, much more than others do, and this is likely to be reflected in the correlations and factors.

Identification of Factors. How factors should be identified and named is a somewhat controversial point. According to Guilford (1940) the factorist studies the common material, formal and functional features in the tests which are loaded with a factor and from this deduces its nature. Most factors are defined by material (e.g. verbal, mechanical information, etc.). The form of the test—whether apparatus or paper-and-pencil, choice-response or creative-response—has not yet been proven to have much influence. Functional factors involve consideration of the testees' mental processes, by means of introspections or job analysis procedures or both (e.g. reasoning, attention, etc.). Bentley (1948) and others have criticized the looseness of factorists' terminology, and the subjectivity of their guesses about the nature of some of their factors. We agree with him that it is better to avoid names of hypothetical functions or faculties, but would claim that the old-fashioned procedure (still common among some vocational psychologists, psychiatrists, teachers and others) of assuming